P9-DFP-878

With warm regards,

Pere

June 2014

POLICY-DRIVEN DEMOCRATIZATION

Also by Peride K. Blind
Democratic Institutions of Undemocratic Individuals: Privatizations, Labor and Democracy in Turkey and Argentina, 2008.

Policy-Driven Democratization

Geometrical Perspectives on Transparency, Accountability, and Corruption

Peride K. Blind

POLICY-DRIVEN DEMOCRATIZATION
Copyright © Peride K. Blind, 2014.

All rights reserved.

First published in 2014 by PALGRAVE MACMILLAN® in the
United States—a division of St. Martin's Press LLC, 175 Fifth Avenue,
New York, NY 10010.

Where this book is distributed in the UK, Europe and the rest of the
world, this is by Palgrave Macmillan, a division of Macmillan Publishers
Limited, registered in England, company number 785998, of Houndmills,
Basingstoke, Hampshire RG21 6XS.

Palgrave Macmillan is the global academic imprint of the above
companies and has companies and representatives throughout the world.

Palgrave® and Macmillan® are registered trademarks in the
United States, the United Kingdom, Europe and other countries.

ISBN: 978-1-137-29477-7

Library of Congress Cataloging-in-Publication Data is available from the
Library of Congress.

A catalogue record of the book is available from the British Library.

Design by SPi Global

First edition: April 2014

10 9 8 7 6 5 4 3 2 1

This book is dedicated to the loving memory of my grandmother,
Azime Kiymet Ozakman

This book is also dedicated to all the cancer patients who, like my
grandmother, have bravely defied this terrible illness, notably:
My beloved father, Seydi Vakkas Kaleagasi
and
My wise director, Haiyan Qian

CONTENTS

List of Figures and Tables

Figures

Tables

PREFACE

In the summer of 1991, I had the opportunity to present my Turkish-French High School, *Galatasaray Lisesi*, at an international film festival for teenagers. The festival took place in Paris. I was only 14, so it was a great honor for me to represent Turkey, particularly because my knowledge of cinema was close to nil. But being fluent in French always has its perks. At the end, the festival was impressive: we got to meet friends from all around Europe and the Middle East, interact with the famous actress Sophie Marceau and visit the then French President's wife, Dannielle Mitterand, at the Champs-Élysées as well as take lunch with the then Mayor of Paris and former President of France, Jacques Chirac.

As impressive as the Festival was, my most vivid memory of this experience, was an ephemeral discussion I had with a fellow international participant, also 14, who was convinced that his uncle lost, or almost lost, his hand in Turkey, or "in one of those countries" because he was believed to have stolen something. I was irritated by the denotation "one of those countries;" I was obviously right in staunchly arguing that it could not have been Turkey, and I remember forcing my brain to find as many forceful arguments as possible about how rule of law based on written and nonviolent punishment including habeas corpus existed in many countries in the Middle East.

And of course, we ended up losing our group and our way to our youth hostel, wandering for a while in the streets of Paris. He was not convinced; I was frustrated.

When I went to pursue my undergraduate and graduate studies, I continuously searched for an answer to the question of democratization. I wondered how one could decide which country is democratic. I wrote about Uzbekistan's entrenched patron–client nexuses and their pernicious effect on its democratization process only to hear at an international conference in New York that "Uzbeks are not interested in democracy to start with." I examined the consolidation of democracy in Greece only to be challenged that "the tardive introduction of electoral democracy and the pernicious corruption make the consolidation of democracy irrelevant there, except maybe for *consolidation of the transition to democracy*." The list could go on.

My research on the Turkish case of democratization painted an even more complex picture since patron–client attributes, corruption, successive coups d'état, the place of Islam in politics and ethnicity issues were all present and vigorous there. Hoping to find solace and perhaps clearer answers, I decided to compare the most incomparable cases I could find: Turkey and Argentina. *Democratic Institutions of Undemocratic Individuals*, which came out of Palgrave in December 2008, analyzed the Turkish and Argentine labor unions' strategies in the face of privatizations. The book concluded that institutions could democratize to adjust to the changing rules of the economic game, and therefore contribute to the overall democratization process, while individuals by themselves rarely did.

At that point in time, I had understood that deciphering democratization analytically was clearly an arduous task: not only were the constituent and adjacent concepts many and complex, so were the levels of analysis at which we could situate and examine its various processes and several implications.

Joining the policy world at the United Nations and looking at governance issues globally and from the more applied perspectives of public administration, I became more and more convinced of the necessity to merge political science with public policy in order to better understand democratization. After all, political scientists could well spend hours debating whether democratization is the most appropriate playfield of elites or of the masses, or a combination of both. They could investigate the details of myriad possible critical junctures on the path from authoritarianism to a possible democracy, itself defined procedurally or substantively, or simply differently from case to case. They could go on pointing to evidence that economic development strategies undertaken by authoritarian as opposed to democratic governments could produce more fruitful results in terms of democracy, or the other way around. Regardless, what matters for both the processes and the outcomes of democratization at the end of the day are the policies that governments and other governance actors design, develop, implement and, perhaps also, internalize.

Shifting the focus to public policy and acknowledging the multiplicity of complex issues involved in democratization processes, this book represents the next level of my continuous thinking on democratization. It attempts to bring political science closer to public administration through a focus on how policies of transparency, accountability and anti-corruption may play significant roles in democratization endeavors from early on.

My hope is that this book benefits those policy-makers who are attempting to make sense of the multiple challenges faced in democratization and development as well as the scholars and students of democratization and democratic governance who are looking for a synthesis of a variety of approaches and explanations found across disciplines. I also hope that it helps providing new perspectives on the assessments of democratization processes in countries like Turkey, Ukraine and myriad others where the sociopolitical turmoil that exists at the time of this writing has its causes deeply rooted in issues pertaining to transparency, accountability and corruption.

I thank the blind peer-reviewers and the Palgrave Macmillan team for their support for this project. I am also appreciative of the great assistance received from the librarians at Princeton Public Library. Last but not least, I thank my wonderful husband, Sebastien, and my two lovely sons, Teohan and Ozan, for their love and support. As always, all errors and ideas contained herein are mine, and do not represent the position of any of the organizations I am associated with.

INTRODUCTION

This book has two aims. First, it tries to construct a comprehensive synthesis of the complex social science concepts of democratization, transparency, accountability and corruption. These are much-debated notions that lie at the rarely explored intersection of political science and public administration. They can be defined, understood and applied very differently, even inconsistently, from each other depending on the ideological and methodological lenses worn by the scholars who study them. This book attempts to combine various perspectives, from different fields and subfields, on each one of these notions to arrive at comprehensive and interlinked understandings.

Second, this book also attempts to link democratization to the policies of transparency, accountability and anti-corruption. It asks the following questions: Can emphasizing transparency, accountability and corruption control early on in democratization processes—rather than later and only when issues arise or become overtly salient—contribute to healthier democratization processes and outcomes? Should explicit focus be given to these policy fields by democratizers, including the ruling and/or the contending elite, civil society representatives, grassroot organizations and external democracy promoters and donors? In the same way that free, fair and periodic elections are the minimum requisites for a *procedural* democracy, can certain policies that promote openness and transparency of government, responsibility and answerability of government institutions and representatives and corruption control become the minimum requirements for a *substantive* democracy? Hence, shifting the focus to public policy and acknowledging the multiplicity of complex issues involved in democratization processes, this book attempts to find the most common drivers of democratization detectable and significant across all or most phases, types and levels of analyses of democratization.

With that aim, the first chapter undertakes the task of synthesizing the numerous understandings and definitions of democratization found across disciplines. Three policy fields—transparency, account-ability and corruption control—are emphasized as common drivers of democratization across its multiple stages, phases and types. The second, third and fourth chapters examine and attempt to offer com-prehensive definitions of these three concepts, respectively. They also detect the theoretical and empirical linkages posited in the litera-ture between each one of them and democratization, understood simply as moving from a lack or low level of democracy to a begin-ning or higher level of democracy, or, to put it differently, the estab-lishment and the upgrading of democratic governance. The final chapter attempts to link these three concepts to each other, juxtapos-ing the potential areas of incompatibility and overlap with conse-quences on democratizations.

Chapter 1, harking back to the early Stoics of the fourth century BC, introduces the *oikeiosis* idea of democratization as the basis for substantive democratization. The conceptual tool of *Concentric Circles of Democratization* tracks the dominant understandings of democratization since the 1950s to the present. The exercise dem-onstrates the prevalence of structural over individual explanations. It also finds that throughout all layers of the circle, a common emphasis exists on the importance of transparent governance, accountable policy making and corruption control without, however, an analytical attempt to link them with each other or with democra-tization. The chapter suggests that comparing different policies aimed at democratization through these common policy areas can help illuminate how they may shape democratization differently in similar structural contexts, and how they may perhaps produce similar outcomes in dissimilar contexts.

Chapter 2 draws attention to the lack of attention that transpar-ency has received as a component of democratization in either political science or public administration. It introduces two tools: one to conceptualize transparency better, and the other to show linkages with democratization. The first didactic tool, Transparency Triangle, disaggregates the concept in terms of its *inputs*, i.e., its possible causes and catalysts, its *outputs,* i.e., its various definitions and types, and its *outcomes*, i.e., its potential and actual impact, including on democratization. The Transparency-Democratization Matrix, in turn, illuminates the direct-indirect and positive-negative linkages between transparency and democratization. The chapter concludes that transparency becomes important with the first elections, and can effectively contribute to democratization thereafter when effectively accompanied by accountability measures.

Chapter 3 highlights the unequivocally positive association posited between accountability and democracy in the literature. It delineates three mechanisms for making sure that the association works as such: *justice* to prepare the ground for democratic account-ability, *transparency* to ensure credibility and legitimate representa-tion and *deliberation*, to maintain a continuous discussion, including the needed justifications and explanations. The chapter likens the multifaceted concept of accountability to a cube of eight corners, four at the bottom and four at the top. The four corners at the bottom constitute the *hard accountability surface* because each corner repre-sents the more material and institutional understandings of account-ability as *answerability*. The four corners at the top constitute the *soft accountability surface* because each represents the more ethical and social understandings of accountability as *responsibility*.

Chapter 4 stresses the need for a multiscalar understanding of corruption whereby its micro-, meso- and macro-level determinants are delineated and linked together. With that aim, it introduces the Corruption Pentagon, which lists the structural conditions that may lie at the root of corruption (Seed) as well as those that tend to nourish it (Feed). Factors that may lead to corrupt transactions among individuals acting out of material necessities (Need) or moral insatia-bility (Greed) are also covered, as are the legal and administrative control mechanisms of corruption (Wield). The chapter concludes that democratization and corruption should be seen as two sides of the same coin rather than two identical but separate coins. It suggests that tackling corruption early on, before it arises, could constitute the stepping stone to a more enduring and healthier democracy.

The main thrust of this book is that democratization has been analyzed from myriad perspectives to be subsequently couched in several cognitive heuristics that appeal mostly to our intuitive System I rather than the more analytical System II, to borrow an analogy created by Nobel Prize-winning psychologist Daniel Kahneman.[1] Scholars have leaned on the side of political procedures and socio-economic structures to explain democratization as an electoral or party competition among different actors, institutionalization of rules and procedures, structural change and/or cultural values. They have then engaged in long discussions about the sequencing, the relative significance and the implementation of these procedural or structural explanations. Scant attention was paid to concrete policies designed, developed, implemented, reconfigured and continuously debated by myriad actors in different governance settings. Yet, when it comes to getting things done with an eye toward long-term success, the question becomes whether the right actions were undertaken, implemented on time and if they were done adequately.

In this respect, transparency, accountability and corruption control policies could be as pertinent to democratization as are elections, political parties and civil society. Their content, timing and implementation patterns could have an important impact on democratization. Further research would thus benefit from a deeper, empirical analysis of policy pathways, from openness to integrity in democratization processes taking place in settings with different structural attributes, levels of development and stages of democratization. After all, if elections are the "procedural minimums" for defining a democracy,[2] certain basic transparency, accountability and corruption control policies could qualify as the "substantive minimums" for defining, and making it work, better.

CHAPTER 1

---※◈※---

THE CONCENTRIC CIRCLES
OF DEMOCRATIZATION: TEASING
OUT THE COMMON DRIVERS

The Stoic philosophers of the fourth century BC believed in the idea of *oikeiosis*. Oikeiosis proposed to gradually expand one's closest attachments to oneself on to the family, society and eventually all of humanity. The early Stoic philosopher Hierocles depicted the idea of oikeiosis through his *concentric circles of identity*: the innermost circle represented the individual; the surrounding circles stood for immediate family, extended family, local group, citizens, countrymen and humanity, in this order. The objective of oikeiosis was to draw in people from the outer circles into the inner ones, based on the assumption that all human beings belong to one single and universal community with a shared morality at the core. As such, oikeiosis became the basis of cosmopolitan ethics.[1]

The definitions and the various understandings of democratization since the 1950s can be likened to Hierocles' concentric circles. The search to define and understand democratization shows an overall tendency to move from the outer layers to the inner layers of the *concentric circles of democratization*. Democratization, which sprang as a corollary of overall socioeconomic development, moved from the outmost circles of cultural and structural change to systemic and institutional reorganization, and from there to individual elite interactions, and their dealings with mass society representatives, and from there back to mid-level circles of state–society dealings and community-led projects of sociopolitical liberalization.

The move through the concentric circles has neither been constantly unidirectional from the outer to the inner layers nor has one circular layer been the only level of study of democratization at any given point in time. Often, fragments from different layers of analysis have coexisted, one layer dominating rather than excluding others at any given time. The individual-level understandings of democratic transitions in the 1980s, and the following institutional analyses of democratic consolidation in the 1990s, for instance, have culminated in the eclectic democratization studies, including historical, structural, cultural and agency-based explanations in the 2000s.

The increasingly eclectic definitions of democratization conform to the oikeiosis idea of democratization. The rising appreciation of the multifaceted nature of democratization implies that teasing out the common ingredients across all circles, rather than trying to prove the most adequate circle(s) of democratization, could benefit the democratization literature and policy making. If delineated properly, these common elements could be the drivers of democratization rather than its immediate or deep-rooted causes, yet still exert significant impact on the processes and outcomes of democratization. Such an exercise, reminiscent of the System II Model by Kahneman (2013), could take us closer to a more consensual and applied understanding of democratization.

The model of concentric circles of democratization is an exercise in approaching *politics* of democratization to its *policies*, thereby contributing to a more policy-driven understanding, and hence a more effective implementation of democratization. Preliminary research shows that open communication and free flow of information, answerability to citizens and accountability, and corruption control are essential ingredients of democracies. Yet, they are seldom studied systematically in a comprehensive work whereby they are interlinked with each other and with democratization. This book proposes to focus on these three common drivers across all circles of democratization to offer an oikeiosis definition of democratization.

The Idea: Oikeiosis of Democratization

An oikeiosis understanding of democratization implies adopting a holistic view on the processes of attaining, maintaining and developing democracies. Despite its inherent complexities, this book adopts the Occam's Razor principle to define democratization simply as moving from a lack or low level of democracy to a beginning or higher level of democracy. Democratization, for our purposes, is thus the establishment and the upgrading of democracies. Such a definition consciously repudiates the segmented view that has dominated the literature. As shown in Figure 1.1, the segmented view of democratization includes mainly four conceptual categories: (i) *process-led differences* or the *democratization versus democracy* debate; (ii) *scope-led differences* or the *procedures versus rights* debate; (iii) *stage-led differences* or the *transition versus consolidation* debate; and (iv) *degree-led differences* or *democracy versus democratic quality* debate.

Regarding *process-led differences*, there is a tendency in the literature to associate *democratization* with the *origins* of a specific regime type, and *democracy* with the *stability* of this regime. While such theoretical distinctions and arbitrary thresholds are useful for didactic purposes, they are not empirically verifiable. This study assumes that disassociating the later phases of democracy from the overall process of democratization is unproductive, at the very least because the process has no end point to it. Ideally, a democracy, or polyarchy, depending on the extent to which one deems full democracy to be attainable, should be continuously democratizing regardless of whether it is a new or established democracy. This study, therefore, does not separate the origins of a democracy from its stability. It assumes that democratization is a continuous endeavor, and not only restricted to newly emerging democracies.

Regarding *scope-led differences*, there is voluminous research on whether democratization should include political rights in addition to fair, free, regular and competitive elections, and whether political rights should be accompanied with social and/or economic rights for full(er) democratization. This study adopts a holistic rights-based approach to view democratization as expanding social and economic rights in addition to political and human rights. Neither elections nor the number of turnover of governments, distribution of land or income equality are by themselves sufficient to make democratization a success. Procedures are crucial but are not sufficient by themselves to offer a complete understanding. Democracy as such is not simply about the choice of procedures that regulate access to state power (Mazzuca 2007) or the effectiveness of the executive to rule (Collier and Levitsky 1996). It is instead a situation of human dignity

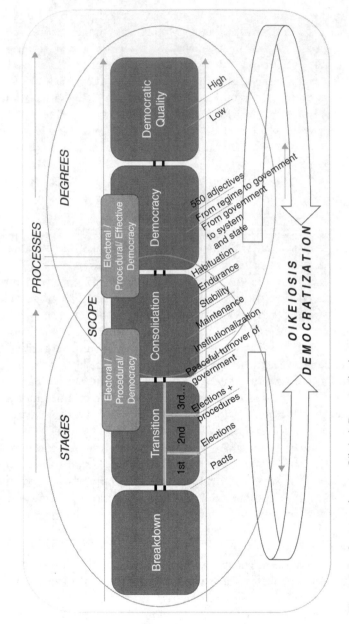

Figure 1.1 Segmented versus Oikeiosis Democratization

and political equality ensured by socioeconomic forces, including issues pertaining to distributional conflicts and resource endowments (Acemoglu and Robinson 2006, Vanhanen 2007).

Regarding *stage-led differences,* most studies are prone to impose temporal frontiers to democratization. For instance, there is significant consensus in the literature that the beginnings of a democracy, or democratic transitions, have different causes and consequences than its later stages referred to as democratic consolidation (Shin 1994: 151). The theoretically useful distinction between transition and consolidation has monopolized the democratization debate to the extent that the real endeavor to understand democratization for what it really is has been lost. It might thus be more beneficial to devote time and energy to see the actual policies that have fostered and advanced democratization throughout rather than figuring out where to draw the line between the breakdown of autocracies, the start and end points of democratic transitions, when democratic consolidation starts and ends, and whether it can be equated with democratic stability, maintenance, persistence, endurance or habituation.[2]

Regarding *degree-led differences,* there have been distinctions in the literature drawn between democracies, and democracies with low and high qualities. Many scholars have differentiated between democratic consolidation and democratic quality by associating the former with temporal stability and the latter with regime characteristics such as corruption, weak rule of law, class and other types of persistent or intermittent conflict. The same scholars, though, have also tended to use the two concepts interchangeably. Furthermore, such characteristics associated with democratic quality, particularly corruption and the weak rule of law, have been cited extensively as the main reasons for failures of democratization, by the same and other scholars. This study does not view the adjacent notion of democratic quality as separate and distinct from democratization. The assumption is that democratization will succeed only if high quality democracies are targeted earlier rather than later. According to this degreeless understanding, low quality democracies might not be democratizing at all, and transparent and accountable systems with minimum corruption are seldom non-democracies—even when procedurally deemed undemocratic or of a certain degree of democracy.

THE MODEL: CONCENTRIC CIRCLES
OF DEMOCRATIZATION

Democratization emerged as an independent field of study with the transitology literature of the 1980s; however, this is not the first time that scholars have addressed democratization. The search for understanding the nature and processes of democratic governance, including a democratic regime, government and state, was very much the spotlight of policy-makers and scholars during the first decolonization wave in the 1950s and the Cold War. The early studies that covered democratization did so only indirectly, however, and as part of their larger quest to understand economic development. Joseph Schumpeter, Friedrich Hayek and Karl Polanyi offered some initial perspectives on democratization as an upshot of socioeconomic development.

Having started as a corollary of economic development, democratization was mostly studied from structural perspectives. The move from economic to social structures and from there to political systems, state institutions, individual elite negotiations and social movements can be visualized through the model of concentric circles of democratization. The direction of the dominant perspectives is from the outer layers of structures to individual action and attitudes, with intermittent spikes to adjacent or outer circles. The counter-moves back to mid-circles of institutional analysis in the 1990s, and the eclectic focus of the last decade on socioeconomic structures, history and civil society show that democratization studies are at a crossroads. A useful exercise for democratization studies could be to find those elements that are significant across all layers of the circles of democratization rather than simply combining different layers of analysis. The Concentric Circles Model of Democratization is depicted in Figure 1.2.

Genesis at the Outer Circles: Democracy as a Corollary
of Economic Structures

As early as 1942 Schumpeter constructed his theory of democracy in his *Capitalism, Socialism and Democracy*. Although democratization was not his immediate concern, Schumpeter offered the most influential definition of a *procedural* democracy. He equated it with competitive

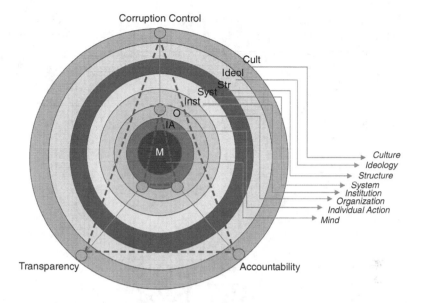

Figure 1.2   Concentric Circles of Democratization

elections toward the selection of a government. He enumerated five conditions to make a democracy successful over time: high quality and resourceful politicians and political institutions; an independent judiciary; a cohesive and well-trained bureaucracy; transparency and honesty; and tolerance for differing points of view (290).

Schumpeter's contemporary, Hayek, also associated democracy with competition, albeit of a different nature. His model of democracy revolved around free markets and market-based competition rather than electoral contestation. It required a comprehensive rule of law system seeking to limit arbitrary government interference in the economy, and the expansion of individual freedoms, including, notably, entrepreneurship. Their differences notwithstanding, both Schumpeter and Hayek were interested in understanding development rather than elucidating how democracies develop overtime. For Schumpeter, elections sufficed to qualify a regime as a democracy. For Hayek, free markets were enough to instill and safeguard democracies.

Individual initiative and free markets were nowhere enough for democratization according to Hayek's contemporary, Polanyi (1944).

He argued that the only way to advance freedoms in societies toward greater democratization was to countervail the market-propelled inequalities with social reforms, including particularly distributive policies.[3] As a precursor of the theory of radical democracy, Polanyi's ideas pioneered the recent "networked" understandings of democratization based on bottom-up social mobilization and resistance politics, particularly against economic globalization and neoliberalism (Munck 2002, 2004, 2006).

First Spike to the Inner Core in the 1950s: Democracy as an Individual Attribute

A more direct and less economic approach on democratization was adopted briefly in the 1950s by Lasswell (1951). He conceived democracy as an individual attribute rather than a structural appendage of economics. In his *Democratic Character*, he associated democratization with the innate characteristics of open-mindedness, self-esteem, empathy and optimism. He argued that certain general and deep-seated psychological dispositions toward life, such as humanism, philanthropy, versatility, inclusiveness, tolerance and benevolence would lead individuals, communities and societies to democratize.[4] Adorno (1950) showed the other side of the coin in his *Authoritarian Personality*, where he enumerated the undemocratic predispositions of fatalism, dogmatism, rigid reverence to authority, obsession with rank and power, traditionalism and ethnocentrism.

In these first and short-lived individual-level analyses of democratization, modern, open and tolerant belief systems were assumed to lead to democracy, while traditional, closed and rigid values brought authoritarian or totalitarian regimes (Rokeach 1960). Later Sniderman (1975) verified that there is indeed a connection between an individual's character and his/her regime preferences even though it was not utterly clear which one was the cause, and which one was the consequence. That is when the influence of structures regained importance, yet this time leaning toward sociopolitical rather than overtly economic models.

Back to the Outer Circles: Democracy as a Corollary of Sociopolitical Structures

Owing its genesis to Parsons' *Social System* (1951), structuralists focused on the ways in which the Lasswellian traits of democracy could be initiated and shaped by certain social structures. Marrying the individual-empiricism of Lasswellian democracy with the collective-structuralism of Parsons, the influential modernization theory of the 1960s asserted that all attempts to nurture democratization without modernization, and vice versa, were bound to fail.

Modernization theory found its strongest voice in Lipset's *Some Social Requisites of Democracy* published in 1959. Lipset associated democracy with rule of law, legitimacy, effective performance, social mobility, cross-cutting cleavages, limited inequality, political modera-tion and the gradual incorporation of the newly mobilizing groups into politics (Diamond and Marks 1992). He maintained that democ-ratization was brought forth not so much by some apolitical psycho-logical attributes but economic and sociopolitical development, itself propelled by open-minded, middle-class entrepreneurs.[5]

In Lipset's framework, the low income and the high economic insecurity of the lower classes often went hand in hand with low literacy and inadequate education, authoritarian family patterns and limited participation in political and/or voluntary organizations. Democratization occurred when industrialization increased the gross domestic product per capita, creating a wealthy and educated middle class, and the subsequent incorporation of the working class into the system through the institutionalization of socioeconomic and political concessions, such as voting in the elections and other participatory mechanisms.

Lerner (1958), another modernization theorist, enumerated three consecutive steps of modernization toward democratization: First came urbanization—since only cities could give rise to the complex skills and resources necessary for modern industrial economies to emerge and function. Second was education—since only well-off urbanites could have the means and the will to educate themselves to acquire more wealth and knowledge. Third on the list was media—since the quest of the urban middle classes for higher knowledge would be fuelled by newspapers, radio networks, television and other media channels to ultimately increase the quantity and the quality of citizen participation.[6]

The emphasis of the modernization theory on social structures as determinants of democratization was kept by Easton (1953) but specified in terms of political processes, including interest articulation, aggregation and adjudication, policy formulation, implementation and evaluation. Accordingly, how people reacted to these processes and how their feedback was channeled into and used by governing institutions to effectively respond to citizen demands determined the *political support*—the backbone of democratization for Easton (1965). If support corroded due to societal divisions or the state–society chasm, legitimacy of the entire political system and democratization suffered.[7] Democratization, in this sense, was the general acceptance of the formal and informal rules and norms of the system (Bachrach and Baratz 1962).

Almond and Verba (1963) also refined the structural basis of modernization. They adopted a more specific focus on political systems pointing specifically at state–society interactions within a political system rather than political processes in general, as the precursor to democracies. Therefore, for Almond and Verba (1963), it was not as much the long-term economic development, deep-seated social class formations and interactions, or gradual political liberalization and participation that paved the way to a stronger democracy, but how citizens viewed and interacted with their governing institutions. Democratization occurred if and when citizens were mature enough to know when to decrease and increase their participation in relation to the level of the effectiveness and legitimacy of the state. If the state was aloof and inefficient in all or certain policy areas, citizens were to increase participation. When the state was open and efficient, they were to decrease their activism. Eventually, such systemic, regular and balanced state–society interaction culminated in civic cultures, which propelled democratization.

As much as Easton, Almond and Verba and other systems theorists converged on their eclectic views of democratization as a system of processes between state and society, deep-seated structures and social constructs continued to play a major role in the developmental field during the second half of the 1960s. What was slightly different was the methodological gateway to these structures. Moore's *Social Origins of Dictatorship and Democracy* (1966) used macro-historical comparative analysis rather than structural-functionalist lenses to understand the different pathways to democratization. His focus was not only on the rapid economic modernization of societies and their healthy participation in politics but on class conflict. Democratization, according to him, occurred when the democratic urban intelligentsia prevailed over the undemocratic rural aristocracy.

Moore agreed with Lipset that industrialization was a necessary precondition for democratization, and that a middle-class bourgeoisie was the driving force behind it. He distinguished, however, that things were neither as simple as attaining a given percentage of GDP/capita nor raising the literacy level and media outreach in cities. Instead, capitalist development that led to democratization was one where revolutions led by the bourgeoisie could uphold the benefits and the beneficiaries of economic development, and subdue the innately undemocratic landed aristocracy. Accordingly, England, France and the United States democratized as opposed to Japan and Germany where the bourgeoisie lost its battle against an undemocratic gentry, and ended up with fascism, and Russia and China, where the lack of bourgeoisie led to the empowerment of the peasantry, and ended up with communism (Wiener 1975).

Structural explanations and historical accounts of development continued in the 1970s with the neo-Marxist dependency development theorists like Cardoso (1972) and Evans (1979). Like their structuralist predecessors, dependency scholars covered issues related to democracy and democratization only as part and parcel of their overall quest to understand socioeconomic development. They believed that all types of development in every sphere, including political development and democratization, depended on when and how states were incorporated into the international capitalist system.

In the developmentalist perspective, democratization was equated with the willingness and the ability of the state to express the voices of the popular forces in the society (Cardoso and Faletto 1979: 216). Many of them later referred to a "globalized social democracy," which was characterized by openness to international markets, robust social policies that promote social justice and an accountable state as well as global agency by the South (Evans 2009). Like dependency scholars, world-system theorists also equated democracy with political universalism (Amin 1973). Although they seldom touched upon democracy directly, they tended to associate it with anti-capitalist social movements and resistance politics by the masses (Wallerstein 1974).

Second Spike to the Mid-Circles: Democratization as Institutional Strength of State and Groups
Huntington's *Political Order in Changing Societies* (1968) was the last grand theory explaining political development at a global scale.

Huntington moved one circle closer to the inner core of the concentric circles and identified political and public institutions as the main determinants of democratization. Suspicious of any hard-to-pinpoint socioeconomic structure or political process to breed democratization, he stressed the need for strong, stable and predictable state institutions to initiate and sustain democratization.

According to Huntington (1968), democracy and a weak government could not coexist. Democratization occurred only in environments where state institutions were adaptable, complex, autonomous and coherent. Only then government would be able to effectively respond to the needs and demands of vibrant associations at the grassroots level, and only then, trust would ensue. Like Moore, he pointed at the need to successfully include the rural forces in democratization processes. For democratization to succeed, social mobilizations at the rural level in the developing world had to be channeled adequately *into* rather than *against* the system through strong political institutions. If not, much like Apter (1965) had done a few years back, Huntington warned that modernization could lead to soaring corruption, violence and instability; not democratization.

The shift from the larger socioeconomic development patterns to the institutional strength of state in explaining democratization was followed by yet another move closer to the inner circles in the 1970s. Democratization was defined as a conscientious project of regime change launched and maintained by national actors in Rustow's *Transitions to Democracy* (1970), Dahl's *Polyarchy* (1971), O'Donnell's *Bureaucratic Authoritarianism* (1973), Schmitter's *Still the Century of Corporatism?* (1974) and Lindblom's *Politics and Markets* (1977). While Rustow emphasized national unity as a precondition to establish democracies, Dahl (1971) stressed public participation and political contestation. O'Donnell (1973) and Schmitter (1974) underlined actors' political organization, policy orientations and negotiations to explain variants of democratization. Lindblom (1977, 1979) associated it with partisan mutual adjustments and incremental policy making by interest groups with constricted volitions of the masses.

Rustowian struggle for democracy was to be staged by a *newly emerging social group*, much like Lipset's middle class and Moore's manufacturing elite. The struggle was followed by a *decision phase* where the contending elite factions negotiated, compromised and consciously opted for democratic rules. Democratization became enduring

during the *habituation phase* when democratic rules and norms were made an integral part of the system. This agent-driven account of democratization—where the actions and decisions of the governing and the contending elite were considered key for democratization— constituted the basis for the first explicitly democracy-focused studies of the 1980s.

Rustow (1970) pointed at polarization, not pluralism, as the defining characteristic of the emergence of democracies (354). Democratization for him was revolutionary at its genesis, and evolutionary later on, as pluralist modes of decision making and negotiation took hold. Democratization as such was about "the habit of dissension and conciliation over ever-changing issues and amidst changing alignments" (363). Contemporary pluralist theorists like Lindblom (1965, 1979) and Dahl (1971) could not agree more with this evolutionary view of democratization.

Lindblom (1965) associated democratization with incrementalism rather than revolutions. Incrementalist democratization for Lindblom was about a few significant policy changes rather than one sudden push for democracy. He explained that democratization was mostly about decentralized political decision-making models of partisan mutual adjustments on the part of all concerned actors. For Lindblom, democracies differed from non-democracies in that they made several small changes to the existing policies rather than opting for infrequent, major and often disruptive change (Lindblom 1979).

Dahl (1971) likewise conjured democratization as a process of power bargaining among different groups from the governmental and non-governmental sectors. He believed that a liberal market economy with a high GNP per capita and high cultural homogeneity, or such economy with subcultural pluralism and the effective institutions of representation provided the most propitious conditions for democratization (115–123, 203). Numerous actors with bounded rationality and facing complex challenges made cost-benefit analyses to arrive at decisions that could at best approximate but never fully equate democratic systems. Dahl called this near-perfect democratic system a "polyarchy." Polyarchies were made up of two essential parameters: public participation or inclusion, and public contestation or liberalization.

Polyarchies based on public inclusion and public contestation included several characteristics including freedom of organization, freedom of expression, the right to vote, broad eligibility for public office, the right to compete for support and votes, the availability of alternative sources of information, free and fair elections, and the dependence of public policies on citizens' preferences. Depending on which parameter occurred first historically, democratization could take a different pathway.

This pluralist understanding of democratization and its axioms of contestation and participation provided the basis for democracy data-bases such as the Freedom House, Polity and others, which opera-tionalized and quantified democracies.[8] Dahl's work also contributed to the formulation of various other studies that expanded on the shortcomings of polyarchies. One such study by O'Donnell (1973) examined the opposite case of polyarchies, and shed light on the dif-ferent variants of authoritarianism. Another work by Schmitter (1974) rejected pluralism, and analyzed the institutionalization of interest group representation in the form of corporatism.

Following up on Dahl's agency-based analysis of democratiza-tion, but contesting the democratic outcome of elite negotiations, O'Donnell (1973) showed that delayed economic development, and more specifically the end of the first easy phase of Import Substitution Industrialization (ISI), could lead to the unlikely alliance of the military with the bureaucracy and international economic actors, as happened in Latin America in the 1960s. The emergence of the "bureaucratic authoritarian" regime was the diametric opposite of Lipset's positive association between growth and democracy.

In bureaucratic authoritarianism, all political or public issues were reduced to technical problems and addressed by state technocrats excluding, demobilizing and repressing citizens. Although bureau-cratic authoritarianism was later extended from a mere regime type to a form of state and political system, it was better understood as an analytical construct where both elite agency and socioeconomic structures interacted to affect democratization, in this case negatively (Remmer and Merkx 1982).

Schmitter (1974) also studied the involvement of different groups, both from the state and society, in policy formulation pro-cesses. The end result of these processes was neither democratiza-tion nor bureaucratic authoritarianism but corporatism. He defined corporatism as "a system of interest representation in which the constituent units are organized into a limited number of singular, compulsory, non-competitive, hierarchically ordered and functionally differentiated categories, recognized or licensed by the state and granted a deliberate representational monopoly within their respective categories in exchange for observing certain controls on their selection of leaders and articulation of demands and supports" (93–94).

Corporatism had statist and societal variants.[9] Statist corporatism was a system of interest representation by monopolistic, centralized and internally non-democratic associations. Societal corporatism, later called neo-corporatism by Schmitter (1984), was associated with a policy process of dialoguing, concerting and partnering between state and less hierarchically organized societal groups. Democracy and democratization were associated with this type of policy making, and the statist corporatist structures were linked with authoritarianism (Western 1991, Baccaro 2003).

Authoritarianism, corporatism, their variants and associations to democratization gave way to the debate about the role of state in politics and policy making. O'Donnell (1976) defined corporatism as "a set of structures that link state with society" (47) and specified that "bureaucratic authoritarianism" both repressed civil society (statizing) and opened state areas to civil society organizations (privatizing). Malloy (1976) defined his hybrid concept of "authoritarian corporatism" as enforced limited pluralism by state and its partners. Authoritarian corporatism came about not so much as a result of either developmental conflicts, elite negotiations, certain socioeconomic structures or state; instead, it was a product of ingrained populist ideologies and movements typical of Latin America since the 1930s.

Going beyond coalition politics and interest group negotiations, Skocpol (1979, 1985) synthesized the corporatist and authoritarian notions to bring the state back into analysis. She focused on the autonomy and capacity of state institutions in not only making decisions, but creating the very meaning of politics. Stepan (1985) demonstrated how even the strategies of political opposition are defined and shaped by state structures. While authoritarianism, and not democratization, was the gist of the debate in bureaucratic authoritarianism, corporatism and the state-centered accounts of political development, as Schamis (1991) later summarized: "Authoritarianism in the 1970s does not constitute a separate topic from that of democracy in the 1980s" (202).

Growth at the Inner Circles: Agency-led Democratization with Constant Spikes to the Mid-Circles of Institutions

The third wave of democratization that started in Spain and Portugal in the mid-1970s, continued in Latin America in the 1980s, and Asia and Africa in the 1990s, provided the impetus for the shift in the studies of democratization from the macro-structural and meso-statist explanations (1950s–70s) to meso-organizational and micro-individual definitions of democratization (1980s–2000s). One such transitional analysis from the structural to the individual accounts of democratization was produced by Inkeles (1978, 1983). Focusing on individual modernity, he rejected the Laswellian mind-studies of democracy as well as Lipset's structuralist accounts of modernization and Almond and Verba's systemic links between modernity and democracy. He maintained instead that modern orientations like open-mindedness, secularism, positivism, meritocracy, rationality or nationalism could satisfy the requirements of a dictatorship as well as those of a democracy (Inkeles 1969, 1978).

Like Inglehart's analysis on post-materialist values (1977, 1990, 1997), Inkeles' objective was to understand how modern identities emerged as a result of socioeconomic forces (Welzel 2009). Democratization was not a direct part of the analysis but was included later as an indirect component when Inglehart made linkages between the socioeconomic structures and the prerequisites for democracy at individual and cultural levels of analysis. Accordingly, economic development created changes in individual values through increased social complexity and autonomy. In the second phase of modernization also called post-industrialization,[10] these emancipative values triggered by socioeconomic development triumphed over those maintained by the authoritarian elite (Inglehart et al. 2003, 2005, 2008).

A more direct and analytical turn to the agency-based explanations of democratization came with the *Breakdown of Democratic Regimes* by Linz and Stepan (1978). They explained that democracies were instituted and maintained not by certain structural (pre) conditions or institutional attributes but by the deliberate decisions and actions of individual political leaders (40). Both performance and legitimacy were necessary for democratization. The material means of incorporating disloyal and ambivalent groups into the system as well as the use of symbols and myths to strengthen support and legitimacy were essential. If and when democracy failed, it was not because the structural conditions were not met, but because the democratic leadership failed to strategically negotiate amidst the uncertainty of the transition.

The thirteen authors who contributed to the four volumes that made up the *Breakdown of Democratic Regimes* seldom pursued a uniform approach to democratization. O'Donnell and Schmitter's (1986) *Transitions from Authoritarian Rule* had a common approach and one decisive factor for democratization: rupture between the authoritarian hard-liners and the more liberal soft-liners of the non-democratic elite when faced with the threat of a violent insurgency by the masses. Such rupture could end up in elite negotiations or *pacts* defined as procedural arrangements between the soft-liners and the hard-liners who negotiated and bargained away sacrifices in exchange for a possible compensation in the post-authoritarian regime, such as an office and/or avoiding persecution (Przeworski and Wallerstien 1982).

Transitional scholars agreed on the central impact of pacts on democratization. The agency and the short-term strategic calculations of the hard- and soft-liner authoritarian elite, not structural limitations, mattered (Karl 2005). Palma (1990) characterized democratization as the "crafting" of alliances in the transition process. Burton and Higley (1987) and Burton et al. (1992) attributed democratic consolidation to "elite settlements" and "elite convergence." What the transitologists disagreed on was the impact of the pact depending on its type (Stradiotto and Guo 2010). Some argued that pacted transitions offered the most viable path to democracy (O'Donnell and Schmitter 1986, Karl 1990, Karl and Schmitter 1991, Higley and Burton 2006). Others claimed that pacts, whether driven by the old elite or the opposition, threatened long-term democratization by working against party system institutionalization and political competition, and by sowing the seeds of patronage and corruption (Przeworski 1991, Hagopian 1996). Still other transitologists focused on foreign-led transitions such as those in Grenada, Panama, Afghanistan and Iraq. Finally, some transitions were categorized as multiclassed or simply as unclassifiable.[11]

The pro-pact transitologists differentiated between incumbent versus opposition-led transitions as viable paths of democratization.

Incumbent-led transitions were top-down regime conversions by the authoritarian elite perceiving the threat of violent overthrow. They seldom led to full-fledged democratization since the structures of the old regime were kept and the opposition was too weak to contest the outcomes. Some examples were Spain, Brazil, Taiwan, Hungary, the USSR, Bulgaria and Chile. Opposition-led transitions were based on the cooperation of the old authoritarian elite and the new elite of the mass-based movements in determining the conditions of transitions (Stradiotto and Guo 2010, Nilsson 2012).[12] Cycles of protests and repression eventually led to negotiated agreements between government and opposition in Poland, Czechoslovakia, Mongolia, Nicaragua, Uruguay, Bolivia, Honduras, El Salvador, South Korea and South Africa.

Some non-pact transitologists pointed at revolutions, not pacts, as the most propitious starters for democratization. The suddenness of revolutions was associated with a complete break from the authoritarian past thereby allowing the opposition to push for unrestricted elections and to restrict the ability of the old elite to interfere in the democratization process (Munck and Leff 1997). Other non-pact transitologists argued that revolutions produced enduring patterns of domination that are often undemocratic due to the isolation of the incumbents (Karl and Schmitter 1991). The examples of violent transitions in Nicaragua, Iran, Portugal and Romania offered scanty evidence of easy success since the reliance on force during the transition continued in the post-transition period (Ward and Gleditsch 1998). For these transitologists, the "relatively peaceful, but threatening mass mobilizations from below" that many associated with the post-communist world were the preferred route to democratization (McFaul 2002, Bunce 2003).

Whether pro- or anti-pact, the first democratization scholars of the 1980s, inspired by Rustow's emphasis that the initiation and the deepening of democracies abide by different logics, divided the democratization process into two specific, yet interrelated phases. The first transitional phase denoted to the "time between the breakdown of a dictatorship and the conclusion of the first democratic national elections" (Bermeo 1997: 305). The essential ingredient of a democratic transition was that political authority was now to originate from the free decision of an electorate (Przeworski 1986, Linz 1993, Welsh 1994). The subsequent consolidation phase referred to the lengthy post-transition process whereby democratic structures and norms were learned and accepted as legitimate by state and society. Democratic consolidation was deemed to be achieved if: (i) two free and fair elections took place; or (ii) a government lost in the elections and gave up power peacefully one time (Przeworski et al. 1996: 50–51); or (iii) two consecutive turnovers of power (Huntington 1991). Pacts marked the beginning of the opening of the authoritarian regime, or the transition, and the first national elections signaled the end of the transition, and the beginning of democratic consolidation (Przeworski 1986, Welsh 1994).[13]

Although the initiation of a democratic regime and the subsequent deepening of democratic rules and norms were separate, they were also intrinsically related. From a path-dependent perspective, the way in which democratic transitions happened could shape the types of institutions established afterward. Going further back in the past, the ways in which the previous authoritarian regime ruled could also affect the democratic transition and consolidation patterns. Democratization in this understanding was more than a two-stage procedural negotiation, and much more so than free, fair, regular and competitive elections.[14] It was a continuous process of institution-building and political change toward a democratic political regime and governance (Potter et al. 1997). It was equivalent to the gradual application of the rules and procedures of citizenship to political institutions previously governed by other principles, such as coercive control or social tradition (O'Donnell and Schmitter 1986). It entailed liberalization but included more than just a relaxation of repression and the granting of certain freedoms (O'Donnell et al. 1988). It was about the institutionalization of these freedoms, and of the very right to have rights.

First Spike to the Mid-Circles: Democratization as Institutional Development

The rights-based institutionalist focus adopted by democratization scholars in the 1990s coincided with the rising interest in the consolidation of democratization. Democratic systems were founded upon well-functioning organizations like stable, responsive and accountable political parties and party systems, an effective judiciary and representative legislature, free trade unions, free professional associations, free press, free universities and research institutes, and free religious organizations (Snow and Manzetti 1993). Increases in the rights and freedoms enjoyed by these organizations were deemed important for the consolidation of democracy.

Weak institutionalized party systems with weak ties to citizens lay at the root of consolidation problems in the developing world, according to Mainwaring and Scully (1995) and Mainwaring (1998). The lack of linkages between vulnerable populations—such as women's groups and rural workers—and civil society was stressed as a factor hampering the sustainability of democratization (Grzybowski 1990, Paré 1990, Waylen 1993). From an empirical perspective, disciplined political parties were contrasted with clientelist politics to provide reasons for the lack of democratic consolidation in Africa (Sandbrook 1996). Institutionalized party rules as opposed to personalist dealings as well as the place of vulnerable groups in the overall sociopolitical system were also instrumental in examining democratization patterns in Arab countries (AbuKhalil 1997).

Judicial independence also entered the lexicon of democratization in the 1990s. The formation of impartial, respected and autonomous court systems was associated with strong and durable democracies (Larkins 1996, Pilar 1999). Some linkages between judicial independence and democratic consolidation consisted of higher respect for the constitution, rule of law and accountability. A non-independent judiciary, in turn, was associated with "delegative democracy" defined by excessive presidentialism and weak horizontal accountability among political institutions (O'Donnell 1994).[15]

Trade and labor unions were also studied for the first time in the democratization literature in the 1990s. Defying the one-sided focus on government elite, Rueschemeyer et al. (1992), and Rueschemeyer et al. (1993) argued that capitalist development led to democratization, not through increase in the literacy rates of the middle class or the victory of the manufacturing elite over the landed gentry, but through an increase in the capacity of the collective organization of the working class.

Labor union-led protests often contributed to delegitimizing the authoritarian regime and furthered transitions through increased contestation. The mobilization of trade unions against the dictatorships in Uruguay and the Solidarity movement in Poland were underlined as "new social movements" (Pelczynski 1988). Levitsky (1998) showed the significant role of labor unions in the Polish democratic transition vis-à-vis the Argentine case. Collier and Mahoney (1997) demonstrated how the oppositional role of labor unions contributed to the democratic transitions of Southern Europe and South America. Labor activities were also found to be instrumental in legitimizing the democratic left and labor-based parties during democratic consolidation (Collier and Collier 1991, Collier 1995, 1999).

Institutionalist analyses of democratization also focused on technical questions such as whether a presidential, semi-presidential or parliamentarian system, or if a majoritarian versus proportional electoral system would produce better outcomes in terms of consolidation. Actor-centered institutionalist approaches or *new institutionalism* proposed to combine structures and actors in explaining democratization (Scharpf 1997). It brought in the influence of institutions on the preferences and choices of individual and collective actors. Linz and Valenzuela (1994) assessed the actions of presidents and of the congress within presidentialist versus parliamentarian systems to conclude that presidentialism is less favorable to democracy than parliamentarianism. Mainwaring and Shugart (1997), on the other hand, elaborated that a potential switch from presidentialism to parliamentarianism could implicate even more problems for democratization in the long run.[16]

Similarly, Lijphart (1984, 1999) and Powell (2000) contrasted majoritarian or Westminster style democracies with consensual types based on proportional representation found in Continental Europe. They opted for the latter as being more beneficial for democratization in the long run, particularly for ethnically, culturally and linguistically divided societies, mainly due to the larger focus on minority rights in proportional representation. Institutions such as multimember districts, more so than two major parties, coalition cabinets, bicameralism and decentralized or federal political systems were preferred for democratic consolidation in multiethnic societies to the first-past-the-post and winner-take-all electoral systems with only two major political parties, single-party cabinets, unicameralism, and a unitary and centralized government. Mainwaring (2001) showed correlations, not causations, between consensual democracies and better government performance, economic management, control of violence and inequalities, minority representation, citizen satisfaction, environment protection and social welfare.

Decentralization policies and programs implemented across the world since the mid-1990s gave prominence to local governments as agents of democratization within a dominantly institutionalist perspective. Decentralization and local governance reforms were associated with democratization and even made their way into national constitutions, notably in Africa (Crawford 2009, Ojambo 2012). The causal linkages between decentralization, local governance and democratization included increased accountability, easier communication and better allocation of resources with increased public sector efficiency and alleviation of poverty. Most recent research on decentralization and democratization, however, produced ambivalent results. They also raised the need to combine institutionalist analyses with interest-driven individual analyses to get a fuller picture of democratization in different settings.

Accordingly, starting with the mid-2000s, it was not increased participation or inclusion of the vulnerable, but tighter patron–client nexuses and local elite politics that became associated with decentralization efforts in Asia and Africa (Hetland 2008, Bénit-Gbaffou 2011, Imai and Sato 2012, Simandjuntak 2012). Increased accountability and citizen-centric service delivery were attributed to central authority and institutionalized party systems, and the overall democratic regime in Latin America; not to decentralization (Goldfrank 2011). O'Dwyer and Ziblatt (2006) found that the positive impact of decentralization on higher government efficiency was valid only for high, and not for low GDP/capita countries, thereby bringing back the structural conditions of development, including political development, in democratization. These and other studies demonstrated the utility of analyzing decentralization processes, not only in terms of institutional reforms, but also in terms of interest calculation and preferences of the actors involved in decentralization processes (Johnson 2001, Kubal 2006, Mansrisuk 2012).

Maturation of Democratization: Eclectic Processes with Structuralist Overtones

Agency-led transitions and institution-driven consolidations of democracy, and the perceived need to combine both, soon culminated in an era of eclectic democratization with overall structuralist tendencies. This eclectic phase, which brings us to the current stage of democratization studies, can best be characterized as maturation since it is underlined by a common quest for converging democratization parameters beyond some arbitrarily set theoretical thresholds. Three main groups of eclectic democratization studies can be detected from the 1990s and onward.

The first group of eclectic democratization studies looked at the omitted or less-favored actors of transitions, to ask "Who initiates and leads democratization?" The move from the Mid-Circles of Institutions to the *Inner Circles of Individual Agency* meant a new emphasis on new democracy activists such as the civil society and grassroots (McFaul 1997, Carothers 2000, 2002) as well as external actors (Huntington 1991, Przeworski et al. 1996, Brinks and Coppedge 2006). These accounts showed that not just elite settlements, but social movements, associationalism and globalization are also integral parts of democratization (Collier and Mahoney 1997).

The second group of democratization studies reverted to the *Outer Circles of Structure* yet restricted its analysis to economic variables while adopting a more eclectic methodology including a combination of structural-cultural analysis with a degree of agency-based preferences in studying the linkages between economic development, growth, inequality, democratic transitions and consolidation (Przeworski 1991, Haggard and Kaufman 1995). The main question was "How does economics affect democratization?" The double-edged sword of the relationship between economic factors and democratization often stemmed from the different conceptualizations and operationalizations of these vast concepts.

The third group of democratization studies from the 1990s onward went further outward along the concentric circles of democratization, and revisited the role of previous state structures, legacies, values and cultures in understanding democratization (Luebbert 1991, Rueschemeyer et al. 1992, Linz and Stepan 1996). The question asked at this layer of *Outmost Circles of Culture* was "What legacies and values determine the prospects for democratization?" The historical approach adopted by this line of studies demonstrated how elite negotiations were not immune to the historically ingrained patterns of authority, as documented in the cases of Brazil, Peru, South Korea and the Philippines (Hagopian 1990).

Inner Circles of Individual Agency: Who Initiates
and Leads Democratization?

Starting with the 1990s and peaking in the 2000s, transitologists' focus on the attitudes, acts and actions of the authoritarian incumbents and the elite from the opposition parties expanded to cover other governance actors such as civil society, people's or social movements, foreign governments and regional and international organizations. Each one of these actors was studied both in terms of their role in transitional pacts and their organization for and during democratic consolidation.

Civil Society

The demise of the USSR, the collapse of communism and the end of the Cold War in the beginning of the 1990s precipitated the quest of scholars and practitioners for a new actor in democratization. The hard-liner and soft-liner divide in the ruling authoritarian regime as the launch pad of democratization gave way to the role of organized society in bringing about and sustaining democratization. Concomitantly, the focus shifted from elite-driven pacts to mass-driven coalitions with a reformist state in ending authoritarianism and strengthening democratization. Przeworski's (1991) model of democratization attributed the main cause for democratization to the cooperation between the democratic civil society leaders and key elite actors willing to liberalize, all in a context where the state was at least minimally capable to lead. Lipset (1994), the father of modernization theory, also added civil society to his list of necessary conditions for democratization when he revisited his 1959 thesis *Some Social Requisites of Democracy.*

Civil society was put in the spotlight both theoretically and empirically in the 1990s. It became equated with democracy because civil society meant an implicit rejection of military governments and a demand for the right to have rights, including particularly the respect for human rights (Lechner 1991, Seligman 1992, Blaney and Pasha 1993). Different definitions of civil society were given and distinct linkages were made to democratization depending on the chosen paradigm and the political convictions of scholars (Cohen and Arato 1992). Three main categories among these definitions stand out: (i) *civil society as voluntary associations;* (ii) *civil society as communities;* and (iii) *civil society as public space.*

The first understanding of civil society as voluntary associations put emphasis on voluntary action and social trust as the main links with democracy (Putnam et al. 1993, Putnam 2000). Civil society consisted of groups of citizens, spontaneously and freely emerging and associating in the tradition of John Locke (Scholte 2002). It was equivalent to a network of voluntary associations composed of private individuals pursuing their own special interests *against* an overarching state. It was assumed that a multitude of dynamic secondary associations formed by individuals interested in their own freedoms brought democratization through instilling the "habits of the heart," such as tolerance, cooperation and norms of reciprocity through face-to-face communication and horizontal bonds of social trust.

The second communitarian understanding of civil society stressed political trust (Booth and Richard 1998) as well as human capital (Becker 1993) and cultural capital (Bourdieu 1990) in linking civil society with democratization (Edwards and Foley 1998: 135).[17] Civil society was understood as an ally of a supporting state and constitution, all working together for the public good, much in the spirit of Montesquieu (Katz 2002). Its main role was to be an instiller of civic virtue and active citizenship toward the building of institutional democracy where formal and informal state institutions mattered more than voluntary associations.

The third public space definition of civil society combined both social and political trust in linking democratization with civil society, itself characterized by institutionalized civic deliberation and political participation (Benhabib 1992: 75, Dryzek 2000: 74–75, Young 2000: 167). Defined as an arena for deliberation among individual citizens as well as for institutional collaboration, civil society included both voluntary associations and civic communities pursuing the public good while at the same time avoiding co-optation by state (Thomas 1997). The progression from collective action and voluntary associations to democracy was ensured through civic engagement, social networks and innovative policy making. Democratization occurred when civil society contributed to making the state more deliberative, inclusive, open, transparent, accountable and better connected with society. The three definitions of civil society and their relation to democracy are illustrated in Figure 1.3.

The role of civil society in democratization was also examined empirically. In South and Central America, Pereira (1993) showed that the rise of social movements and citizen organizations and their effective alliance with the soft-liners in the ruling elite were crucial in countering the military and bringing down authoritarian regimes. Kamrava and Mora (1998) argued that the absence of a democratically

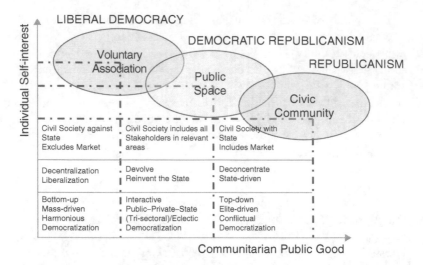

Figure 1.3   Three Conceptions of Civil Society and Linkages to Democratization

inclined civil society in the Middle East hampered democratization prospects there, even when compared to Latin America where the traditions of bureaucratic authoritarianism and state corporatism were hostile to civic initiatives. In Asia, Uhlin (1993) explained how the emerging Indonesian civil society was able to override class differences in effectively voicing its common support for democratization. In Africa, Oquaye (2000) offered vivid accounts of the Ghanaian civil society in resisting both the divisiveness of multiparty systems and the repression of the authoritarian regime. Wiredu (1999) went as far to advocate replacing the originally Western idea of political party competition with a more consensual, cooperative, deliberative and an essentially African form of voluntary political organizations by civil society (42–43).

The focus on civil society as a significant agent of democratization continued in the 2000s but was diversified and deepened through structural, cultural and institutional explanations.[18] Reminiscing Lindblom's argument for "muddling through" democratic policy making, Weyland (2012) claimed that people's participation and mobilization produced more successful results in terms of democratization when undertaken in politically incremental rather than abrupt fashions. Chen (2011) showed that the pact-led transition in Taiwan was neither a top-down nor a bottom-up process, but both. Ljubownikow et al. (2013) depicted how changes in Russia's economic, political and legal environment replicated similar shifts in its civil society and democratization processes. These area specialists illuminated the inevitable connection between historical development, civil society agency and democratization.

With time, the constituting units of civil society and its scope received greater attention. The question arose as to whether the private sector and trade unions were part of the non-profit third sector. The United Nations Environment Program (UNEP) included business, trade unions, non-governmental organizations, faith communities, parliamentarians, journalists and academicians in its definition of civil society (Spencer 2000). The European Commission embraced business and trade unions along with non-governmental organizations in its list of "social partners." The Organization for Economic Cooperation and Development (OECD) created a formal structure for consulting businesses and trade unions along with the non-profit organizations. World Bank's new country assistance strategy made civil society into a vital partner alongside the private sector and international organizations. Civic Solidarity Platform, a network of several dozens of human rights NGOs from throughout the Organization for Security and Cooperation in Europe (OSCE) region, was created to make recommendations to the governments of the OSCE participating States and institutions.

Trade unions, labor organizations and the private sector started cooperating with civil society organizations, often in the form of national, regional and global social movements, to express their support for democratization. Trade unions participated in social movements like Brazil's Rural Landless Workers Movement, the Unemployed Workers' Movement of Argentina, the Zapatista National Liberation Army, Mothers' Movements in the United States, labor unions in France and burial societies in South Africa. Their activism contributed to the building of social capital among the clusters of their members, and supported the building and the consolidation of democracy (Munck 2003).

The convergence of markets and state in the 1990s also blurred the border lines between civil society and the private sector. The conditionality of international lending policy on fair and free elections, human rights, transparency in political institutions and other dimensions of democratic governance made civil society into the new partners of the private sector. In their new role, civil society organizations often acted as intermediaries in channeling development aid to state institutions (Tandon and Mohanty 2003). A significant percentage of non-profit NGOs promoted for-profit activities such as micro-enterprises and community-based enterprises of inclusive finance (Fisher 2003). Corporate responsibility, the role of transnational corporations in democratization and their cooperation with civil society organizations—locally, nationally, regionally and globally—are continuously shaping the meaning and practice of democratization and development (Sorcha and Douglas 2004).

More recently, hybrid organizations comprising tenets of civil society associations also became part of the democratization literature. Truth commissions, formed as a result of consultative processes between governments, civil society and victims' groups in conflict and post-conflict settings, were linked with democratization, albeit often in contradictory terms. Taylor and Dukalskis (2012) found a positive relationship between truth commissions and democratization. They claimed that the transparency and the publicness of truth commissions positively influenced democratization. Brahm (2007), on the other hand, found that truth commissions have either inconsequential or negative effects on long-term democratization and human rights.

These and similar debates in most democratization studies point at the need to shift from theoretical approaches to empirical analyses, especially vis-à-vis the study of the linkages between civil society and democratization. Policy-driven perspectives can be instrumental in contributing to such a shift. Comparing different policies aimed at civil society development and integration can help illuminate how the latter may impact democratization in different ways in similar structural contexts, and how similar policies may produce similar outcomes in dissimilar systems. Perhaps civil society's contributions to democratization are stronger when transparency, accountability and/or anti-corruption policies are adopted early on, and/or if they make explicit references to the role of civil society in specific terms, or perhaps separate civil society legislation is more effective in supporting democratization along with these policies.

Timing of policies is also important in addition to their contents and inter-linkages. Politics and policy can be brought closer together with a focus on the timing of certain civil society development and integration policies, public administration and governance policies, and their implementation. Moreover, the introduction of pertinent policies can be juxtaposed and compared with the strategic negotiations undertaken by the elite at key points in time throughout the democratization processes to note the differences, if any, in the processes and outcomes of democratization. Perhaps if transparency, accountability and anti-corruption policies are enacted with different levels of participation by civil society and/or at specific conjectures in relation to the timing of the elections, or the honeymoon period of democratically elected governments or during the rule of incumbent regimes, they can shape democratization in different ways.

Democratization Agents Other than Civil Society
Agents of democratization other than civil society—such as the parliament, the executive, the judiciary, political parties, central banks and many others—are also covered by democratization studies. With the increasing spread and impact of globalization, and the ensuing tighter links between political and economic development and governance, external factors of democratization—such as regional, interregional and international organizations—also received attention, particularly within the framework of foreign-driven democratizations.

The focus on the external factors of democratization originated with Whitehead's *contagion theory* or Huntington's *snowballing concept* as a result of what is also referred to as the *demonstration effects of democratization*. They maintained that increase in one nation's level of democracy leads to increase in its neighbors' democracy while decrease may "infect" them and reduce their democraticness. Starr and Lindborg (2003) referred to the same idea as the *democratic diffusion* or the *democratic domino theory*. They added that at the end, global democracy as a whole could deteriorate, albeit at exponentially infinitesimal degrees at each successive domino (Leeson and Dean 2009). For others democratization by external pressure did not go beyond small countries with a weak international clout. Because such countries preferred to bandwagon in general, they would democratize as a result of their bigger neighbors' democratizing. Bigger countries with a stronger say in international politics, such as Russia and China, however, would tend to balance and consolidate against external factors of democratization (Mullerson 2009).

Multilateral institutions also came to the spotlight of democratization studies in the past few years. It was argued that, under favorable conditions, they could foster democracy by combating special interests, protecting individual and minority rights and facilitating collective deliberation (Keohane et al. 2009).[19] The *democratic functionalism theory*, for instance, maintained that democracy is part and parcel of the logic of European institution-building and governance process through mainly a collective learning process of democratization (Trenz and Eder 2004). Accordingly, the diffusion of democratic norms, principles and laws by the European Union (Dominguez 2010),[20] particularly through its political conditionality approach of *acquis communautaire* for candidate countries, was linked with democratization. Gherghina (2009) found that the prospects of access to the European Union along with economic development were the two major causes for successful democratization in the post-communist countries in Central and Eastern Europe. Tudoroiu (2010) also linked the democratization of the latter to the incentive schemes and strategies used by the Organization for Security and Cooperation in Europe (OSCE), the European Union's Europe Agreements and NATO's Partnership for Peace.

One must emphasize that the democratizing impact of external organizations has rarely been a uniform trend while the internal democracy of these very organizations has also been subject to fierce debate (Decker and Sonnicksen 2009).[21] Some scholars attributed the deficiencies of democratic consolidation in Central America to the outside influence of international economic actors and their collusion with the local oligarchies (Cannon and Hume 2012). The democratizing impact of the European Union has also been non-uniform across different non-eligible members, such as those in Latin America (Dominguez 2010).

External factors of democratization other than multilateral institutions, including particularly foreign-led and foreign-supported processes of democratization, were also highlighted in the recent democratization literature. They focused on the use of both peaceful and non-peaceful means of implanting and maintaining democratic governments. Foreign-supported democratization through "democracy assistance" or foreign-aid has often targeted governmental entities such as the parliament, the judiciary, national and local governments and civil society organizations. Given the increasing number of empirically relevant cases, democratization through the use of military force has also been analyzed.

Foreign-supported democratization through aid was found to work both positively and negatively for democratization. Knack (2004), for instance, found no significant relation between democracy aid and democratization in his multivariate analysis of 76 recipient nations over the 1975–2000 period. Savun and Tirone (2011), on the other hand, found that democracy aid decreases the risk of conflict by reducing the uncertainty of transitional elite-led pacts, and therefore plays a positive role in democratic transitions. They also found that democracy aid contributes positively to democratic consolidation, specifically through its impact on the strengthening of the parliament, judiciary and civil society. Sardamov (2005) and Hearn (2000) supported the thesis on the positive impact of foreign aid on democratization but questioned the over-reliance on local civil society organizations to deliver it effectively. McKoy and Miller (2012) linked the prospects for successful democratization not to foreign aid *per se* but to the donor's beliefs about the *policies* of the recipient country rather than its *values*.

Foreign-military-initiated democratic transitions received increasing attention starting with the United States' invasion of Iraq in 2003. Some focused on the positive liberalizing effects of this type of external democratization (Walker 2012). Others emphasized their downsides (Stradiotto and Guo 2010), often based on more recent empirical studies such as Haiti, where the intervention of the United States resulted in civil unrest and the quick collapse of the incipient democratic rule; and Afghanistan and Iraq, where the new governments still face legitimacy problems due mainly to internal, tribal and ethnic clashes. The studies on foreign-military-initiated democratization came to the consensus that although foreign interventions typically come with large sums of aid for rebuilding the target country, additional factors, such as a certain degree of national or cultural homogeneity, are needed for successful democratization.

Other actors of democratization that received attention in the past years are the national military and international migrants. Civil–military relations have been part of the democratization studies since Rouquié's (1987) seminal study on the role of the military in authoritarian regimes in Latin America. The importance of the civilian control of the military in the newly emerging democracies in Asia (Pion-Berlin 2011a, Chambers 2011, Croissant et al. 2012) and in Africa (Williamson 2010, Said 2012) as well as during democratic consolidation in Turkey (Harris 2011, Heper 2011, Pion-Berlin 2011b) and in Latin America (Mani 2011, Zirker et al. 2011) have been continuously stressed in the literature.

Migrants' role in transitions to democracy and its consolidation also received attention recently, albeit less so when compared to the other actors of democratization. Their direct impact on democratization worked through their role in diffusing knowledge, including about democratic ideas, norms and innovations (Perez-Armendariz and Crow 2010). Their indirect impact on democratization worked through their remittances and their impact, therefore, on poverty alleviation (Brinkerhoff 2012). The overall consensus among scholars was that the supporting structures such as state-supported macroeconomic policies, local integration and linkages of migrants with civil society were important factors in ensuring that migrants contribute to democratization positively rather than negatively (Popkin 2003).

Outer Circles of Structure: How Does Economics Affect Democratization?

Our analysis of the democratization literature from the 1950s to our days through the analytical tool of the Concentric Circles of Democratization demonstrate that democratization as a concept and a field of study is grounded in economics. Often, the same economic variables are related to democratization in contradictory ways due to their dissimilar conceptualization and operationalization by different scholars. In linking inequality to democratization, for instance, Przeworski et al. (1996) differentiated among three measures of inequality: (i) the Gini coefficient; (ii) the total income gap between the richest and the poorest ten percent of the population; and (iii) income produced in manufacturing that accrues to the income of workers. They found only the latter to matter for democratization.

The different definitions of democratization also determined the direction of the relationship posited between it and economic variables. Acemoglu and Robinson (2006) argued that democratization is more likely when inequality is at middling levels because they defined democratization as a function of the autocratic elites' fear of the extent to which a future median voter would redistribute votes under different levels of structural socioeconomic inequality. Ansell and Samuels (2010), on the other hand, defined democratization as a function of the demands for protection directed to the state by the rising economic groups. This definition yielded that land and income inequality are what together determine democratization: Autocracies with equal land distribution were predicted to democratize, but contrary to the conventional wisdom, income inequality was found to promote democratization in contexts with equal land distribution.

Other scholars made economic rights part of their definition of a democracy refusing to restrict the latter to a procedural understanding where only competitive elections or political participation mattered. Such an assumption influenced their assessment of the relationship between economic development, distribution, inequality and democratization. Others, in contrast, argued that non-political rights can easily be provided by non-democracies or that many would not protest against the lack of political rights provided that they are prosperous and receive efficient public services. Habermas (1996) summarized the lack of the relationship between economic and democratic logics when he said that "in principle, the constitutional state and the welfare state can be implemented without democracy" (78).

Some of the economic concepts and variables linked—positively, negatively or neutrally—to democratization, both in its transitional and consolidation phases and its variants of democratic quality, included: economic development, prosperity and growth; economic inequalities; and economic crises and reforms.

Economic Development, Prosperity and Growth
It was the father of the modernization theory, Lipset (1959, 1960) who said that "the more well-to-do a nation, the greater the chances that it will sustain democracy" (75, 48–50). For Lipset, economic development and industrialization led to social conditions that were conducive to the establishment and maintenance of a democracy. Przeworski's dictum (2000) that "no democracy ever fell in a country with a per capita income higher than that of Argentina in 1975, that is $6,055 per 1985 purchasing power parity dollars" gave some concrete figures in terms of the needed economic development for making democratic consolidation certain and democratic breakdowns unlikely. Although at first Przeworski maintained that economic development does not lead to the emergence but only to the stability of democratic regimes, many scholars demonstrated

linkages between economic development and the emergence of democracy, i.e., democratic transitions (Feng and Zak 1999, Gill 2000, Epstein et al. 2006, Wucherpfenning and Deutsch 2009).

Despite voluminous work on economic prosperity and democracy, the links posited between the two were seldom consensual. Some scholars maintained that economic development leads to democratization, in its various phases and types—transition, consolidation, longevity and/or quality. Others added that the reverse was true as well, that poor countries tend to become undemocratic because of the links between poverty, and malfunctioning bureaucracies and corruption. Some disagreed. They claimed that that economic development, particularly if delayed, could deter democratization, again in its various forms and stages. Some maintained that economic development both engenders and prevents democratization depending on the country's starting level of economic development. Others upgraded the notion of economic development to human development, and linked the latter to democratization, not economic development (Diamond 1992).[22]

Among those who believed that higher economic development leads to democratization, income was among the most significant determinants, particularly when compared to explanatory variables affected by income such as education, or social variables such as ethno-linguistic homogeneity (Przeworski 2006). Higher income brackets and affluent societies were associated with democratic regimes while lower income brackets and poor societies went hand-in-hand with authoritarian types of governance. This relationship was verified empirically except for the interwar period in Germany, India, Mongolia and some oil-rich Arab countries (Stradiotto and Guo 2010).

Among the scholars who argued that higher economic development does not lead to democratization were de Mesquita and Downs (2005). They pointed to China where economic development has not been matched by democratization so far, at least at the national level. Acemoglu et al. (2008) also showed weak correlations between income and the likelihood of democratic transitions, and a strong correlation between income and democratic breakdowns. Acemoglu and Robinson (2006) demonstrated that relatively prosperous countries with a relatively equal distribution of resources can have stable authoritarian regimes instead of democracy.

Among the scholars who maintained that economic development leads to both democratization and authoritarianism were Lipset et al. (1993). They argued that the relationship between economic growth and authoritarianism was an N-curve. Economic growth in poor and lower income countries led to democratization as did growth in high income countries, specifically those above $6,000 per 1992 purchasing power parity dollars. However, those countries in the mid-levels of development were more likely to note regress in democratization as a result of further growth.

Some scholars distinguished economic growth from economic development. They argued that the rate of economic development, and not economic development *per se*, made the difference in terms of successful democratic patterns and outcomes. They maintained that rising living standards, growth of private ownership and increased industrialization were found to be conducive to democratization. Evans and Whitefield (1995) found that higher economic growth rates were associated with higher democratic quality and longevity. Barro (1999) associated the increasing rate of economic growth with the "gradual rise in democracy" and the decreasing rate of economic growth with the "breakdown of democracy." Acemoglu and Robinson (2006), on the other hand, determined that the countries that have grown faster in the past 25–30 years have not become more democratic.

Economic Inequalities
One of the most influential economic variables to influence democratization was income inequality or the Gini coefficient, which measures the ratio of incomes to top-to-bottom-quintile. Przeworski et al. (1996) concluded that "democracy is much more likely to survive in countries where income inequality is declining over time." They found that "the expected life of democracy in countries with shrinking inequality is about 84 years, while the expected life of democracies with rising income inequality is about 22 years (299)." Boix (2003) demonstrated that higher levels of economic equality and capital mobility promote democratic consolidation whereas higher levels of inequality foment political instability, thereby increasing the likelihood of transitions to democracy. Lower levels of inequality, in turn, were found to lead to the prevalence of authoritarian regimes (Muller and Seligson 1987, Alesina and Perotti 1996).

Przeworski (2004) agreed with Boix (2003) that democracy is more likely in countries with declining inequality, but underlined a different inequality measure: the labor share of value added in manufacturing. He found that democracies are four times more likely to survive in countries where this share is greater than 25 percent. Ansell and Samuels (2010), on the other hand, pointed at land inequality as the most important determinant of democratization. They maintained that income inequality is more likely to promote democratization in authoritarian contexts where land is distributed more or less equally. Still others found no relation between income inequality and democracy (Bollen and Jackman 1985).

Acemoglu and Robinson (2006) also linked economics and democracy both positively and negatively. Their curve had an inverse U-shape, and linked inequality, defined more comprehensively in terms of a society's assets, and not just income or land inequality, with the two separate stages of democratization. Higher structural inequality increased the chances of democratic transitions in very unequal contexts but decreased the chances of consolidation in initially equal settings. Boix (2003) explained the lack of democratization in oil-rich Arab countries by combining agency-driven analysis with structural analysis. He included both income equality and asset-specificity in his analysis. He argued that the dominance of the largely immobile economic assets that are easy to tax, make the Arab elite feel threatened by the perceived cost of a potential democratization.

Economic Crises and Reforms

More recent studies defined democratic transitions as a strategic response to weak economic conditions and pointed at economic downturns and crises—not economic development, growth or growth rate—as precipitators of democratization.[23] Haggard and Kaufman (1995, 1997) were two pioneers in linking economic crisis with democratization. Arguing that not the strategic elite negotiations *per se* but the economic resources and interests of the pact-making elites are the primary drivers of democratization, they examined the impact of sudden economic downturns on the bargaining power of authoritarian incumbents and pro-democracy opposition leaders. Comparing democratic transitions that occurred during economic crises versus those that took place during economic prosperity and growth, they found that the former does not cause but intensifies the rifts among the authoritarian elite, thereby increasing the relative strength of the opposition, and the likelihood of successful democratic transitions.[24]

While agreeing with the above assessment of the impact of economic incentives of pact-makers on democratic transitions, Yap (2012, 2013) found democratization over the long run in Taiwan, South Korea and the Philippines was better explained by political trust rather than material interests. Kalinowski (2007) found that economic crises might trigger democratic transitions but they hamper established democracies even though the latter are better able to manage the crises than are authoritarian regimes. Others argued the opposite and found democracies to breed economic and financial crises due ironically to some of their intrinsically democratic attributes, i.e., their transparency, frequent executive turnover, openness to international markets, credible commitment, capacity and financial freedoms (Lipscy 2011).[25]

The nature of the relationship between economic crises and democratization is certainly not a black or white debate. Gasiorowski (1995) demonstrated that economic crises can both encourage and discourage democratic transitions and consolidation depending on the type and degree of the crisis, and the kind of sociopolitical crisis they may or may not ignite. Freedman (2005) put emphasis on the impact of the internal political dynamics, coalition-making trends and leadership factors in determining the nature of the impact of economic crises on democratization. Tedesco (2002) and Kiki (2008) showed the inseparability of factors that lead to economic crises from those that also cause political instability.

Many scholars focused on the solution rather than the problem. They dwelled on specific economic policies undertaken to respond to the economic crises when assessing the overall impact on democratization. The "shock therapy" approach of economic policy making typical of belt-tightening neoliberal models of development were found to be incompatible with political democracy because their closed-door technocratic decision-making styles were intrinsically exclusive (Naím 1994). Others went further to claim that "unbridled markets and democracy are not natural partners" (Chang 2007). Conversely, others measured and found economic liberalism to be a strong associate of transitions to democracy, but less of consolidation measured as starting after ten years following the end of the transitional period (Rode and Gwartney 2012).

More specific economic policies of welfare, unemployment, women's inclusion into the labor force and the availability of adequate financing for small and medium enterprises as well as the relative weight of pro-business versus social policies and their implementation were also linked to democratization (Fishman 2010). Whether the economy relied on oil-based or other extracted industry revenues and the associated labor scarcity leading the country to import foreign laborers led to triangular arguments about the abundance of natural resources, increased immigration and the often negative outcomes for democratic transitions (Bearce and Hutnick 2011).

The sequencing of political and economic reforms was also a big item in the democratization literature of the past two decades. Modernization scholars had long argued that economic development precedes democratization. Yet scholars in the late 1990s and the 2000s often adopted the "democracy first, development later" approach (Halperin et al. 2005). Accordingly, better protection of property rights in democracies was seen as a consequence, and not a cause of higher economic growth (Leblang 1996). The free flow of information and transparent policy making also worked to eliminate economic asymmetries more easily than under authoritarian regimes where opacity was the rule. Last but not least, it was argued that the relatively higher rates of social expenditures during economic hardships helped economies recover faster in democracies (Brown and Hunter 1999). The move was thus toward a more eclectic approach. Sociopolitical norms and institutions, particularly state reconstruction, thus gained in importance as possible movers of economic reforms that are needed for democratic consolidation (Linz and Stepan 1996: 11).

Outmost Layers of Culture: What Legacies
Influence Democratization?

Transitologists focused exclusively on strategic elite bargaining in which each actor carefully weighed costs and benefits associated with continued allegiance to the authoritarian regime versus defection given an imminent breakdown of the authoritarian regime and the uncertainty about its aftermath. Many scholars criticized that the choices that the actors made were assumed to reflect their attitude *ipso facto*. The main criticism concentrated on the absence of analysis regarding the factors that determined why the elite made the choices they did to start with. Those scholars followed the historical approach adopted by Moore (1966) and Skocpol (1985) to show that the choices themselves were grounded historically, and determined by the structures within which the elite operated.

In addition to the perceived need to understand how preferences were formed, there were several other reasons for the post-transitology move back to the outer circles of culture. For once, it became empirically clear that the procedural move toward electoral systems and constitution-writing did not equate to democratic transitions. A multitude of adjectives were added to the term of democracy to try to decipher the new regime breed that sprouted across the globe since the first wave of democratizations in Western Europe and North America in the 1800s. Collier and Levitsky (1996) identified over 550 examples of adjectives qualifying democracies including those that do not employ the term "democracy," such as hybrid regimes, semi-competitive polity and partially illiberal regimes, to name a few.

The increasingly detailed analyses of democracy types and subtypes were the first signs of scholars' realization that democratization was not a dichotomous event with clear-cut thresholds from its beginnings to its later stages. Instead, it was more adequately conceived as a continuous process carried out by a multitude of actors with irrational preferences and sticky institutions. In such process, institutionalized "gray zones" between dictatorship and liberal democracy (Carothers 2002) could persist, even though multiparty and electoral politics were present and functioning fairly well. In fact, certain types and degrees of liberalization could be used as autocratic means to limit full-fledged democratization (Karl 2005). It was thus understood that to better assess democratization, a history-driven account was needed.

In explaining history-led democratization, scholars put emphasis on a plethora of factors, including the nature of the previous regime (Linz and Stepan 1996), its coercive capacity,[26] whether the country in question has had a prior democratic experience, whether there was a healthy balance of power among the components associated with democracy such as electoral competitiveness, contestation, civil rights, social, political and economic rights, and the autonomy of governmental entities, civil society and organizations in the social, economic and political sectors. Often the cases analyzed from this perspective were hybrid regimes. The goal was to account for the deviance and understand how and why it occurred.

The outmost layers of concentric circles of democratization often examined the democratization experiences of such cases ranging from Azerbaijan and Turkmenistan in the Caspian Sea basin to Cambodia in Southeast Asia and Nigeria in West Africa. Much like Hagopian did in the case of Latin America in the 1990s, Carnegie (2012) argued that the legacies of the authoritarian rule and the discriminatory practices of the colonial period persisted in the post-election period in Indonesia. Mamdani (1997) did the same in Africa where colonial legacies promoted ethnic rivalries to set one group against another, thereby justifing the authoritarian state. *Façade* or *sham democracy* were terms used to refer to the cases where histori-cally ingrained authoritarian habits of mind coexisted with elections, as in Algeria, Jordan and Egypt (Milton-Edwards 1993). *Tutelage* or *guided democracy* or *borderline democracy* denoted system-wise dem-ocratic regimes where certain groups, like the military, kept anti-democratic privileges, as in post-1990 Chile and, until recently, Turkey (Rabkin 1992).[27]

The move back to the outer circles of democratization was galva-nized by the perceived need to re-emphasize political culture, state legacy and history. A "renaissance of political culture" (Inglehart 1988) took place as economic and institutional explanations failed to fully capture democratization experiences. (Granato 1996,[28] Jackman and Miller 1996).[29] Whether in influencing the structure and func-tioning of institutions or shaping the actions of leaders in mobilizing civil society, political culture was seen as a significant factor for both the onset and the sustainability of democratization. Economic growth, crisis and inequality variables thus gave way to nationalism and ethnicity as important drivers of democratization. History-led analyses of democratization also put emphasis on the scope, types and the sequencing of rights that democratization processes should cover. Religion and democracy linkages were also stressed. In the same way that the economic variables' relation to democratization went both ways, these socially constructed phenomena were also linked both positively and negatively to democratization.

On the positive side, national sovereignty was seen as a precondi-tion of democratization (Caspersen 2011). Nationalism, in the sense of collective identity, shared legacies and an imagined community (Anderson 1991) was found to co-exist with democracy (Rowley 2012). Taylor (1999) argued that nationalism contributed to democ-ratization by fostering debate in civil society (141). Yack (2001) claimed that national identity strengthens popular sovereignty, which lies at the core of any democracy (517). On the negative side, scholars stressed that it was not nationalism that breeds democracy but democracy that generates national unity. Still others maintained that the two are not always related to each other or that they could be negatively interlinked. Denk and Silander (2012) showed that democracy almost always transpired as result of ethnic cleansing. Keyman and Kanci (2011) gave accounts of nationalism associated with ethnic upsurge and irrational behavior.

Different variants and degrees of nationalism were shown to interact differently with democratization (Helbling 2009).[30] *Civic nationalism* based on territoriality, for instance, was associated positively with democratization while *ethno-nationalism* based on kinship ties was linked negatively with it (Resler 1997, Snyder 2000, Berglund et al. 2001). Yet, other research showed that the ethnicity factor does not have to hamper democratization since it can be controlled through economic development as well as policy (Mousseau 2001). Supporting evidence came from the cases of post-Soviet Estonia and Ukraine (Surzhko-Harned 2010).

Different brands of nationalism were associated with the different phases of democratization. For instance, nationalism, including its ethno-variants, was found to be useful for democratic transitions in terms of their contributions to building unity and solidarity (Surzhko-Harned 2010). Bunce (2003) argued that nationalism can benefit democratization if nationalist mobilizations begin at the time when the authoritarian regime is weak (Bunce 2003). Democratic consolidation often was linked with post-nationalism, or loyalty and adherence to constitutions (Spinner 2008). Other scholars found nationalism to contribute effectively to both phases of democratization through two factors: *stateness* defined as the ability of the state to formulate and implement policies independently (Nettl 1968), and inclusive decision making to stimulate and integrate the formerly inactive social and political groups.

In addition to nationalism, history-led perspectives on democratization also prioritized the debate over rights and their relation to democratization. They emphasized two issues among others. First, whether liberalization, defined as extended civil and personal liberties, should precede procedural democracy and political participation as it did in Western Europe at the time of the first wave of democratization, or whether it should succeed it. Scholars questioned whether political participation should be seen as an end in itself or as a means to protect one's civil liberties (Held 2006: 231). Opting for the latter, many claimed that democratization is jeopardized simply because political participation happens before the extension of liberties (Denk 2012).

The second issue stressed by the history-led democratization scholars concerned the question of whether civil rights should be complemented with political, social, economic and human rights in defining and progressing toward democracy. The emphasis on the rule of the people in defining democratization, shifted from representation through universal suffrage to inclusive participation, and from there to mutual consultation and individual rights and freedom. Tilly (2007) characterized democracy as "a regime where the political relations between the state and its citizens feature broad, equal, protected and mutually binding consultation" (14). Article Twenty-Five of The International Covenant on Civil and Political Rights (ICCPR) adopted by the United Nations General Assembly in 1966, emphasized the role of elections, not for civic participation or consultation *per se*, but to ensure the accountability of representatives for the exercise of their legislative and executive powers. It underlined that citizen's participation in the conduct of public affairs must be supported by freedom of expression, assembly and association.

A parallel issue to the question of the weight and timing of the rights in the democratization process was whether individual freedoms were sufficient to instigate and maintain democracies, or whether socioeconomic equality and the associated distributive policies should also be part of democratization (Arat 1991, 1999, Acemoglu and Robinson 2006, Boix 2003). These are important distinctions in terms of their implications for democratization since "*freedom* calls for a government that governs least; and *equality*, for a government that governs most" (Barzun 1989).

Last but not least, religion and democracy have been an unavoidable pair in the outer circles of democratization. Religions that prescribe a holistic view of society, such as Catholicism, Orthodoxy and Islam were often claimed to restrict the emergence and development of civil liberties and liberal democracies. Dating back to Weber's *Protestant Ethic and the Spirit of Capitalism* (1905), scholars made different associations between belief systems and democracy. Weber had found Protestantism to lead to democracy particularly through its emphasis on hard work, frugality and efficiency. Other scholars attributed democratic values to Catholic doctrines only after the Second Vatican Council and the Church's changed focus on human rights and economic development in the 1960s (Wiarda 1981, Novak 1989, Troy 2009). For Huntington, the third wave of democratization in Southern Europe in the 1970–80s was proof of the synergy between Christianity, Western values and liberal democracy.

Confucianism did not bode well with democracy according to Pye (1988, 1999) mainly because of its focus on rigid hierarchies and unquestioned compliance with authority. Islam also was often depicted as being inherently un- or anti-democratic due, inter alia, to its overemphasis on the afterlife, its strict Sharia principles governing state matters, the original tax system, which failed to protect property rights, and the *waqf*,[31] whose rigidity hampered the development of civil society and private commercial enterprises (Kuran 2013). According to Kuran, these institutions contributed to high corruption, low trust, and widespread nepotism sustaining autocracies and making democracies unstable.

In all of the above religion–democracy linkages, studies of both qualitative and quantitative nature demonstrated that there can be both democratic and undemocratic traits in every belief system at different points in time, and in their different applications in numerous contexts. Ackerly (2005) argued for the democratic traits of Confucianism explaining how Confucian political thought allows for public spaces, political interaction and contestation. Keqian (2006) specified the Confucian values of moderation, rectitude, objectivity, sincerity, honesty and propriety toward democratization in Asia. Likewise, Minkenberg (2007) showed that Islam was not the reason for the lack of democratization—patriarchal orders, geopolitical and regional factors were.

CONCLUSION

Subjecting democratization literature to the concentric circles model teaches us two things among others, which can reconfigure the way we think about, and study democratization. First, it is clear that democratization was often seen as an upshot of economic development at its birth, and has been studied predominantly from structural perspectives all along. The short-lived mind-driven analyses of the 1950s, the ephemeral interest-groups approaches of the 1970s and the relatively longer but still limited focus on agency-led democratization of the 1980s have been dwarfed by the explanations given by economic development, class analysis, state capacity and state-society relations, institutional development, historical legacies and culture. Contrary to the overwhelming criticism raised against the transitology literature from the mid-1990s onward for taking a one-sided view of democratization as elite games with static preferences, there might be still unearthed relations and key areas of significance to examine at this individual level of analysis.

Second, agency-driven democratization seems to follow a cookbook recipe. It is mainly concerned with defining, refuting and then redefining and further debating the dosages of certain ingredients needed for a good start, the right temperature for a thorough cooking, and the adequate timing and degree of heating for a well-cooked democracy. Since it is ubiquitously acknowledged that each country has its own national cuisine, thus different recipes with different ingredients, dosages, temperatures and cooking periods, the aims of the scholars to standardize the recipe focus mostly on the main ingredient, i.e., elections, and the actions of the cook in preparing the meal—breakdown, transition, consolidation, quality of democracy, rather than a complete list of the necessary ingredients or preparation methods and seasoning. There might be value in examining the ingredients and finding those common spices which act as the significant catalysts throughout the cooking process—from start to end. The increasingly salient emphasis on the eclecticism of the approaches and methodologies of democratization studies since the 1990s also point to this need.

A policy-driven approach to democratization can be just what is needed to realize the shift in focus from the constituent to the catalytic ingredients. Whether one chooses to define democratization through elite-led pacts, civil society movements, state structures, economic development, historical legacies or cultural change, and regardless of whether the case in question is one of a newly emerging democracy or the consolidation of existing democratic institutions and norms, three common catalytic ingredients manifest themselves across all layers and phases of democratization: transparency, accountability and corruption control.

Comparing different policies aimed at democratization through these common policy areas can help illuminate how they shape democratization differently in similar structural contexts, and how they produce similar outcomes in dissimilar contexts. In addition to asking when transitions occur and through what kinds of dynamics, one may question whether states enacting and effectively enforcing transparency policies early on achieve better democratization outcomes over the long run. Likewise, it would be pertinent to examine if better results in terms of increased legitimacy, higher participation and enhanced trust ensue if accountability politics are made explicit parts of democratization reforms in their initial stages and continuously from then on. One can also wonder if anti-corruption laws, policies and institutions should be considered only to enhance the quality of democratic regimes, or if they can also be effective for democratic transitions and consolidation as opposed to a truncated emphasis on elections first, procedural institutions second and corruption control last.

The oikeiosis idea as the foundation of *cosmopolitan ethics* implies drawing people in from the outer to the inner circles. The oikeiosis idea of democratization as the basis of *substantive democratization* also implies that the presence and degree of transparency, accountability and corruption affect citizens' everyday lives; not elections or some other milestone event deemed theoretically significant for democratization. To put it differently, one can debate whether elections are or are not enough for democratization to occur, or what type of institutions or level of economic development or equality are required for minimum or maximum levels of democracy. But it would be highly improbable to disagree on the importance of transparency, accountability and control of corruption for democratization—across all phases and degrees.

Making transparent policy making, accountable governance and corruption control integral parts of the democratization projects, legally, institutionally and early on, can be the "substantive minimums" of (effective) democracies—in the same way that elections are the "procedural minimums" of (electoral) democracies. The next three chapters examine the definitions, applications and limitations of these three democratic catalysts or the substantive minimums—transparency, accountability and corruption control—in democratization. The idea is to emphasize and relate the common ingredients of democratization processes across all layers of the concentric circles model and, doing that, to bridge public administration and politics together.

CHAPTER 2

———◆◆◆———

THE TRANSPARENCY TRIANGLE:
DIFFERENTIATING INPUTS, OUTPUTS
AND OUTCOMES

Transparency is not a commonly studied concept in either political science or public administration, especially when compared to the voluminous research on democratization, accountability and corruption. Its entry into the social sciences lexicon can be traced back to the end of the Cold War in the 1990s and the third wave of democratization. The concomitant formation of the European institutions and the renewed interest in state at around the same time also contributed to the increased saliency of transparency in policy circles and the academia. As a result and with time, information disclosure and dissemination of data to citizens were hailed as significant tools for fighting corruption (Ball 2009). As a matter of fact, government transparency was first defined as a possible means of controlling corruption (Mauro 1995, Ades and Di Tella 1999, Sandholtz and Koetzle 2000, Treisman 2000, Montinola and Jackman 2002).

Starting as an anti-corruption tool, the understanding and applications of transparency were extended and elaborated with time. Transparency was recognized to be a multifaceted value, norm and policy for governing, including but not limited to controlling corruption. This expansion and deepening of the meaning of the term went hand in hand with its increasing association with accountability. In later stages, transparency was seen as both a necessary step to accountability, and its consequence. In its fullest sense, it was defined as citizens' control over policy and decision making toward legitimate and effective governance, encompassing corruption control, law, order and bureaucratic quality, among other things (Knack and Keefer 1995).

The pairing of transparency with accountability often occurred within the larger framework of good governance. Often, it was also through the good governance paradigm that transparency was linked indirectly with democratization. The few direct linkages posited between transparency and democratization were either theoretical, thus without sufficient empirical evidence, or were confined to the cases of transitional democracies equated with electoral politics. It is thus safe to conclude that transparency has not been a direct concern either for democratization scholars or for democratizers in the field. It emerged and stayed as one of the many items on the list of public administrators who wanted to streamline administration, maintain credibility and join the "right to information" bandwagon at the end of the 1990s and the beginning of the 2000s.

This chapter attempts to fill in the transparency lacuna in democratization and public administration literatures by drawing a definitional map of the term. Doing that, it aims to go beyond the dominating debate about its often overestimated positive and underestimated negative attributes, and understand transparency for what it is. The conflated understanding of transparency is disentangled through the "transparency triangle" shown in Figure 2.1. The triangle is a didactic tool that differentiates among the *inputs* of transparency, i.e., its possible causes and catalysts; its *outputs*, i.e., its various definitions, types, policies and legislation; and its *outcomes*, i.e., its potential and actual impact on democratization. The relationship between transparency and democratization is also illuminated through a matrix of direct-indirect and positive-negative linkages.

INPUTS OF TRANSPARENCY: WHAT LEADS TO TRANSPARENCY?

Possible causes and drivers of transparency can be distinguished from sector to sector. In the public realm, Stirton and Lodge (2001) defined four mechanisms to make the public sector more transparent: *voice*,

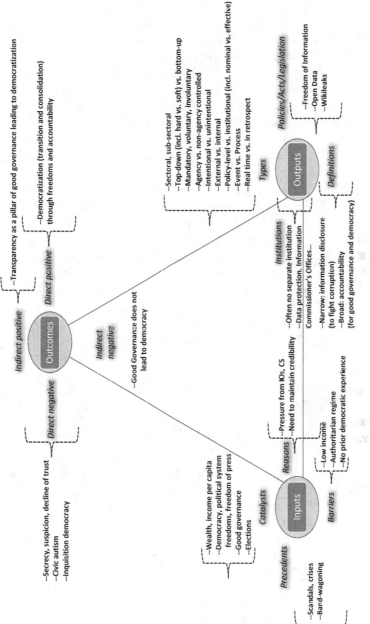

Figure 2.1 Transparency Triangle

representation, information and *choice*. Public organizations first had to give *voice* to their citizens and allow their effective *representation* in the processes of designing and creating public services. They then had to provide effective *information* to citizens and their organizations, and offer them *choices* of public services. In the economic domain, higher wealth and standards of living were associated with increasing transparency. In the political realm, the factors that lead to transparency could be of domestic or international origins. At the domestic level, structural causes such as regime type, political system, prior level of democracy, including particularly the freedoms of expression and press were deemed important. A culture of democracy was also stressed as providing a propitious context for transparency to emerge, develop and persist. Instrumentally, elections were examined as a possible enabler for transparency. At the international level, the acts and actions of international and regional organizations were emphasized as important promoters of transparency. At both the domestic and international spheres, scandals and crises of all types and different magnitudes were found to precede the adoption of transparency policies, acts and laws.

From a political perspective, transparency was often associated with new or established democracies as opposed to non-democratic settings. Preliminary research suggested that transparency can be unproductive or inconsequential in non-democracies, which were often defined by the absence of contested elections (Malesky 2012). Among democracies, the type of the democratic political system was a determinant of transparency (Geddes and Neto 1992). In a given democratic system, if the legislature is controlled by a political party other than the one controlling the executive, as often happens in the United States, it was found that the legislature would be more amenable to adopt transparency laws. In contrast, in democratic systems where the same political party holds the majority in both the legislature and the executive, as in the United Kingdom, transparency policies would be less likely to be adopted by the parliament (Blanton 2002).[1] The forty-year difference between the initial adoption of the Freedom of Information Laws between the United States (1960s) and the United Kingdom (2000s) illustrates the plausibility of this argument (Finkelstein 2000).

Elections were linked with transparency in the democratization literature. Electoral incentives, and particularly economic voting, were found to be highly correlated with greater openness in democracies (Rosendorff and Doces 2006). For Hollyer et al. (2011) transparency would be the result of elections regardless of whether the latter were conducted in a transparent fashion or not. For others, the transparency of elections itself was a determining factor for both the transparency of the system overall and for good governance in the newly democratizing states (Debrah 2011). Transparency was conceived therefore as both an intrinsic and an extrinsic attribute of elections, which could lead to new or more transparency later on.

From an economic perspective, it was argued that it is relatively easier for wealthier countries to adopt and implement transparency laws and regulations because of the relatively lower cost of gathering and disseminating the required information (Kaufman and Siegelbaum 1997, Hellman and Kaufman 2001). Another asserted linkage consisted of the psychology of governance: during economic booms, governments have the confidence to disclose information as opposed to times of economic deterioration when they become defensive and secretive unless transparency has been institutionalized previously (Grigorescu 2003). From the standpoint of these economic and psychological links, participation in capacity development programs was also associated positively with increasing transparency in recipient countries. Overall, lower income and lower democracy levels meant lower degrees of transparency.

From a cultural perspective, political traditions and bureaucratic systems that included transparency and accountability as local practices were associated with higher transparency. Cultures and historical legacies with highly centralized and discretionary power, low trust, endemic corruption and exclusive decision-making processes were associated with low public transparency. To provide some empirical examples, Indonesia's Dutch colonial legacy and weak democratic traditions were deemed to be at the root of the consistent lack of effective transparency there (Kristiansen et al. 2008). In Kenya, it was the externally imposed transparency rules linked with ineffective vertical accountability (Githinji and Holmquist 2012). Right before the start of the civil war, Syria's culture of corruption was said to perpetuate artificial transparency to the detriment of long-term political and economic reform there (Borshchevskaya 2010). In the case of Samoa, Amosa (2010) maintained that the embracing of the local practices of governance led to higher transparency and accountability there.

At the international level, the transparency of international or regional organizations such as the United Nations, World Bank, International Monetary Fund, the Organization for Economic Cooperation and Development (OECD), the European Union, the Council of Europe, and the Organization for Security and Cooperation in Europe (OSCE), to name a few, was found to be instrumental in increasing the transparency of the member or to-be-member governments. It was shown that the increased transparency and the adoption of information disclosure policies by these organizations put more pressure on the national governments to do the same. Even though the areas of information flow have been narrow and limited to a few policy areas, such as defense budget (NATO), and economic and environmental data (IMF), the transfer of information from national governments to international organizations has increased over the years in tandem with the increased demands for transparency in the running of these organizations (Florini 1998, Mitchell 1998, Grigorescu 2003). Often, national governments have released the requested information to their citizens after having conveyed it to the pertinent international or regional organizations since not doing so would jeopardize their credibility.

Social, political and economic crises and scandals, of domestic or international origin, were stressed as the most immediate factors preceding the actual adoption of transparency clauses. Grigorescu (2007) claimed that the higher the impact and the visibility of the scandal, the more immediate is the adoption of the freedom of information acts and laws domestically. A sizeable scandal was found to precede the establishment of an internal control system, change to the access-to-information rules and other means to improve the efficiency and the legitimacy of governments and government agencies. To provide some empirical examples, the United States' freedom of information law came into effect as a result of the protests spurred by the Vietnam War and the Watergate scandal at the end of the 1960s. The 1997 Asian economic crisis led to the adoption of the freedom of information law in Thailand. The 1998 United Nations' Security Council Report, which revealed South Africa's sale of weapons to Angola despite a UN embargo, brought forth the increased dissemination of defense information in South Africa, which then adopted its first comprehensive freedom of information law in 2000.

In Romania, the precursor to the 2001 access to information legislation was also a domestic environmental crisis that led to a European Union task force investigating the Romanian officials' response. Romania was quick to adopt a transparency law to prevent its citizens from obtaining information from the European institutions. The institutionalization of transparency in Romania went parallel to the European Union's own strengthening of transparency in the wake of the 1999 financial mismanagement and corruption scandal of the European Commission (Grigorescu 2003). The Aarhus Convention on Access to Information, Public Participation in Decision-making and Access to Justice in Environmental Matters was held and enacted in 1998, and entered into effect in 2001.[2] The European Transparency Initiative of 2004 followed this chain of administrative reforms. The United Kingdom made its Parliament subject to its 2000 Freedom of Information Act as late as in 2009 when the expenses scandal of several members of the House of Commons damaged the public trust in legislative delegates (Kelso 2009).

Overall, the two main barriers to transparency have been: (i) barriers to access information; and (ii) government agencies' resistance to disclosure. In general, large and wealthy international organizations and national governments that deal with a few and technical issues and work with a multitude of transnational and national non governmental organizations were deemed more likely to have public information disclosure policies as opposed to those that have less resources, and work on multiple, complex and political matters without or scanty involvement of the non-profit sector (Peters 1989, Abbott and Snidal 1998: 10, Barnett and Finnemore 2004).[3]

OUTPUTS OF TRANSPARENCY: DEFINITIONS, TYPES, POLICIES, INSTITUTIONS

Definitions

At its emergence in the 1990s, transparency referred to the need to report data and information with the aim to address corruption (Cooper 2004, Lewis and Gilman 2005). The documents pertaining to the founding of the European Union, the General Agreement on Tariffs and Trade and Transparency International, defined transparency as sharing information about results, policies and findings (Cooper and Yoder 2002, Holzner and Holzner 2006). The transparency in political and policy studies was defined more specifically as a government's willingness and ability to disseminate policy-relevant data, including policy decisions, results and processes (Stasavage 2003). More analytically, it was understood to be "the ability of actor B to receive information from actor A, even when A is not offering it" (Grigorescu 2007: 626). The full range of factors that affect the information flow, including its accuracy, reliability, timeliness, accessibility, consistency and regularity, were broadly referred to as transparency (Mitchell 1998, Vishwanath and Kaufman 1999, Heard-Laureote 2007, Neyland 2007).

With time, operations and processes that *lead to* policies and results, and not just the policies and results themselves, were deemed important for transparency. That is how and when transparency came to be associated with accountability. Transparency as such was defined as a means to achieve the accountability of any organization (March and Olsen 1994, Florini 2002)—since policy processes were key to evaluating the relevant institutions and keeping them accountable for their performance and responsibilities (Florini 1999, Bellver and Kaufman 2005). The 1994 Summit of the Organization of American States and the 1997 Convention of the Organization for Economic Cooperation and Development against Bribery and Corruption started using transparency in tandem with accountability to ensure "credible conflict-of-interest policies, open preparation and execution of budget, participation of citizens in the formulation and implementation of public policies, and the creation of official accounts of decision making through open meetings and citizen oversight of the government" (Hollyer et al. 2011: 296).

In this broader understanding, transparency was not a black or white issue of giving out or retaining such and such information. It was a continuum from supreme secrecy, where no one outside the government circle could know about anything, to public meetings where nothing would be spared to open communication (Florini 2002). Transparency, in this sense, was equated with the "legal, political, institutional structures that make information available about the internal characteristics of government and societies through free press, open government, public hearings and healthy and effective civil society" (Finel and Lord 1999: 316).

Linking the narrow and the broad understandings of transparency together, Stone (2002) conjured it as a metaphor or symbol for a host of ideas, indicating and interlinking four components. First, it indicated that a problem existed: corruption. Second, it offered a solution: information, offered through open decision making, meetings and actions. Third, it contributed to the creation of formal and informal accountability. Fourth, it became an all-purpose value to incorporate in all policies and policy-making processes, including design and formulation, implementation, monitoring and evaluation. Scholars thus broadened the meaning of transparency, moving it from a simple anti-corruption tool and greater accountability mechanism to an attribute of policy making.

The move from the narrow information disclosure focus to the broader open decision making structures of transparency raised questions about its supply and demand dimensions. Fung (2013) maintained that democratic transparency involved four consecutive steps: *information disclosure, information quality, access to information and usage of information.* First, government had to provide adequate information about its operations and actions. Then, such information had to be made readily available. Third, the information had to be organized and provided in accessible ways, and last but not least, the supporting sociopolitical and economic structures had to allow citizens to act on the available and intelligible information.

It was emphasized that the quantity of information that is made public does not equal transparency if the information is irrelevant, low quality, invalid, unverifiable and untimely (Martin and Feldman 1998) or if its access by the public is limited. In this sense, meaningful transparency was deemed to transpire not when governments provided such information, but when the public understood and acted on it (Piotrowski and Van Ryzin 2007, Maguire 2011, Grimmelikhuijsen 2012).

From a disciplinary perspective, different definitions of transparency were offered. In legal studies, transparency was a form of regulation which pressured organizations to reveal certain data (Etzioni 2010, Shkabatur 2012). In political science, government transparency meant the existence of institutions and policies that allowed citizens to gain access to government information (Otenyo and Lind 2004). In policy studies, transparency was not a stand-alone norm but one of the several components of a legitimate and effective governance plan (Van Doeveren 2011). In public choice, transparency was defined as a tool to decrease asymmetries of information and discipline institutions (Ferejohn 1986, 1999). In organizational theory, it referred to how organizations were expected to manage their day-to-day activities. In corruption studies, it was often associated with the lack of corrupt practices (Robins and Coulter 2007, Gartner 2013). In international relations, transparency was seen as a factor of peace and prosperity for its positive impact on interstate cooperation, and negative influence on security dilemmas and conflict spirals (Florini 1997, Finel and Lord 2000, Ritter 2000). In security studies, transparency was conjured as a strategy to signal benign intentions and to constrain one's ability to undertake aggression.

More specifically and in line with a disciplinary perspective on transparency, Libich (2006) differentiated among political, economic, procedural, policy-driven and operational transparency.

- *Political transparency* was defined as the provision of effective information on the mission of any given organization. It required accountable leadership and open decision making toward pre-defined and shared goals. Hirsch and Osborne (2000) defined political transparency more specifically as a means to improve governance outcomes such as administrative or policy effectiveness.
- *Economic transparency*, including fiscal and budgetary transparency, referred to the provision of information regarding the expenditures of governance programs and projects.
- *Procedural transparency* required open decision-making processes about the procedures and steps, and not just disclosure of results, findings and reasons of decisions undertaken by leaders and organizations.
- *Policy-driven transparency* meant specifically the open meetings involved in processes of formulating, implementing, evaluating and monitoring public policies.
- *Operational transparency* was about performance measurement in business administration and public management.

Transparency was also defined along more specific sectors. Fiscal transparency was about how governments managed public finances and handled public money (Alt et al. 2002, Alt and Lassen 2006).

Budget transparency was especially important since it was agreed that an open budget[4] that allowed for unlimited and free insight from civil society and the public at large into all its features and phases (Renzio and Masud 2011) was deemed crucial for the overall transparency and the performance of the economic and political systems. In other sectors, however, such as in environment, in extractive industries, and in social protection, the data disclosed by governments has been less voluminous, particularly when compared to fiscal and economic data (Sanchez et al. 2013)[5] even though the potential impact for economic development and democratization may be equally significant (Mol 2010).

A few quantifiable studies undertaken on transparency defined the latter as "visible decision-making" (Haque and Pathrannarakul 2013). It was measured as broadly as corruption, law and order, bureaucratic quality, expropriation risk in the Transparency Index by the International Country Risk Guide (ICRG), and as narrowly as newspaper circulation to operationalize the flow of information—as a proxy for transparency (Adsera et al. 2003). In between, transparency was operationalized, *inter alia*, as: (i) data dissemination and presence/absence of policy and information on specific issues, including economic, fiscal and debt-related data (Stasavage 2003); (ii) timeliness of government data provision and variation in the scope and content of freedom of information laws across countries (Islam 2006); (iii) freedoms of expression, association, media and press, including the laws and regulations that influence media content; and (iv) the structure of media ownership and the degree of political control over news media (Kaufmann et al. 2008).

International organizations have emphasized the different dimensions of transparency in their definitions, often depending on their own preferences regarding the type and level of transparency they are willing to abide by. The World Bank, for instance, increased its transparency by publishing post-project assessments rather than disclosing information on project formulation, implementation or on its internal processes. In July 2011, the World Bank unveiled a major initiative to make its funding processes more transparent. Information about specific funds supported by member countries, and the disbursement and repayment status of thousands of projects were made available. The World Bank's definition of transparency as "release of information by institutions, which is relevant to evaluating those institutions" has clearly taken on an institutionalist perspective has been linked more closely with accountability.

The United Nations opened up its processes of decision making for capacity development projects by accrediting and involving civil society organizations around the world into the project formulation and implementation in addition to post-project evaluation and monitoring. There is still scope for improvement, however, when it comes to the transparency of its internal governance. Taking this into account, the United Nations Transparency and Accountability Initiative (UNTAI) launched by the United States in 2007 sought to increase the internal accountability and transparency of the UN system. The UN (1997) defines transparency more generally as "enough information made available, accessible and understandable through different means of media to those who will be affected by it."

Some argued that the progress toward transparency achieved by the World Bank and the United Nations has not been matched by the International Monetary Fund (Gartner 2013). The IMF (2001) has a sector-specific definition of transparency as "openness in economic policymaking and in disseminating data on economic and financial developments." The OECD and the EU associate transparency with openness in communicating to the public.[6] The OECD (2010) offers a more elaborate definition as "an environment in which the objectives of policy, its framework, policy decisions and their rationale, data and information related to monetary and financial policies, terms of agencies are provided to the public in comprehensible, accessible, timely manners."[7] The Organization for Security and Cooperation in Europe (OSCE), like the European Court of Human Rights, goes a step further to equate access to information and transparency with human rights (2004).

Typologies

In addition to its disciplinary and sectoral definitions, transparency was typologized regarding its operational attributes. Transparency requirements mandated or proposed from the central government down to the local governments were categorized under *Transparency from Above* or *Top-down Transparency*. Transparency policies that are locally grown and requested to be issued and implemented by citizens were referred to as *Transparency from Below* or *Bottom-up*

Transparency. Within top-down transparency, *Transparency Upward* referred to within-government transparency linkages whereby a hierarchical superior/principal could observe the conduct, behavior, performance and/or results produced by the hierarchical subordinate/ agent. Within bottom-up transparency, *Transparency Downward* referred to instances when citizens could observe the conduct, behavior, performance and/or the results produced by the government (Heald 2006).[8]

Within the transparency from the above category, government-mandated and legally binding transparency policies were referred to as *Hard or Public Transparency* as opposed to those that are voluntary and informal called as *Soft or Social Transparency*. Many scholars pointed to the first type of mandatory transparency, such as annual auditing of statements and finances, disclosure of terms of contracts and privacy policies, online notice and comment and requests based on the Freedom of Information Acts/Laws (FOIA/Ls) and online disclosure of federal spending, as effective mechanisms of good governance for their instrumentality in disciplining government agencies and putting a barrier against capture and collusion (Etzioni 2010, Shkabatur 2012).

The second type of soft or social transparency, also called discretionary transparency, included techniques such as naming and shaming, and open data, and was deemed less effective in increasing transparency but more in promoting policy innovation. Others argued that there was not a significant difference between hard and soft transparency in terms of success of adoption and implementation. For instance, both mandatory and voluntary transparency policies imposed by the provincial government of Ontario[9] on its local municipalities engendered negative reactions on the part of citizens while their success rate of adoption and implementation depended on the financial resources and human capital of the municipalities.

Soft transparency was exemplified best in the United States' government's *Open Government Directive* and *Memorandum* directing all federal agencies to publish at least three high-value raw datasets of their choosing at www.data.gov. The ensuing open data movement has not culminated in increased transparency regarding govern-ment decision processes nor has it prompted the release of sensitive information. It has, however, led to a user-centered innovative pro-duction or crowdsourcing, and the development of a multitude of applications. Many have referred to this new era of transparency as the *democratization of innovation* (von Hippel 2005) where both a more engaged government (Newsom and Dickey 2013) and a better connected citizenry may lead to the strengthening of participatory democracy (Noveck 2010).

Within the category of Transparency from Below, Shkabatur (2012) emphasized the type of *Involuntary Transparency* equated with *whistleblowing*. Whistleblowing is understood to be the disclosure by a person—usually an employee in a government agency or private enterprise—to the public or to those in authority, of mismanagement, corruption, illegality or some other wrongdoing. Involuntary transparency or whistleblowing gained significant importance since Wikileaks in 2010.[10] Deemed as an effective external and independent check on agencies' behavior, yet questioned in terms of security and privacy issues, Wikileaks transparency has ushered in a new era of institutional openness when compared to the more conventional and limited transparency spurred by the FOIA/Ls (Hood 2011). In this respect, social-media based transparency whereby citizens are able to point to issues of concern before they actually become full-blown scandals, has also been part of the evolving meaning of transparency (Lathrop and Ruma 2010).

Operationally, transparency was also categorized regarding who the government provides the information to. *External Transparency* referred to situations where a government releases information to international organizations, and *Internal Transparency*, when it does so to its own public (Mitchell 1998). Grigorescu (2002) documented, for instance, that Eastern and Central European countries often released sensitive information to the European Union, Council of Europe and NATO, but less so to their societies. It has been argued that the IMF has bailed out countries based on information that governments have provided to the international financial institution without their citizens being aware.[11] With time, and in parallel to globalization and the increasing interconnectedness, external and internal transparency have shown tendencies to converge—since failing to provide the information to citizens directly has often meant a potential loss of credibility for national governments.

Transparency was also categorized according to the transparency policy on paper and transparency implementation in practice. Although often measured as formal rules of access to information

(Florini 2007), transparency in actual practice has often diverged from what is written in the books since there is a time lag between the introduction of the policy, called *Policy-level Transparency*, and its habituation, called *Institutional Transparency* (Kaldor and Vejvoda 1997). Freedom of information, access to information and press freedom laws could exist in paper but prove to be ineffective when devoid of institutionalization and enforcement.

Institutions created based on incomplete or imperfect policies, could eventually improve and effectively ensure transparency toward democratization (Martin and Feldman 1998). As such, partial transparency and transparency policies devoid of full institutionalization were often seen as paths to full transparency based on the reasoning that even partial transparency could deter conflict of interest and corrupt behavior (Hollyer et al. 2011). In both cases, transparency policies and institutions could be manipulated to appear as façade transparency such as when information is offered for propaganda purposes. Heald (2006) called this distinction *Nominal* versus *Effective Transparency*.

The way in which transparency rules and regulations are enforced led to yet another operational categorization: *Agent-Controlled Transparency*, defined as transparency requirements that are implemented and enforced by a given governmental or independent agency; and *Non-Agent Controlled Transparency*, defined as transparency requirements that are not within any specific agency's immediate control, such as freedom of press and whistleblowing. Agent-controlled transparency was deemed less effective than non-agent controlled transparency, particularly in fighting corruption, including when controlling for the influence of electoral democracy (Lindstedt and Naurin 2010).

With the rise and spread of the Internet and its significant impact on transparency, a new categorization of *Intentional* versus *Unintentional Transparency* emerged. Intentional transparency referred to cases where the principals deliberately chose to disclose information about the internal workings of their organizations and other things. Unintentional transparency occurred when information was divulged unwillingly, including through the Information and Communication Technologies (ICTs), which can store and track data automatically, and instantly calculate and compare measurable outputs. The result could either be democratization through increased transparency or the creation of a culture of suspicion due to misinformation or excess information. Unintentional transparency leading to a culture of suspicion could also end up in tighter control of information by the central government, hence ultimately a potential decrease in transparency (Hood and Heald 2006).

Other categorizations of transparency in terms of its implementation included the level of details provided regarding its results versus its lifecycle. *Event Transparency* and *Process Transparency* referred respectively to the information related to the results of policies, and the processes of decision making, acts and actions leading to these results. The importance of the timing of information release was also stressed in yet another operational categorization of transparency. *Transparency in Retrospect* versus *Transparency in Real Time* referred to after-the-fact disclosure of information as opposed to making policies and government decisions open and accessible as they are taking place (Heald 2006).

Policies

Transparency was put into practice generally through legislation of freedom of press, and more specifically through legislation of Freedom of Information or Access to Information, including Sunshine policies, acts and laws. Freedom of Information was defined as an extension of freedom of speech, and at times, as a human right to know. Freedom of Information Acts and Laws (FOIA/Ls) put the burden on government and its agencies to respond to citizens' needs to obtain government-held information, freely or at a minimal cost, and in ways that are easily accessible and understandable. Some FOIA/Ls have included privacy and/or open data protection laws, others not. Some have had extended mandates to the private sector, others not. Sunshine acts and laws have made it mandatory for government entities to have public meetings.

The content, scope, enactment and success of implementation of FOIA/Ls change from country to country. A comprehensive FOIA/L generally has a clear content and allows for a comprehensive access to government data with only a few and precise exemptions. It either does not charge a fee or does so minimally, and allows for effective appeal mechanisms as well as an independent review of denials of access to information. Comprehensive laws are often found in democratic states while democratizing states might have incomprehensive FOIA/Ls before possibly adopting fully functional and comprehensive acts and laws of transparency. Some newly democratizing states, particularly those in Africa, have taken the strict legal measures to entrench transparency in their national constitutions.

Some of the traditional problems associated with FOIA/Ls are that they are costly,[12] subject to significant delays and numerous exemptions, and suffer from a lack of specific expertise in government agencies. In addition to a common list of exemptions including confidential state secrets related to national security, all FOIA/Ls include what is called the "deliberative process privilege," which means that inter- and intra-agency communication is exempt from disclosure so as to allow government agencies to maintain confidentiality in their internal decisional processes. FOIA/Ls also make the disclosure of classified information exempt. This could include information about law enforcement procedures if such disclosure creates safety hazards.[13] FOIA/Ls are also subject to the implementation gap—between what the law says and how it functions.[14] Unintentional consequences are also a matter of concern. The implementation of FOIA/Ls have often led to the strengthening of groups and organizations with the technical expertise to understand the disclosed information and ask relevant questions. FOIA/Ls have thus not led to increased public accountability at all instances.

The first FOIA/Ls phase of transparency policies was succeeded, and at times, superseded by the Open Data Movement and its associated policies. Contrary to the FOIA/L, Open Data puts the responsibility on the government to provide data rather than on the citizen to request it. It does not, however, specify to the public bodies which datasets to disclose. It only encourages them to voluntarily expose data of their own choosing. Citizens can then freely access and use this data to solve problems, hold the government to account and participate more effectively in policy- and decision-making processes (Maguire 2011). Many datasets on gifts received by governmental departments, tender contracts, information on real estate records, salaries and spending patterns of government officials, certain performance indicators such as prison costs, donation data as well as political campaign contributions and expenses have been made public thanks to the open data movement.[15]

In difference from the traditional freedom of information, the objective of the open data movement has not only been transparency but transparency through participation, collaboration and innovation.

Citizens are not only empowered to request and access government information but considered as co-decision-makers in a collaborative movement of data democratization and shared governance. David Cameron, the Prime Minister of the United Kingdom, has likened open data to a smaller state bigger society agenda. Debates have centered on making open data more democratic by opening up the *policy lifecycle* to the public rather than just disclosing *policies as fait-accompli*, and/or *post-policy monitoring and evaluation* (Luna-Reyes and Chun 2012).

Manipulative disclosure, abundance of exemptions, window dressing or fake transparency, reliance on intermediaries are some of the criticisms raised against both freedom of information and open data movements (Ripken 2006). The open data movement was criticized in addition for causing or exacerbating: (i) quantity-quality divide, defined as the increased quantity of illegible information leading to civic autism, i.e., uncertainty, unpredictability and distrust, rather than public accountability, good governance or democratization (Moore 2011); (ii) public-programmer divide, defined as the ability and ease of the computer experts in reading and using open data versus the lay citizens' inability to do so; and (iii) voluntary-mandatory data divide, defined as the full discretion of the government over which data to retain and release as well as when and how to disclose it. The latter has meant that performance data on federal contractors and grantees is often off public scrutiny.

Wikileaks signaled the beginnings of a third phase in the transparency movement. The Freedom of Information phase consisted of regular laws and codes that formally oblige government entities to disclose specific information while balancing against concerns of security, confidentiality and privacy. The Open Data phase excluded such concerns since no requirement was made vis-à-vis the content of the data to be disclosed. Wikileaks, on the other hand, originated directly from citizens' initiatives to reveal data beyond what is required in freedom of information legislation, and what is offered in open data disclosures. As such, the Wikileaks phase has meant a blurring of the lines among transparency, privacy and secrecy.

While governments often conceal sensitive data to circumvent freedom of information requirements and simply choose not to reveal it in open data disclosures, eschewing Wikileaks has been trickier. Technical fixes such as stronger firewalls, and/or legal and cyber counterattacks such as the denial of web-hosting service and online donation instruments are some of the strategies used by governments to countervail Wikileaks transparency.[16] Wikileaks also highlighted the following transparency paradox: believing in the value of transparency does not mean support for the activities of transparency in all situations. In other words, government and non-government actors can support greater openness, and at the same time support privacy and secrecy (Fung et al. 2007). This is because greater openness can make negotiations lengthier and less sincere. Interest groups with greater access to discussions can derail, disrupt or change the agenda. More transparency can bring more regulation causing the syndrome of "compliance with rules" rather than a focus on the public good and/or genuine problem solving. The asymmetry of information between democratic and non-democratic nations may also put the democratic nations at a disadvantage since they have to abide by several rules of disclosure and compliance before acting (Florini 1998, Finel and Lord 1999).

Institutions

Many transparency initiatives undertaken by governments and international/regional governance institutions worldwide have stayed at the policy level. There is no central and separate governmental unit that is in charge of Freedom of Information Acts and Laws and their implementation, for instance. The same is generally true for the Open Government and Open Data Initiatives. Instead, there are officers in charge of overseeing these acts and initiatives, and the timely production and publishing of the associated reports and other relevant data in each governmental agency or department. Overall, however, the monitoring and evaluation of the effective and legitimate implementation of transparency policies are often couched in the executive, such as the Presidential Office of Management and Budget (OMB), which scrutinizes the performance of federal agencies in the United States. At the parliamentary level, committees and commissions are charged with the monitoring and evaluation of the implementation of transparency policies. The Transparency Oversight Commission in the United States monitors the implementation of federal spending for transparency laws, and disciplines agencies that fail to comply with these laws by facilitating public litigation and by using budget allocations as sticks and carrots. The Inspector General's Office, complements the Transparency Oversight Commission, and is mandated to prevent and detect fraud, waste and abuse. Together, they can solicit non-compliance reports from the civil society (Shkabatur 2012). Last but not least, Government Accountability Office in the United States and the Government Accountability and Transparency Board work to ensure that transparency is integrally linked with accountability and corruption control. Focusing on government spending and public expenditures, they audit, inspect, monitor and display relevant data on government agencies' spending with a particular focus on fraud detection and prevention. The same task is undertaken by the Public Sector Transparency Board appointed by the Prime Minister in the United Kingdom.

These relatively new institutions dating back to 2010 onward in the United States can be considered for possible replication in other contexts where transparency, accountability and corruption control are made integral parts of democratization, governance and development plans and programs. Across countries, there is also the Data Protection and Information Commissioner's Office that handles citizens' complaints about their access to information under the FOIA/Ls. Information Commissioners may or may not handle the open data and privacy issues related to transparency, and they often act as a special type of ombudsman. Their functioning, independence and comparative performance would also help better assess the role of transparency in democratization.

OUTCOMES OF TRANSPARENCY: CONSEQUENCES AND IMPACT

Transparency is a janus-faced concept. On the positive side, its immediate outcomes are greater public awareness about what the government is doing, and informed decisions about education, health, employment and any other sphere affecting citizens' everyday lives. Further down the road, transparency is often expected to lead to strengthened public accountability, when supportive conditions are in place. On the negative side, promoting transparency is costly, and may increase uncertainty and unpredictability (Moore 2011). It can also impede efficient law enforcement while invading individual privacy, overriding national security, and jeopardizing free deliberation among policy-makers (Shkabatur 2012). Often, both faces of transparency are simultaneously visible. More transparency in local governments in Holland, for instance, led people to believe that local government was honest and benevolent but incompetent (Margetts 2011).

On the positive spectrum, transparency was deemed to be the solution to cure all ills, including lack of accountability, economic inefficiency and deficit, institutional sclerosis and bureaucratic inertia (Moore 2011). As early as in the 1960s, Almond and Verba (1963) wrote that transparency increased public trust in government. Weber (2008) maintained that transparency increases civil society mobilization, and strengthens civic development and political participation. Transparency was proposed as an antidote to global economic and financial problems, and international money laundering (Tanzi 1996); it was deemed to be a catalyst for trade liberalization (Qureshi 1990). It was shown to decrease corruption and increase economic performance in democratic and democratizing states (Kopits and Craig 1998, Hood 2001). Etzioni (2010) pitted transparency against excessive regulation, secrecy and conflict-of interest.

On the negative spectrum, the manipulation of transparency policies in the hands of bureaucrats was associated with increasing bureaucratization (Piotrowski and Van Ryzin 2007). Transparency was associated with rising alienation and a culture of suspicion and confusion due to the misinterpretation of complex data or its oversimplification (Githinji and Holmquist 2012). Transparency was linked with group and formal thinking thereby decreasing the analytical and overall quality of decision-making processes (Maguire 2011). Last but not least, any positive impact that transparency could have on political development was deemed insufficient and/or ineffective compared to the overarching influence of historical legacies, cultural attributes of lack of trust and corruption.

TRANSPARENCY AND DEMOCRATIZATION LINKAGES

The janus-faced transparency is fully at play when it comes to its linkages with democracy and democratization. Some scholars assume that democracies are more transparent than non-democracies because information is an intrinsically necessary component of political and economic freedoms, hence both a cause and a consequence of long-term stability, peace and prosperity. Transparency is associated with democratic peace theory, the idea that democracies do not fight each other, through its mitigating impact on security dilemmas (Florini 2002). Other scholars claim transparency can lead to political cynicism, "civic autism" and "inquisition democracy" because the information is too much, overly technical, low quality, impertinent, not contextualized enough, oversimplified, too negative (Fung et al. 2007: 107) or used as a strategic tool to curtail civil society activism and to capture votes (Bertelli 2008).

Separate from the two opposite views over the linkages between transparency and democracy, transparency is most often linked with good governance positively. Then, the question is not as much how transparency is associated with democratization but how it contributes to it through good governance, and what the relationship is between good governance and democratization. Among the scholars who link transparency with democratization through good governance, the main assumption is that transparency is a requisite of good and democratic governance. Scholars who question the indirect linkages between transparency and democratization usually maintain that good governance and democracy are separate and not significantly related to each other.

Dissecting these directly and indirectly positive and negative linkages between transparency and democratization can be done through a *two-by-two transparency-democracy matrix* shown in Figure 2.2.

On the direct-positive spectrum, some authors see transparency as an intrinsic element of democracy and assume a perfect correlation between the two.[17] This position is well depicted by the dictum that democracies die behind closed doors, or that a democracy is a house of glass, and equal to public knowledge (Bodei 2011). Democracy is also equated with transparency on an individual basis since policy-makers in democracies can never be entirely free from commitment to truth-telling (Shapiro 2003: 20). The causal links between transparency and democracy in this understanding are often basic freedoms and rights (Van Belle 2000: 50) and accountability (Shkabatur 2012).

The first causal chain comprising freedoms and rights are in conformity with Dahl's theory of democracy (1971). For Dahl,

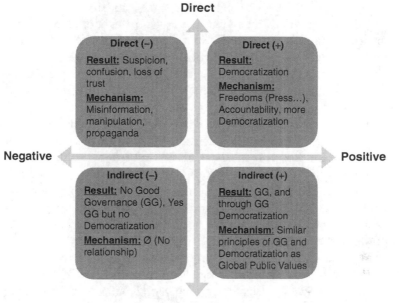

Figure 2.2 Transparency-Democratization Matrix

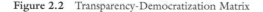

procedural democracy leads to substantive democracy when citizens benefiting from the free flow of information and armed with a host of freedoms can make informed decisions at the ballot box. Democracy is thus conjured as an extension of the democratic values such as free speech, free expression and free press, and the right-to-know. In this broader understanding of democracy, transparency is characterized as a human right, also indirectly referred to in Article 19 of the *Universal Declaration of Human Rights* by the United Nations (GTI 2003, Birkinshaw 2006, 2012,[18] ICHRP 2009, Edel 2011).

The second causal chain involving accountability is in line with Bentham's (2001) motto that "The more strictly we are watched, the better we behave." If politicians and bureaucrats know that their actions are made public, or could be so in the future because institutions and/or policies allow for such possibility, then they will act in the public interest, and not their private interest. Transparency thus helps to: (i) promote impartiality by suppressing self-interested behavior by officials (Vermeule 2007: 182); and to (ii) create the propitious conditions for public control, participation and government accountability (Fenster 2010, Aftergood 2009).[19] In this understanding, transparency is a toolbox to lay down the institutional rules to promote government accountability (Stirton and Lodge 2001). And government accountability is a sign of a democratic polity (March and Olsen 1994: 162–165).

Transparency is important for democracies from the first elections on. Since democracy is based on the ability of citizens to monitor and complain, and that of governments to respond to them, even the minimalist understandings of democracy based on electoral competition and contestation require free flow of information and transparency (Mueller 1992). Stressing transparent elections[20] from early on in new democracies, and not later for consolidation purposes only, was considered an important success factor for overall transparency and democratization in the long run. For instance, the transparency factor duly emphasized and applied in the founding and the functioning of the electoral commission in Ghana was pointed as one of the main reasons as to why this country was able to hold five successful general elections with marginal errors, with two of them ending up on peaceful turnover of power (Debrah 2011).

Once a procedural democracy is established, transparency is important for increasing the likelihood of survival of the new democracies and their progress toward more substantive democratization. This is because transparency and democracy are endogenously related with each other: it is not only transparency that promotes democratization, but democratization that breeds transparency. The two-way relationship works at both the individual and institutional levels. At the individual level, transparency benefits from leaders who have been socialized in democratic systems:[21] they effectively uphold transparency rules and norms. At the institutional level, as democratic institutions and norms develop, there is a spillover, albeit slow, that leads to the (further) adoption of transparency institutions.

The spillover includes, *inter alia*, the mechanism of empowered societal actors who eventually break the government's monopoly over information. One then can argue that legislation that supports government transparency, such as FOIA/Ls and open data protection, is more likely to be adopted in democratic systems where basic freedoms, including particularly the freedom of press, have already been adopted—since it is these general freedoms and laws that empower the social actors to pursue more information.[22]

Among the measures recommended to increase the direct-positive impact of transparency on democratization, one can find the strengthening of a healthy civil society, the creation of independent enforcement agencies that are also open to public scrutiny, the presentation of information in lay terms in addition to the technical datasets when necessary and adequate, including the creation and updating of indicators.

On the direct-negative spectrum, scholars seem to agree that transparency is necessary for accountability, and therefore for democracy, but simply insufficient if pursued for its own sake. Transparency, in this understanding, cannot lead to increased public accountability if the supporting courts, cooperative administrations and experienced and democratic intermediaries are absent, inadequate or inefficient.[23] Other scholars focus on transparency side effects such as secrecy, suspicion and trust issues.[24] Still others point at the cases of traditionally democratic states which either have not adopted institutions and practices of transparency (Grigorescu 2002) or have done so relatively late, such as the United Kingdom.

Cases such as Singapore with high transparency and low corruption trends, but a relatively low democratic score have also received attention in directly but negatively linking transparency with democracy. Another example of introducing transparency in legislative decision-making processes in authoritarian settings comes from Vietnam, a single-party authoritarian regime. The findings showed no evidence of direct impact of transparency on the performance of delegates even though the starting assumption was that it could do so since non-governmental organizations and the media were expected to substitute for the incentives otherwise created by the voters, competitive elections and contestation in democratic settings. The Vietnamese delegates who received intense training on transparency ended up damaging their re-election process (Malesky 2012) instead of supporting transparency and/or furthering democratization.

These empirical examples and the associated theoretical debates point to the possibility that transparency legislation can: (i) benefit newly democratizing states and already democratic states—not authoritarian states; (ii) be introduced together with, and not before, the founding elections; and (iii) be introduced preferably together with or after the introduction of basic freedoms including particularly the freedom of the press.

A group of middle-ground scholars argue that it is unproductive to search for either the positive or the negative effects of transparency on democracy. They maintain that the nature of the impact of transparency on democratization depends on the policy area where it is applied. Accordingly, governments can have incentives to promote opacity for less visible matters, for potentially controversial decisions including those that concern resource allocation and distribution, and those where their action goes against the will of the majority. Conversely, governments often encourage transparency in already highly visible policy areas, and where they expect that their actions would be awarded with votes during elections (Mani and Mukand 2007).

On the indirect-positive spectrum, transparency is often seen as a pillar of good governance and therefore, amenable to democracy, but not as a direct corollary of it. In this understanding, the underlying assumption is that neither elections nor administrative reform is necessary *per se* to promote democratization. What is needed is high-quality governance, which mostly depends on the underlying power structures. Transparency is one of the pillars of good governance policies, and a globally acknowledged public value instrumental in instilling, maintaining and enhancing these democratic structures (Besley and Burgess 2002, Adsera et al. 2003, Jørgensen and Sorensen 2012–2013). To work efficiently, however, it has to be accompanied by a whole set of other good governance factors and policies, including: accountability, predictability and participation (Kopits and Craig 1998: 158); efficiency, effectiveness and rule of law (Rothstein and Teorell 2008: 167); efficient public service, reliable judiciary and balanced state-society relations (Williams and Young 1994); political stability, control of corruption and regulatory quality (Kaufmann et al. 2008); decency, fairness and participation (Overseas Development Institute 2009); and coherence (European Commission 2011: 1).

The concept of governance can best be defined as a process of decision making by governmental and non-governmental actors (Hirst 1994, Kickert et al. 1997). Currently, one can find as broad a definition of governance as "who gets, what, when and how" (Maogoto 2007: 380); "schemes of collaborative efforts, policy entrepreneurship and participatory initiatives" (Duit and Gulay 2008: 329); mechanisms for steering social systems toward their goals (Roseneau 2005) or the sum of ways that individuals and institutions in both public and private spheres manage their affairs (Knio 2010). More instrumental understandings of governance often refer to it as "the method of public sector management, including financial accountability" and as "internal and external control mechanisms" (Thirkel-White 2003: 107). A more recent and multidisciplinary analysis of the evolution of the concept and practice of governance by Blind (2011) shows that the term has been conflated with "development" and "democratization." Its use has even extended to the issues related to human rights, well beyond its initial usage in the literature as aid conditionality.

While governance is an analytical concept that makes us aware of how decisions are made, good governance is a prescriptive notion that stresses the values considered important for decision-making processes undertaken in different contexts and by different institutions with different goals and agendas. When defining good governance, the World Bank emphasizes political stability and the lack of violence; the IMF stresses the importance of tackling corruption; the UN underlines the consensus orientation and the EU makes linkages with democracy, human rights and respect for minorities. OECD (2007) defines it as the sum of participation, transparency, accountability, rule of law, effectiveness and equity. OSCE (2012) makes a more direct link between good governance and transparency to juxtapose them together rather than subsuming the latter under the former.

Often, good governance is based on the notion of public values (Kernaghan 2003), i.e., principles to be followed when producing a public service and providing direction to the behavior of public servants (Jørgensen and Andersen 2011). Common global public values exist despite the multitude of national political cultures and institutional heritages. They include transparency along with accountability, effectiveness and the rule of law. These values of good governance are similar to those that are associated with democratization.

Among the measures recommended to increase the indirect-positive impact of transparency on democratization are the issuance of mandatory as opposed to discretionary transparency requirements on public agencies, and increased focus on process rather than event transparency only provided, of course, that the deliberative process privilege of elected and appointed officials is respected.

On the indirect-negative spectrum, one can find those scholars who maintain that transparency will not lead to high-quality governance if it is included only implicitly and/or as an ad hoc, and not as an explicit and persistent, objective of governance programs, and others who completely delink good governance from democratization. For Rosenau (2005), Bang (2008) and Bang and Esmark (2009), for instance, good governance is not a necessary requirement for democratization. They argue that governance is apolitical and good governance is mainly about risk management policies in a globalized society. Democracy, on the other hand, is the formal party system and politics of interest formation, aggregation, contestation and adjudication.[25] For Stockemer (2009), it is not good governance that leads to democracy but democracy that promotes good governance. Likewise, CDL by the Council of Europe, does not find resemblance between good governance, understood as *participative deliberation* (2011: 12–14), and democratization, which, in addition, includes *economic and social rights*.

CONCLUSION

The transparency triangle shows that the inputs of government transparency include economic, political and contextual factors at the national and international levels of analysis. As with the modernization theory of development and democratization, higher economic and political development, including particularly the substantive attributes of democratization such as the basic rights and freedoms, are associated with higher transparency and vice-versa. In addition, circumstantial factors such as scandals of corruption, and external demonstration effects, such as the adoption of transparency policies by national governments and regional/international organizations, are found to lead to the instilling or furthering of transparency.

More specifically, the inputs of transparency range from a democratic culture and system including the non-agency transparency enablers such as freedom of press, to economic variables of income and growth. The more immediate propellants of transparency legislation and institutions include scandals and crises of social, economic and political nature and of significant magnitude. The impact of international organizations and of other governments undertaking transparency initiatives also push countries to adopt more open communication and information sharing methods in order to maintain credibility.

The outputs of transparency, including its definitions, types, policies and institutions, respond to a variety of needs, and operate through a variety of channels with different degrees of effectiveness, compliance, enforcement and institutionalization. Sectoral, sub-sectoral and instrumental definitions go hand-in-hand with the different typologies of transparency depending on who initiates transparency toward whom, when, in what ways and degrees of clarity, quality, institutionalization and enforcement. More specifically, the definitions of government transparency range from the use of open communication tools and strategies to fight corruption to the use of transparency as a public value to instill and maintain an accountable government.

As the outputs of transparency, the policies of transparency often include FOIA/Ls, open data legislation, and others pertaining to involuntary transparency or whistleblowing as demonstrated recently by the Wikileaks incident. The rise of the Internet, and of ICTs in general, have greatly impacted the way government transparency is understood, practiced and enforced.

As for the outcomes of transparency, the most immediate one is increased knowledge and greater awareness even though the way in which information is released may at times produce opposite results. The longer-term outcomes of transparency, including its impact on democratization, are best described as janus-faced. As the transparency-democratization matrix demonstrates, transparency can be directly or indirectly related to democratization, and exert positive or negative effects depending on a host of factors that lead to, support or hamper transparency. Transparency and democratization are positively and directly linked through the first democratic elections and the institutionalization of democratic systems afterward, and not before. This is true whether democratization is understood as a host of social, political and economic rights or as government accountability, including in its minimalist sense of electoral politics and contestation. They are positively and indirectly linked through accountability and the other pillars of the good governance paradigm. They are negatively linked either because transparency has side effects that do not bode well with either procedural or substantive democracy directly, or because good governance and democracy are not the same and/or do not feed into each other.

What seems to be a consensus on the linkages between transparency and democratization is that they are endogenously related. Transparency may lead to democratization, and democratization may breed and further transparency overall or in given policy areas. The key lies in whether the right accompanying conditions, such as the electoral incentives, the basic freedoms of expression, press and association, and the lack of consecutive corruption scandals, are present or absent. In any case, transparency seems unproductive in authoritarian settings defined by the lack of elections. It appears to take on importance with the first elections, and thereafter.

Born as a tool to fight corruption, transparency is intrinsically related to anti-corruption strategies, policies and laws.[26] Transparency and accountability have also been used in tandem in the past few years. Ball (2009), for instance, traced the meaning of transparency from its use by non-governmental and supranational organizations to its use in international relations, non-profit, public policy and administration. She found that the definition of transparency reveals three metaphors: first, transparency as a public value embraced by society to counter corruption; second, transparency as open decision making by governments and non-profits; and third, transparency as a complex tool of good governance in programs, policies, organizations and nations. In the first metaphor, transparency was subtly intertwined with accountability. In the second, as transparency encouraged openness, it also increased concerns for secrecy and privacy. In the third linkage, policy-makers created transparency alongside accountability, efficiency and effectiveness.

To give some empirical examples of transparency-accountability linkages, in the United States, policy-makers have called for greater transparency and accountability in government even though in the past they might have called for greater accountability only (Hartz-Karp 2005). The Federal Funding Accountability and the Transparency Act of 2006 and the Legislative Transparency and Accountability section of the Honest Leadership and Open Government Act of 2007 have used the word "transparency" side by side with "accountability."

Although transparency and accountability have become pairs in international politics and governance, a growing number of studies stress that their positive association is only possible when transparency policies are given the time to get institutionalized, and are supported by a legitimate constitution including basic rights and freedoms, committed leadership and independent and effective control agencies. This again emphasizes that making transparency institutionalization into a minimum condition of substantive democratization early on could potentially multiply the long-term positive influence of procedural and constitutional reforms in democratization.

Although the focus on transparency has increased recently, particularly in tandem with the increasing recognition of the high impact of ICTs on transparency, governance and democracy, transparency is still one of the least-studied areas in public administration and political science (Otenyo and Lind 2004). Early introduction and effective enforcement of certain policies of transparency, and their integration into the political system at certain crucial points of the democratic development process can make the difference between a strong and a fickle democratization process and outcome. Therefore, further research on the direct linkages between transparency and democratization in newly established democracies is particularly needed.

CHAPTER 3

———————✦———————

THE ACCOUNTABILITY CUBE: MOVING FROM DICHOTOMY TO CONTINUITY [1]

As much as the role of transparency in democratization is debatable, the links of accountability with democratization are not—they are unequivocally positive. Accountability is integral to issue areas that are endogenous to democratization, such as deliberative public networks, authority and power relations and participatory policy and decision making (Olsen 2013). Accountability is also indirectly related to democratization because, like transparency, it is a pillar of legitimate and effective public administration and good governance (Head 2012, Crowe 2011).

As opposed to transparency, accountability becomes part of democratization from early on and long before the first elections. It is used as a mechanism of justice in post-conflict societies where a newly ending civil war necessitates reparation and reconciliation before any procedural democratization can even start (Lamin 2003, Kaiser 2005, Crippa 2012, Kim 2012, Pajibo 2012). It is also a tool of public engagement and empowerment later on with its necessary components of free and effective information flow, regulatory transparency and free and fair electoral mechanisms (Ashworth 2012, Shkabatur 2012, Woon 2012). Last but not least, accountability is part of the democratic maturation processes through inclusive policy making and answerability mechanisms in between elections (Sandbrook 1996, Fritz 2008, Good and Taylor 2008, Lange 2008, Le Van 2011).

A conceptual analysis of accountability from a multidisciplinary perspective finds that accountability has been defined in overly dichotomous terms. This can best be illustrated through a cube of eight corners, four at the bottom and four at the top. The four corners at the bottom constitute the *hard accountability surface* for each represents the rational and institutional understanding of *accountability as answerability*. The hard accountability corners are *material, legal, ex-post and horizontal accountability*. The four corners at the top make up the *soft accountability surface* for each represents the more ethical and social understanding of *accountability as responsibility*. The soft accountability corners are *moral, political, ex-ante* and *vertical accountability*.

Each one of the four vertical edges of the accountability cube includes one corner from the soft accountability surface, and another one from the hard accountability surface, i.e., the accountability dichotomies. The accountability cube links the respective dichotomies to show how the two opposite corners from the opposite accountability planes complement each other in a continuous, not dichotomous, understanding of accountability. The four categories (edges) of the accountability cube are the *prescriptive, descriptive, operational* and *longitudinal pillars of accountability*.

The first edge of *prescriptive dichotomies of accountability* describes accountability as moral versus material norms. The second category of *descriptive dichotomies of accountability* explains accountability in terms of its political-administrative versus economic-legal attributes. The third *operational dichotomy of accountability* investigates the internal versus external accountability mechanisms within institutions, and between them and the public. The *longitudinal dichotomy of accountability* pits accountability as a policy tool for effective and legitimate policy making against accountability as a policy tool for compliance with predetermined rules and regulations.

The dichotomous pillars of accountability are neither exhaustive nor mutually exclusive. Their purpose is to meaningfully summarize and make an otherwise large and complex body of definitional analysis more manageable. Focusing on the linkages and the convergences among the edges and the corners of the accountability cube can take us from a dichotomous to a *continuous* understanding of accountability.

THE FOUR EDGES OF THE ACCOUNTABILITY CUBE: DICHOTOMOUS DEFINITIONS

Scholars agree that accountability is an amorphous concept that is difficult to define. This partly arises from its dualistic nature. On the one hand, accountability is abstract and value-ridden because it is associated with the notions of responsibility, integrity, democracy, fairness and justice.[2] On the other hand, accountability is highly concrete and value-free because its etymological origin lies in bookkeeping where account-holders must give justifications of their possessions to pre-determined bodies according to fixed procedures (Boven 2007b). The first approach to accountability is broad as in "state of being responsible" (Black 1979: 18); the second is narrower as in "given obligations to evidence management or performance imposed by law, agreement or regulation" (Kohler 1975: 6).

This inherent dualism of the concept coupled with the necessity for parsimony in social sciences has triggered a predominantly dichotomous analysis of accountability in the literature. As shown in Figure 3.1, the dichotomies can be said to transpire along the *prescriptive, descriptive, operational and longitudinal dimensions*—categories that are neither exhaustive nor mutually exclusive. While useful for didactic purposes, taken separately, these polar perspectives provide only a limited understanding of accountability. Multiple convergences that exist among them, both on theoretical and empirical grounds, can be missed when a dichotomous approach is adopted. Ergo, much could be gained from a continuous understanding of accountability.

Prescriptive Dichotomies

In prescriptive terms, a dichotomous understanding of accountability can best be summarized as the *philosophy* versus the *means* of government. Lloyd (2008), writing on the challenges of embedding accountability into the culture of an organization, refers to the philosophy component as the "software" and the means component as the "hardware" of accountability. The hardware, or the structures of accountability, includes the procedures, mechanisms and processes, while the software, or its cultural precepts, refers to the attitudes and behavior, perceptions and the mindset.[3] Lloyd, while emphasizing

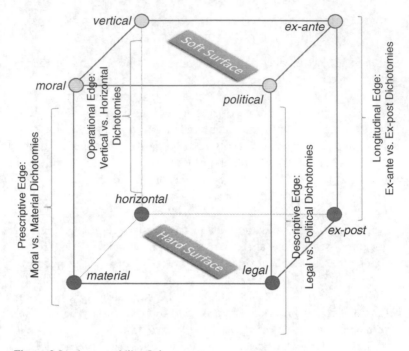

Figure 3.1 Accountability Cube

the need for a balanced approach between the hardware and the software understandings of accountability, also urges the policy-makers to favor the "software" option for two reasons: (i) the hardware approach has already been examined in the literature to a great extent; and (ii) the accountability structures without the supporting culture could be façade accountability.[4]

Boven (2010) is yet another scholar who offers a dichotomous understanding of accountability along prescriptive terms. His dichotomy consists of "virtue" versus "mechanism" views of accountability.[5] While the *virtue* perspective encompasses a discussion about *good governance*[6] and *trust in government*,[7] the *mechanism* view of accountability subscribes to the *public management* discourse, including its old and new variants.[8] In the former case, accountability is seen as a positive quality of organizations or officials whose actual behavior is the locus of attention. In the latter case, it is seen as an institutional arrangement where an *accountee* is held to account by a forum, or the *accountor* (Pollitt 2003: 89). Here, the gist of accountability is not the behavior of public agents, but the way in which the principal–agent nexuses operate.

Ackerman (2005) also stresses two variants of accountability: accountability as "honesty" and accountability as "performance." On an individual level, the first variant is associated with the rule-following bureaucrats who restrain from the non-procedural, and the second variant, with the pro-active public decision-makers who are expected to perform efficiently and effectively. Ackerman indicates that the first "honesty" version is "process-oriented" and "negative" accountability because the public servants are evaluated constantly and according to certain standard operating principles (SOPs). As for the second "performance" understanding of accountability, Ackerman states that the association is with "results-driven" and "positive" accountability insofar as accountability is seen as the ability to produce effective policy outcomes, which are evaluated at project endings (8).

Martin and Webb (2009) are other scholars who adopt a dichotomous approach to accountability. Their juxtaposition consists of the "user-choice" versus the "social justice" dimensions. They demonstrate that, in Wales, as a result of the shifts in the public administration ethos and practice from the competitive/consumer-driven performance management (user-choice) to collaborative/citizen-centric inclusive management (social justice), significant improvements were noted in public service delivery.[9] As enumerated in Table 3.1, these and similar prescriptive dichotomies of accountability have dominated the conceptual literature.

Table 3.1 Prescriptive Dichotomies of Accountability

Accountability as the "philosophy" of government	Accountability as the "means" of government	Authors
Software	Hardware	Lloyd (2008)
Virtue	Mechanism	Boven (2010)
Honesty	Performance	Ackerman (2005)
Social Justice	User-choice	Martin and Webb (2009)

Descriptive Dichotomies

The prescriptive dichotomies have their counterparts in the descriptive domain which, at the risk of oversimplification, include the legal versus the political understandings of accountability. More specifically, the descriptive dichotomies of accountability cover *market-based versus bureaucratic accountability, political versus legal/judicial accountability and social versus institutional accountability*.[10] These comparative categories largely subsume the more enumerative and less analytical categorizations, such as the organizational, professional, managerial, moral and fiscal accountability (Jabbra and Dwivedi 1989, Smith 1991, Romzek 2000) or program, process and outcome accountability (Chandler and Piano 1988).[11]

Market-Based versus Bureaucratic Accountability
Accountability has been described by contrasting its public- and private-sector-like attributes. Market-based accountability consists of perceiving citizens as consumers, who must be accounted to on the basis of the services they receive. Market-based accountability gained currency in public administration when the New Public Management Theory of the 1990s emphasized the transferability of market forces to the public sector toward improving the efficiency, competitiveness and the accountability of government institutions (Bartley 1999). "Reinventing Government" by Osborne and Gaebler (1992) praised an "entrepreneurial" government, which contracted out the production and the delivery of public services to the private sector and/or civil society, and then supervised the process toward ensuring the public interest.

One criticism of market-based accountability comes from Ladd (2008),[12] who examines accountability mechanisms in public education in the United States. He shows that when parents are conceived as consumers or clients, and are given several choices between different schools and school programs, the end result is not the expected school reform toward higher achievement but the further marginalization of the disadvantaged students. As a result, governments have to look for complementary solutions, rather than adopting purely market-based accountability frameworks, such as the establishment of charter schools run by citizens' groups and/or non-governmental organizations.

In contrast to market-based accountability, bureaucratic accountability refers to rules, regulations and norms of hierarchical obligation to answer to one's superior. Although bureaucratic accountability involves answerability to superiors, it is no longer confined to an internally structured chain of command such as internal auditing, evaluation and surveillance (Smith 1991). Market-driven concepts and practices have made their way into bureaucratic accountability, hence the convergence with market-based accountability.

Salient areas of convergence are personnel management, performance evaluation, auditing and monitoring. The overlapping of these bureaucratic accountability mechanisms with those of political and social accountability shows the inadequacy of dichotomous understandings of accountability. These convergences give the signals of potential advantages that may accrue if continuous and graded views of accountability were adopted instead of binary descriptions.

In practice, bureaucratic accountability has also converged with prescriptive accountabilities. For instance, the *internal/formal mechanisms* of bureaucratic accountability, such as the command-and-control elements of public administration, relate to personal and professional ethics. Such informal elements, particularly commitment and anticipated reactions from superiors, can be quite abstract. Yet, their informal character can be formalized through instruments such as the codes of conduct or internal performance evaluations.

Bureaucratic accountability has also merged with political and legal accountability types through its *external/formal mechanisms*, which link public administration with parliaments, advisory committees, ombudsmen, review tribunals and so on. Such institutions of accountability coexist in the domain of political accountability, which is discussed next under the political versus legal/judicial accountability dichotomy. Likewise, bureaucratic accountability is also social through its *external/informal mechanisms* of public opinion and feedback, interest-group pressure, civil society participation and media scrutiny, which are discussed below in reference to the institutional-social accountability dichotomy.

Political versus Legal/Judicial Accountability

Accountability has been defined by pitting its political and legal dimensions against each other. Political accountability is the elected officials' obligation to answer to the public, and of public servants' to the elected officials. Some have differentiated between the "short route" and the "long route" political accountability. The former refers to visible and direct linkages between public service users (citizens) and public service providers (street-level bureaucrats). The latter stresses accountability linkages through public, private or joint providers, between the service-recipient citizens, and the elected politicians and appointed public officials (Joshi 2010). In both cases, political accountability is generally ensured through elections and the legislative system, and is supported by well-functioning political party systems and a healthy executive-legislature division of labor. The three problems associated with political accountability defined as such are: (i) the need for additional accountability measures for periods in-between elections;[13] (ii) the indirectness of public servants' accountability to citizens; and (iii) the increasing power of the executive vis-à-vis the legislative branch, also referred to as "decreetism" (O'Donnell 1994).[14]

Legal accountability is assured by the judiciary, which checks whether politicians and officials act within the confines of their mandates (Goetz and Gaventa 2001). As such, it has more to do with the rule of law and preventing the abuse of public service than efficiency and effectiveness concerns associated with political accountability (World Bank 2004).[15] Ferejohn (2006)[16] distinguishes between political and legal accountability on the grounds that the former is more arbitrary. In political accountability, the political principle (in this case, the elected official) can hold the agent (in this case, the public servant) accountable without providing justifications, such as when he/she punishes an agency by removing a leader, reducing budgets and/or limiting its jurisdiction. In contrast, legal accountability must be based on proof that in the case of a perceived breach of established rules and regulations, the agent is put on notice, through the enactment of prior law/standards.

Partly to resolve the above-mentioned problems associated with political accountability, and partly to approach it with legal accountability, innovative practices, strategies and tools have emerged at the intersection of political and legal accountability. Some of these innovations include the creation of independent/external accountability agencies including corruption-control bodies, independent electoral institutes, auditing agencies and ombudsmen. Research has shown that the strength of these agencies depends on their interconnection and coordination of respective activities as well as their relationship with society, including whether they include civil society organizations and citizens' groups into their decision-making processes and activities.[17]

Institutional versus Social Accountability
The institutional-social accountability divide, also called the *supply-versus the demand-led* or *top-down versus bottom-up* accountability, is more recent than the two previous descriptive sub-dichotomies of market-bureaucratic and political-legal/judicial accountability divides.[18] Institutions of accountability include the parliament, electoral system, the judiciary and the myriad audit organizations, therefore constricting institutional accountability largely to the political and legal realms. Social accountability, on the other hand, is made up of *ad hoc* initiatives of direct and indirect civil society and citizens' engagement in public affairs (Ackerman 2005: 16).

The institutional versus the social divide is more implicit than explicit in the literature. Goetz (2003), for instance, separated the traditional institutions of accountability, namely the electoral systems, legal and judicial entities (e.g. human rights commissions or gender-sensitive bodies, civil service reforms) from the more modern institutions of oversight (e.g. anti-corruption commissions) and the "new accountability agenda" defined as "rights operationalized" (4).[19] Likewise, Joshi (2010) maintained that the new social accountability mechanisms have "little traction" unless they trigger "conventional" accountability processes such as investigations, inspections and audits with formal sanctions (14). Social accountability understood as such, was born in the mid-1990s as a result of disenchantment with the new public management's market-inspired forces, such as privatization, contracting out and joint program management and, later on, the public-private-people partnerships (PPPPs) in the public sector.

Social accountability is associated with the drive to ensure effective, sustainable and, more importantly, pro-poor development (Ackerman 2004, 2005, Malena et al. 2004). Some researchers distinguish between the *voice-led social accountability*, defined by citizens' participation in policy making, advocacy and deliberation processes (Arroyo 2004, Malena et al. 2004), and the *control-oriented social accountability*, defined by citizens' watchdog role, often in cooperation with other societal actors, such as the media and professional associations and citizens' organizations (Peruzzotti and Smulovitz 2006, Orlansky and Chucho 2010, Peruzzotti 2012).[20]

Examples of social accountability include protests, advocacy campaigns, investigative journalism, public interest lawsuits, participatory data collection and analysis tools, participatory budgeting, public expenditure tracking, social audits, citizens' report cards, community score cards and other forms of citizen monitoring and evaluation activities in public policy making and service delivery. These tools and processes of social accountability are often portrayed as the non-state domain, although the state has been very much involved in all of them.[21]

Ackerman (2005) proposed three possible paths for the institutionalization of social accountability with linkages with the state: (i) blending participatory mechanisms into the strategic plans of government agencies and the rules and regulations of front-end bureaucrats; (ii) creating specific government agencies with the explicit objective of ensuring and enhancing societal participation; and (iii) legalizing informal participatory mechanisms by requiring specific government agencies or the government itself to engage society in the different segments and phases of the public policy processes—design, planning, implementation and evaluation. He stated that the first and the second paths have been accomplished to a degree as opposed to the third route, which is still uncommon.[22] As examples of hybrid accountability practices, citizens' councils or citizens' advisory boards, which audit government expenditures, supervise procurement and monitor elections, are only some of the visible experiences that point to the stronger interaction between state and society accountability practices.[23]

The tendencies of institutional and social accountability to converge show that citizens' engagement, that forms the core of social accountability, is not independent of state institutions. Coupled with the same convergence patterns among and with bureaucratic and market-based accountability, such inter-linkages shown in Table 3.2 also highlight the emergent need to move beyond dichotomous definitions of accountability. There is thus an opportunity, both at policy and academic grounds, to carry out cross country and cross sector inventories of the different types and degrees of "institutionalized social" accountability practices across time. In this respect, an empirical perspective on the actual tools of social accountability and their

Table 3.2 Descriptive Dichotomies of Accountability

System-based Accountabilities	Institution-based Accountabilities
Market-based Political Social	Bureaucratic Legal/Judicial Institutional (political, legal, market institutions, independent regulatory institutions or IRIs including audit institutions)

implementation patterns can bring a better grasp of the actual time-frames of the initiatives, their degree of embeddedness in state and society, their legality, direct outputs and more indirect outcomes with regard to accountability, governance and development.

Operational Dichotomies

Accountability, either in prescriptive or descriptive terms, operates through "horizontal" or "vertical" channels. *Horizontal account-ability* refers to within-state or *internal accountability* whereby public servants are held accountable to their peers, and public administrators, altogether, are held accountable to the relevant ministers.[24] As such, horizontal accountability is linked with both political and institutional accountability. It is also linked with administrative and market-based accountability because a procedural strengthening of horizontal accountability requires audit reforms and/or the creation of autonomous entities such as anti-corruption or human rights commissions, and a more substantive ingraining of horizontal accountability necessitates periodic measurements of government outputs.[25]

Vertical or external accountability refers to the oversight provided by civil society,[26] citizens' groups, the private sector and the mass media. It includes citizens' electoral choices and the collective exer-tion of pressure by civil society organizations,[27] communities, indi-vidual citizens and the media in-between elections (Goertz and Jenkins 2001, Malena et al. 2004). Informal mechanisms of vertical accountability include public pressure, negative or positive press releases, media coverage, public displays of support or protest movements, interface meetings between citizens and public officials, and petitions. Formal means occur when citizens appeal to the institutions of horizontal accountability as in presenting evidence to a corruption control agency, appealing to a public ombudsman or filing a claim through the court system.[28]

Although the overall effectiveness of social accountability as institutionalized practices have been questioned in the development management literature, new case study evidence from comparative political science and sociology shows that vertical accountability, associated with pressure exerted by societal forces, is growing in importance.[29] Anderson (2006), for instance, argues that vertical, and not horizontal, mechanisms of accountability, have proved efficient in delimiting executive authoritarianism in Nicaragua. Chang et al. (2010) finds that the freedom and strength of the media, measured by the ability to convey regular and extensive information on accountability breaches and corruption, has had significantly positive impact on political accountability in Italy. Although promising, studies on the significance of the new vertical accountability mechanisms and practices are few (Biela and Papadopoulos 2010). Hence, the convergence areas of vertical and social accountability represent yet another sphere ripe for further research to better understand both the continuous nature of accountability, and implications for democratization.[30]

Recently, more hybrid forms of operational accountability have arisen. One is *diagonal* or *transversal accountability*, which refers to the direct participation of citizens in the state's own internal mechanisms of accountability. Ackerman (2004) called this approach "inviting society into the inner chambers of the state instead of sending sections of the state off to society" (448). Fung and Wright (2001) dubbed it "empowered participatory governance," a society in deliberation over the design and operation of basic public services such as schooling, policing, environmental protection and urban infrastructure. Some examples of diagonal accountability are *citizen oversight committees* or *grievance redress mechanisms* with varying degrees of formality and legal authority.[31] They indicate one more convergence area between social and legal accountability.

Trechsel (2010) recently wrote about yet another type of accountability called "reflexive accountability," where citizens are responsible to themselves by initiating otherwise traditional forms of accountability, such as referenda, themselves. Then, the question becomes: are these "postmodern" forms of diagonal accountability[32] or is "reflexive accountability" just one more entry to the jungle of "accountability with adjectives" (101)?[33] What is clear, however, is that the conceptual and the empirical convergences of accountability mechanisms, processes and tools are too many to ignore. Further research is particularly needed on the new experiences and innovative formations in the developing world in order to better understand and redefine accountability and its impact on democratization processes.[34]

Longitudinal Dichotomies

Another dichotomy prevalent in the conceptual studies of accountability concerns its start and end points. This is the *ex-ante* versus the *ex-post* dichotomy of accountability. Some scholars view accountability as an ex-post event of holding actors accountable for past acts and completed projects. In this view, accountability is perceived as a control mechanism, and is performance-related. Others associate accountability with ex-ante occurrences because they perceive it as a process of "responsibility," including government responsiveness to citizens.

Ex-post accountability refers to holding elected officials to account through law, or other sanctioning mechanisms, including through elections. While the sustainability of ex-post accountability depends on the availability of information and the credibility of formal or informal sanctions (Biela and Papadopoulos 2010) as well as the fairness of elections, the viability of the latter as a robust vertical accountability mechanism has been questioned. For instance, experience shows that elected officials who are charged with, or convicted of, criminal wrongdoing are re-elected around the world irrespective of development differences and stages of democratization (Debrah 2009, Chang et al. 2010).

Ex-ante accountability can also be linked to electoral politics as in the elected officials being liable for their actions based on their pre-election promises and knowledge of the needs and wants of their constituents. Likewise, myriad consultation and other feedback mechanisms currently in use make citizens' interests known long before actual policies are formulated and implemented (Moncrieffe 2001: 27). Some examples of ex-ante accountability are the United States'

Administrative Procedure Act (APA) and National Environmental Policy Act (NEPA). Before agencies can adopt new regulations, they are required to give complete information on the prospective content of these regulations, justify them based on cost-benefit analysis, and even defend them in court if questioned by civil society groups (Ackerman 2005). These understandings of ex-ante accountability point to convergences with *operational-vertical* and *descriptive-social accountability* as well as with *prescriptive accountability*.

These and other examples of overlaps among the dichotomies of accountability point to the need for a process-oriented definition of accountability. As Ackerman (2005) affirmed: "To be accountable is to be in motion, not simply sitting in an office while being open to criticism. It is a dialogue, explanation and justification" (5). Likewise, Hernandez (2009) suggested: "Accountability needs reinterpretation in the form of a system which allows a 'process of responsibilizing' the governors, and a significant presence of citizens' and societal groups in the formulation, implementation, evaluation and monitoring of public policies" (61).[35]

While a discussion on the dyadic nature of accountability is useful for didactic purposes, such dichotomous perspectives do not bode well with reality. What are the common phases of accountability policies and institutionalization? How do the different stages of the process of accountability play out in relation to each other in different sectors, developmental settings and governance milieus? These are some of the questions that policy-makers and scholars of democratization need to answer when thinking about how to proceed with substantive democratization.

ACCOUNTABILITY AS A CONTINUOUS PROCESS

Taking stock of the changing nature of accountability, a few scholars have taken the first steps to offer process-based accounts of accountability. Given the complexities involved in finding a common ground between the "responsibility" and the "answerability" dimensions of accountability, however, they have often erred on the side of "workable definitions." Ackerman (2005), for instance, defined accountability as a "proactive process by which public officials inform about and justify their plans of action, their behavior and results, and are sanctioned accordingly" (1). Taylor and Buranelli (2007), drawing on earlier definitions of political accountability, conceived accountability as "ensuring that governments and their agents act in a public-regarding manner" (61). Kpatchavi (2009) talked about the *"obligation* of power-holders to give an account of their actions to service-recipient citizens, and of those citizens' *rights* to ask for this account" (11), and "to assess them in terms of 'availability, continuity and quality'" (9). Cees and Aarts (2010) referred to "decisional accountability" as the process of "ongoing education, internal and external deliberation, and examination."

Goetz and Gaventa's (2001) continuous conceptualization of accountability consisted of the *consultation, presence and influence* stages. In the first phase, the government opens up arenas for dialogue and information sharing. This phase could include one-off consultative exercises, ongoing participatory assessments on any given topic of concern, citizens' juries and/or surveys. In the second phase, society's access to the government is regularized and formalized. This phase could include quotas in local government for the marginalized groups, and structured access of grassroots organizations to local and national governance mechanisms such as budgeting or planning. In the third phase, impact on policy making is evaluated. This phase could transpire in the form of incorporating citizens' preferences into policy or service design, some form of diagonal accountability mechanism whereby citizens or citizens' groups become part of the accountability institutions and mechanisms, such as in financial audits or litigation rights in case of underperformance by specific government agencies, including poor-quality public services.

According to Goetz and Gaventa (2001), these stages do not necessarily take place in the order presented, nor do they ensure impact. Several intervening variables could affect the success that each stage and the process of accountability as a whole could achieve. Some of these intervening variables include contextual factors (state capacity and state autonomy, political system and the regime, economic development and growth, inequality, bureaucratic capacity), structural elements (depth of procedural and substantive democracy, the established roles and the relationship among the executive/legislative/judicial branches, the level of political participation, party system, population, density of the population, ethnic homogeneity) and other more circumstantial issues (unexpected crises or natural disasters, conflict and war).

Taylor and Buranelli (2007), in their study of accountability deficits in Brazil's public administration, broke the accountability process into three phases: *ex-ante oversight, ex-post investigation, and sanction.*

They then traced how core accountability initiatives for each stage would be allocated to specific institutional actors, including the parliamentary commissions of inquiry, independent or quasi-independent regulatory agencies and the judiciary. They showed that although these institutions could be accountable by themselves, their interaction together could nevertheless weaken accountability. They pointed to the politicized nature of accountability mechanisms and the lack of inter-institutional cooperation as potential culprits. They underlined the need to focus on continuous interactions rather than disparate categorizations of accountability.

Joshi (2010) also came close to a continuous view of accountability. Focusing more specifically on accountability in the area of public service delivery, he conceived accountability as a series of the following actions: *setting standards, getting information about actions, making judgments about appropriateness, and sanctioning unsatisfactory performance.* While Joshi was careful not to single out any of these accountability actions to be either sufficient or necessary for successful public service delivery, the questions he asked are pertinent to the changing understanding and practice of accountability: What are the accountability steps to undertake in order to solve the problem of teacher absenteeism? Which additional initiatives can be envisaged toward improving the overall quality of public education and learning?

Like Joshi (2010) and other scholars adopting a continuous approach to accountability, this book takes a step further to link the latter with continuous democratization. It asks: Are there some accountability mechanisms that would yield more effective outcomes if introduced at any given stage of development and democratization, for example before, after or simultaneously with other and comparable mechanisms, such as transparency and corruption control? How can democratization benefit or suffer when different combinations of transparency and accountability policies are introduced and institutionalized at different points in time, and via different modalities of tools and strategies?

ACCOUNTABILITY AND DEMOCRATIZATION LINKAGES

The links of accountability with democratization are almost unequivocally positive, and both direct and indirect. Accountability is directly related to fundamental issues in democratic politics because it is integral to issue areas that are endogenous to democratization, such as formal and informal standards of monitoring and evaluation, information and deliberative public networks, including participatory policy (Olsen 2013). Accountability is also indirectly related to democratization because it is a commonly agreed pillar of good (democratic) governance,[36] and of legitimate and effective public administration and public service delivery (Crowe 2011, Head 2012).

Accountability is negatively linked with democratization often due only to implementation defects. Cheung (2011), for instance, maintained that the increasing political accountability brought a fall in integrity in the public sector in Hong Kong because of the politicization of the Principal Officials Accountability System (POAS)[37] introduced in 2002. Easterly (2010) directed our attention to the gaps in the accountability standards applied toward the more versus the less affluent sectors of society. Schillemans (2010) emphasized the problems associated with favoring one type of accountability over another.

Directly, accountability as an intrinsic element of democratic politics works through three different paths. First, accountability as a mechanism of justice can be used to ensure compliance with formal and informal rules governing the society, including human rights, particularly in post-conflict societies where a newly ending civil war necessitates reparation and reconciliation before democratization can even start (Lamin 2003, Kaiser 2005, Crippa 2012, Kim 2012, Pajibo 2012). Second, with increased flow of relevant information, and enhanced regulatory transparency, the ensuing accountability relations can lead to democratization by empowering citizens and the civil society to ask relevant questions at opportune moments, thereby allowing them to control the governing entities regularly, through free and fair elections (Ashworth 2012, Shkabatur 2012, Woon 2012). Third, accountability ensures the progression of democratization over the long run by making inclusive policy making the hallmark of governance, including through non-electoral mechanisms to hold the governing bodies and representatives to account (Sandbrook 1996, Fritz 2008, Good and Taylor 2008, Lange 2008, Le Van 2011).

Concerning the first path of direct accountability-democratization linkages, accountability works as a mechanism of justice in post-dictatorial and post-crisis contexts where the beginnings of social, political and economic liberalization along with the first national elections are contemplated. In such contexts, accountability becomes part of the paradigms of transitional justice, peace-building and development (Pajibo 2012). It is conceived as a human right and is about the right to truth, the right to justice and the right to effective remedy and reparation (Pillay 2012). Evenhanded prosecution of human rights violations thus goes hand in hand with the adequate control mechanisms on the government in the aftermath of a civil war and before the first elections. Accountability becomes part of democratization processes before and during the elections through the emerging or revamped judicial system (Croissant 2010), as well as the Truth and Reconciliation Commissions (Lamin 2003), and nation-wide consultation processes including the participation of regional and international organizations (Crippa 2012).

Concerning the second path of direct accountability-democratization linkages, accountability, as a consequence and companion of increased flow of information and effective transparency, makes its way into democratization as early as with the first elections. Research shows that the public may vote, based not only on forward-looking selection of candidates, but on their retrospective sanctioning, i.e., by taking into account the past acts and actions of the running candidates and political parties. The idea of electoral punishment implies that voters punish those officials who adopt incongruent policy positions (Gerber et al. 2011).[38] As such, elections become less dependent on traditional voting loyalties (Dagg 2007) and more on holding to account the prospective governors (Woon 2012).

The relationship between accountability and elections is studied by several scholars, who document the variety of linkages that might exist between the two. Svolik (2013), for instance, claimed that elections are used extensively as accountability mechanisms in new democracies because the voters heed the individual reputation of candidates more in these contexts than in established democracies. Ashworth (2012), on the other hand, argued that competitive elections are ubiquitous mechanisms of formal accountability between citizens and policy-makers, including in more advanced democracies. Weale (2011) qualified that elections are particularly useful in providing authorization, and intermittent yet periodic sanctioning, but less so in providing opportunities for continuous explanation and justification for acts and actions of governors.

Different types of electoral systems were also linked differently with accountability by several scholars. Cho (2012), for instance, maintained that majoritarian electoral systems provide more immediate accountability in terms of citizens' control over policy-makers than proportional electoral systems, which favor long-term inclusion or representativeness over short-term accountability. Accordingly, representativeness could lead to greater accountability for multicultural societies over the long run rather than immediately.[39] Likewise, different cultural settings with unique political traditions could benefit from one or the other electoral system to produce the desired accountability effect toward *sui generis* democratization.

There is consensus among scholars on the overall positive impact of freedom of expression and transparency leading to accountability, starting with the first free and fair elections (Callamard 2010). Elections and electoral accountability, however, are found to be insufficient by themselves to ensure the continuity of democratization. One can think of cases where free and fair elections have led to peaceful turnover of governments even though development is dragging, clientelism is soaring and ethnic tensions are spreading (Sandbrook 1996, Fonchingong 2004). Even in the absence of such negative attributes, electoral democracy being the only game in town is suspect to bring about a sustainable substantive democracy (Fritz 2008). Illiberal authoritarianism, elitist top-down structures and excessive presidentialism, all of them plagued with accountability deficits, could hamper the deepening of electoral democracies (Good and Taylor 2008). Accountability, therefore, continues to be the centerpiece of democratization because it provides answers to these and similar problems, mainly through its emphases on deliberation, dialogue, participation and cooperation (Raphael and Karpowitz 2013).

Concerning the third path of direct accountability-democratization linkages, accountability could work at society- and state-levels in the aftermath of the first national elections toward procedural democracy. At the societal level, media and civil society as well as innovative grassroots formations acting in cooperation with other social groups such as the private sector, professional associations and universities are important accountability actors in democratic consolidation. Depending on their level of organization, capacity, skill sets and freedom of participation, they put pressure on governance institutions to ensure that their concerns and demands are taken into account in policy making. They launch or push for the launching of investigations against suspected misadministration and fraud (Steffek 2010). They strengthen participatory policy, collective responsibility and state-society dialogue (Hanberger 2009).[40]

At the state level, more traditional political forces are active forces of accountability in democratic consolidation. Independent regulatory agencies, state inspectors and auditors, specialized integrity agencies make sure that the internal organization and functioning of public and governmental agencies are in line with the written rules and expected outcomes of achievement. They are effective not only in tackling corrupt or fraudulent activities, but also in preventing conflict of interest, thereby contributing to a culture of accountability and transparency (Head 2012). Their accountability to the government and to societal actors of accountability, and their cooperation with parallel accountability institutions such as user committees and social funds at the local level, increase their overall effectiveness and contributions to democratization (Lange 2008, Lloyd 2008, Sosay 2009).

Although both the state- and societal-level accountability actors and institutions are more effective in contexts where prior democratization, including transparency and electoral accountability, has been well established, new research points to the benefits of instituting formal and informal accountability institutions early on, i.e., during or even before the first national elections. Finkel (2012), comparing the cases of Poland and Russia, argued, for instance, that ombudsmen created before the transition to democracy are more effective later on compared to ombudsmen created after the democratic transitions. Hossain (2010) and Chen and Huhe (2013) showed that media and grassroots could be effective in pushing for better public services, and sanctioning poor services in local settings, particularly if the local officials are from the same lineage groups as the communities.

Accountability also contributes to democratization by its very propagation. The multiplicity of accountability links, also called "redundant accountability," means that people and institutions are accountable to several *accountees* from different sources for the same given act. Schillemans (2010) found that the multiplicity/redundancy of accountability mechanisms improved the: (i) reliability by increasing the chances of catching and correcting unwanted behavior; (ii) information asymmetry problem between agencies and their principals by multiplying the points of access to information; and (iii) legitimacy of accountability systems by allowing a better incorporation of diverse values (Dubnick and Frederickson 2011).

Not all consolidated democracies adopt similar accountability systems nor do they implement the same accountability policies or mechanisms. Different types of accountability frameworks can be better suited to different types of democratic systems (Philp 2009). Differences between the accountability regimes of Europe and Canada, for instance, link those divergences to their networked versus entrepreneurial modes of governance, respectively (Millar 2013). In Europe, *public reporting and deliberation* are the preferred accountability methods, with emphasis on political inclusion and citizen engagement typical of the proportional electoral systems and parliamentarian political systems. In Canada, fiscal auditing and performance management mechanisms with emphasis on formal controls and sanctions are the most prevalent accountability mechanisms.

Similar patterns of divergences were also drawn between the transparency initiatives and the ensuing accountability frameworks in the European Union and the United States (Frost 2003). Transparency was adopted as a stand-alone tool to fight corruption through the Freedom of Information Acts and Laws in the United States. In contrast, the European Union adopted transparency as part of all decision-making processes, and linked it with an overall democratization agenda, including particularly through participatory politics and accountability. Typical of the Westminster political systems, East Asian governments also opted for efficiency and sanction-based accountability found in Canada and in the United States over representativeness and responsibility-driven accountability found in Europe (Rock 2013). In both types of governance systems and their associated accountability frameworks, however, concerns over financial accountability have dominated those over programmatic accountability (Martin and Frahm 2010).

Accountability may also contribute to democratization indirectly, mostly through its positive impact on good governance. As a pillar of good governance, accountability in politics and the public sector is likely to lead to healthy participation, pluralism and party system institutionalization. Accountability can also curtail corruption, and contribute to democratization through this indirect channel. Referring to corruption-free public service as a human right, Kumar

(2013) identified the transparency-accountability pair as a democratizer because of its combined effect on corruption prevention, detection and control.[41] In this perspective, a culture of transparency and accountability will lead to the strengthening of *good* or *good enough* governance,[42] which will then fuel potential democratization, provided that political willingness is strong and continuous (Head 2012, Evans 2012).

CONCLUSION

If anything, this chapter justifies Mulgan's (2000) dictum that accountability is an "ever expanding concept," where its myriad forms and varieties almost render the term "meaningless" (Koppell 2005: 95).[43] Perhaps to simplify the complexities involved in understanding accountability, dichotomous explanations have dominated the literature. This chapter introduces the accountability cube as an instrument to organize and simplify this multiplicity of definitions of accountability offered in several (sub)disciplines, and attempts to link them among each other to show their continuities rather than their seemingly dichotomous nature.

The soft plane of the accountability cube consisting of moral, political, vertical/societal and ex-ante accountability corners is complemented with its hard plane consisting, in turn, of material, legal, horizontal/organizational and ex-post accountability corners. Accordingly, each one of the two facing corners of the edges of the accountability cube is seen as a continuous dimension of accountability. As a result, the moral-material dichotomy of prescriptive accountability, the political-legal dichotomy of descriptive accountability, the vertical-horizontal dichotomy of operational accountability and the ex-ante and ex-post dichotomy of longitudinal accountability are the continuous pillars of the accountability cube. They all pit the *responsibility* understanding of accountability against its *answerability* understanding, and link them both together.

This chapter attempts to link the opposite sides of accountability together to offer an alternative view of accountability as a continuous process of both responsibility and answerability. As such, it also links transparency with accountability, and the latter with corruption control. The direct and indirect implications on democratization are teased out to show potential patterns of continuity. Directly, accountability is associated with democratization: (i) through the perspectives of human rights and justice in post-conflict and pre-transitional stages where both institutional and social accountability work to bring reconciliation; (ii) through freedom of information and transparency in transitional stages where electoral accountability feeds into administrative accountability and democratization over the long run; and (iii) through formal and informal mechanisms of deliberation, participation and control in democratic consolidation.

Accountability in promoting justice prepares the ground for democratization to start; accountability through increased transparency starting with the first elections provides authorization and sanction (Weale 2011); and accountability in political governance in between elections ensures explanation and justification through the institutionalization of organizational learning, public deliberation and participation (Ghere 2011). Indirectly, accountability contributes to democratization through its impact on good governance.

There are many accountability-related issues that this chapter does not cover due to scope and space restrictions. For instance, issues abound on accountability deficits in development agencies vis-à-vis the donors, and between them and aid-receiving countries (DARA 2010),[44] internal and external accountability issues in non-governmental organizations (NGOs), civil society organizations (CSO) and citizens' groups (Beck et al. 2007),[45] accountability in public service delivery (Blind 2009) and in local government (Salvochea 2007), the growing impact of information technologies and knowledge management on accountability (UN 2010), and other more general, yet critical concerns regarding the need to establish the "right institutions" (Inforesources 2008) versus the necessity to have "good politicians" in ensuring democratic accountability (Halim 2008).

Each of the above-mentioned issues could have specific, and sometimes contradictory effects on democratization in different contexts. Yet, they would best be answered through accountability perspectives that are comprehensive and continuous rather than scattered and dichotomous. To put it differently, rather than asking if policy-makers should introduce accountability earlier or later on in democratization processes, we might be better off pondering what types and degrees of soft and hard accountability combinations work best for democratization over the long term. Such exercise would not only bridge the gap between theory and practice but could also bring policy closer to politics. More importantly, it could also contribute to surmounting the artificial divide between procedural and substantive democratization.

CHAPTER 4

———•❈•———

THE CORRUPTION PENTAGON:
LINKING CAUSES, CONTROLS
AND CONSEQUENCES

Corruption has been around since prehistoric times but its common understanding as "the use of public office for private or illicit gain" has gained wide currency only since the 1990s (Doig and McIvor 1999). While efforts to arrive at standard definitions for phenomena as complex and multifaceted as corruption are to be applauded, scholars and policy-makers increasingly agree about the inadequacy of such rudimentary descriptions to cover the whole gamut of corrupt acts and dealings. There is a need for comprehensive yet targeted definitions of corruption with emphasis on the analytical linkages among its common causes, controls and consequences. In other words, a comprehensive focus on how corruption may emerge, propagate, soar and recede can illuminate both the theoretical and practical perspectives on corruption.

This chapter attempts to offer a venue for such conceptual clarity by synthesizing a voluminous literature on corruption definitions and measurements. It does this by undertaking a two-pronged analysis. First, the myriad understandings of corruption are compiled and categorized through macro-historical, micro-individual and meso-institutional approaches. The result is the *Corruption Pentagon* proposed as a conceptual tool to interlink the disparate definitions of corruption at these three levels of analysis. Second, the chapter focuses on the consequences of corruption on democratization, both directly through *nomocracy*, referring to rule of law and legitimacy; and less directly through the national integrity systems, or good governance. The results show that transparency, accountability and corruption control feed into democratization in different ways depending on the types and degrees of the specific governance challenges faced at any point in time.

On the conceptual plane, the Corruption Pentagon lists five defining parameters for corruption: *Seed-Feed-Need-Greed and Wield*. On a macro-historical dimension, the Corruption Pentagon examines the conditions that may lie at the root of corruption (Seed) as well as those that tend to nourish or starve it (Feed). On a micro-individual dimension, it lists the factors that may lead to corrupt transactions among individuals acting out of material necessities (Need) or moral insatiability (Greed). Finally, on a meso-institutional level, it considers the formal/legal and informal/social restraint mechanisms against the emergence and spread of corruption (Wield). Although neither exhaustive nor prescriptive, the Corruption Pentagon attempts to bring corruption closer to a more path-dependent and multiscalar understanding, which several scholars have argued is lacking in the current corruption literature (Xin and Rudel 2004).

On the impact analysis, the chapter proposes to take corruption beyond its debate on "democratic quality" to the overall "processes" of democratization. It differentiates between the *direct* and *indirect* connections between corruption and democratization. Directly, corruption prevention, control and sanctioning improve the legitimacy of the government in the eyes of the public while contributing to economic efficiency in the long-run. Indirectly, anti-corruption measures and institutions enhance the quality and the effectiveness of public services and public administration, which then enhance political legitimacy and economic efficiency, contributing therefore to democratization. At a practical level, the cost–benefit model of corruption supported by continuous democratization is found to tackle political corruption at the top, while the principal–agent model supported by coherent governance reforms is better suited to control administrative or street-level corruption (Andvig et al. 2000). Neopatrimonial regimes where corruption permeates all societal sectors and state hierarchies are candidates for comprehensive democratic overhauls based both on answerability through credible sanctions and responsibility through information-sharing. Consistency and credibility are keys.

The chapter concludes that the most successful anti-corruption initiatives are those that adequately combine all pillars of the Corruption Pentagon depending on the type of corruption faced. The structural-contextual determinants of the Seed-Feed pillar, the individual-organizational mechanisms of the Need-Greed pillar and the formal-informal institutions of the Wield pillar must be effectively combined and interlinked to tackle both the ex-ante and ex-post corruption in government and administration, including at all levels of the hierarchy, albeit with different degrees of emphasis depending on the case. In this process-driven understanding, democratization and anti-corruption policies are like the two sides of the same coin rather than two separate or similar coins.

CORRUPTION: A CHRONOLOGICAL OVERVIEW OF DEFINITIONS

Corruption is nothing new. Two bronze urns unearthed in north-west China's Shaanxi province carried inscriptions that tell the story of how, in 873 BC, a nobleman bribed judges in order to escape charges of appropriating farmland (Xinhua News Agency 2006). The 2500-year-old Indian manuscript "Arthshastra" stressed the need for administrators to combat graft (Jain 1998: vii). The idealism of the ancient Olympics was marred by corruption as early as 67 BC when the Roman emperor Nero bribed judges to win chariot races.

Corrupt dealings and measures to fight them only expand in size and kind as we get closer to the present. The French King Louis XIV sentenced his finance minister to life imprisonment in 1661 for mismanagement of funds and personal enrichment. His contemporary, the Chinese emperor Kangxi, raised the wages of civil servants in order to reduce corruption (Etienne 2011). The Ottoman Empire adopted its first Criminal Law in 1840 thereby redefining as corrupt the previously legitimate act of gift-giving to the Sultan (Bedirhanoglu 2007). In the 1920s–1930s, corruption scandals dogged the United States where extensive media coverage by a free press led to the imprisonment of some of President Warren Harding's acquaintances with influential posts in the government (Gentzkow et al. 2006).

Across the border in Mexico, the top decision-makers treated the state as a "milch cow" to advance their individual enrichment, and corruption escalated to violence there in the 1940s (Niblo 1999: 300–303).

Corruption today is only more widespread, diverse and embedded across cultures, systems and economies. First, it is seen as a legal crime, a social deviation or a moral opprobrium. Yet, it could also be acceptable in different social settings depending on its different outcomes relative to the affected groups' losses and gains at any given point in time. Second, corruption is often based on a mix of factors derived from individual interest, institutional parameters, structural conditions, ethical considerations and cultural habits. Different combinations of originating factors can dominate the causes and consequences of corruption in different contexts. Third, corruption often involves a variety of individual, collective and organizational actors of diverse sectoral, professional, political and socioeconomic backgrounds, acting at any level of governance—local, national, regional and transnational. Last but not least, corruption might be overt and systemic but it could also be hidden and sporadic.

The various combinations of the above-mentioned categories of factors can produce diverse sets of corrupt transactions—of different nature, degree and implications. Synthesizing all factors together, three main understandings or phases of corruption are discernible in corruption studies: (i) the social-functional definitions (1960s–1970s); (ii) the behavioral-institutional definitions (1980s–1990s); and (iii) the performance-perception definitions (2000s–today).

Social-Functional Understanding of Corruption (1960s–1970s)

Corruption was first studied as part of developmental studies. Its classical definition was given by Nye (1967) as "any behavior that deviates from the formal duties of a public role (elective or appoint-ive) because of private-regarding (personal, close family, private clique) wealth or status gains (416)." The main debate consisted of its positive versus negative impact on developmental prospects in the developing world, where it was believed to thrive. Corruption, as such, was seen as an instrument of under-development and a problem of modernity. It was believed that corruption could be socially acceptable in traditional societies (social corruption) while being put to good use to help stimulate economic development (functional corruption) until modernization ran its course (Myrdal 1968).

Social corruption meant that certain acts and dealings that could be seen as suspiciously or outright corrupt in developed countries could be conceived as traditionally imposed or expected duties of gratitude and allegiance in developing countries (Ekpo 1979). With time, social corruption was questioned as corruptibility was linked with certain economic, and not solely social, underpinnings (Sherman 1978). *Functional corruption* was the view of corruption as grease to economic efficiency and growth, and characterized as fresh air to those that are politically marginalized in hyper-bureaucratic and oppressive environments (Braibanti 1963, Leff 1964, Abueva 1966, Bayley 1966).

A prominent corruption scholar, Heidenheimer (1970) differentiated among the *"public opinion," "public interest,"* and *"public office"* understandings of corruption. Corruption was what the public believed a given act to be corrupt, according to the first public opinion definition. It was any act that subverted the generally accepted public interest, according to the second public interest definition. It was also any behavior that violated the formal rules of an organization, according to the third public office definition. Heidenheimer (1970) also differentiated between degrees of corruption: *black corruption* referred to overt corruption with punishable outcomes as agreed by everyone, *white corruption* alluded to socially acceptable corruption that is condoned and unsanctioned, and *gray corruption* underlined those actions deemed corrupt by some, but not by others.

In addition to the diversification in the definitions and types of corruption, the 1970s also witnessed the mitigation of the modernity restriction in the understanding of corruption. As consecutive corruption scandals tormented the advanced industrialized countries, corruption definition expanded to include the developed world (Berg et al. 1976, Benson 1978, Dobel 1978, Amick 1976, Mamoru and Auerbach 1977, Sherman 1978, Williams 1981). The universalization of corruption brought forth doubts about its social and functional interpretations (Goodman 1974, Rose-Ackerman 1978).

Behavioral-Institutional Understanding
of Corruption (1980s–1990s)

The debate over whether and how corruption affected the developed versus the developing countries in different ways continued in the 1980s and the 1990s. The arguments for the positive impact of corruption on economic and political development were abandoned to underline its long-term negative effects (Rashid 1981). Alatas (1990) defined corruption as an umbrella term that covered attributes as diverse and negative as "betrayal of trust, deception, secrecy, complicity, and camouflage" (1, 2). Economically, corruption was found to retard growth (Klitgaard 1988, Knack and Keefer 1995, Mauro 1995, Tanzi and Davoodi 1997), lower private investment, reduce the quality of public infrastructure and services, decrease tax revenues and distort the composition of government expenditures (Mauro 1998). Socially, it was linked with declining trust and legitimacy, particularly in newly created democracies (Griffith and Munroe 1995: 368–70, Dominguez 1997, Moran 2001). Politically, it was seen as an impediment to democratic institutionalization (Doig and McIvor 1999). Corruption thus went from being a developmental instrument in the post-colonial period to a developmental disease in the neoliberal era and thereafter (Cockcroft 2010).

The focus on the social distinctiveness of corruption was also mitigated in this period. Corruption was increasingly associated with informational asymmetry and the individual calculations of perceived benefits and associated risks even though social perspectives persisted in some area studies. In patrimonial societies, for instance, any transgression of the legal rules to engage in corruption, such as embezzlement, could be justified by what the society or certain powerful societal groups received as a result of it (Beck 1999: 209). To illustrate this duality in the understanding of corruption, while the developmental delay in the Philippines was partly attributed to the then President Marcos' pursuit of self-enrichment (Hawes 1987), Africa's developmental and governance challenges were still attributed to its social traditions (Moxon-Browne 1987). In both the social and individual understandings of corruption, often the proposed solutions focused on middle-ground organizational change (Williams 1981, Wade 1982, Doig 1984).

One of the most influential individual analyses of corruption called "principal-agent analysis," examined the relationship between three actors: the citizens, the principal (a governor) and an agent (a public official) who managed the relationship between the citizens and their government (Klitgaard 1988). Some of the factors that led to corrupt acts by agents included wide discretion, centralized power and little accountability in decision-making (Riley 1998: 134). Accordingly, Klitgaard's famous corruption formula read: C = M + D – A (corruption equals monopoly plus discretion minus account-ability). In controlling corruption, changes to individual and organi-zational incentives of office-holders were proposed (Rose-Ackerman 1999). These institutional measures aimed to limit official discretion and monopoly of power, increased controls over officials including through bureaucratic oversight and strengthened accountability measures and democratic political processes overall (Kaufmann 1997). They also decreased the marginal benefits of potential and actual corrupt activity vis-à-vis the marginal benefits of legal activity through criminalization (Rose-Ackerman 2010, Persson et al. 2013).

Institutional reforms against corruption centered on the state and specific government agencies as well as the non-governmental orga-nizations. Strategies to increase the horizontal and vertical account-ability of government offices such as the presidency, the legislature, the public agencies and the courts became important policy param-eters (Manzetti 2000: 133). The research and watchdog roles of non-governmental entities in preventing, detecting and controlling corruption directly and indirectly, through their contributions to good governance, also came under the spotlight (Fowler 1988, 1997, Bratton 1989, Korten 1990, Beckman 1991, Clark 1991). Starting with the mid-1990s, organizational and administrative prac-tices of the NGOs themselves, particularly with regard to their enrol-ment in the dispersion of foreign aid, received increasing attention.

Becoming an organizational construct at its core, corruption also became the locus of attention for international organizations in the 1990s. The World Bank and the Inter-American Development launched their anti-corruption programs (Quick 2000, Shihata 2000). One World Bank manager, Peter Eigen, distressed by the Bank's failure to address corruption, formed Transparency International (TI) in 1993, which became an influential interna-tional organization in analyzing and controlling corruption. The United Nations General Assembly passed a resolution against cor-ruption in 1996, and in 1997, another resolution was passed with respect to the code of conduct of public officials.[1] These resolutions defined corruption as the abuse of entrusted power for private or collective gain by public office holders, civil servants and politicians.

Corruption was also on the agenda of regional organizations of governance by the 1990s. The European Parliament passed the International Code of Conduct for Public Officials in 1996. It defined corruption in line with the United Nations' definition of any misuse of power in decision making, committed for illicit gain.[2] The same year, the Organization of American States (OAS) approved the Inter-American Convention against Corruption (Tulchin and Espach 2000). The Council of Europe issued the Model Code of Behavior for Public Officials in 1997. It referred to corruption as "a serious threat to the basic principles of democracy, a danger to rule of law, the negation of human rights, and a barrier to social and economic progress" (Council of Europe 1997). The same year, the Organization for Economic Cooperation and Development (OECD) created a convention that criminalized bribery by OECD-based enterprises abroad.[3] Some African states undertook a series of administrative reforms aimed at reducing government corruption (Riley 1998). The Council of Europe held the Civil Law and Criminal Law Conventions on Corruption in 1999. The same year, the Group of States against Corruption (GRECO) was formed.

Performance-Perceptions Understandings of Corruption (2000s–today)

The mix of individual-behavioral and institutional-organizational approaches continued on in the 2000s. Individual analyses were elaborated through a targeted focus on the different types of individual actors and attributes. Institutionalist analyses expanded their focus from accountability to transparency as a significant anti-corruption factor. This decade gave rise to dichotomous yet eclectic studies of corruption, including ex-ante *corruption prevention* versus ex-post *control*, the *formal* and the *informal* means of corruption control, *integrity systems* versus *legal sanctions* for corruption prevention and the *subjective* versus *objective* methods of corruption measurement.

Individual analyses of corruption merged with gender studies to show how and why women may be less corrupt than men, this giving birth to the new corruption variable of rates of women office holders in politics (Goetz 2007). The "good politician" factor was another individual variable that acquired importance. Anti-corruption measures of electoral accountability and judicial efficacy were linked with their increasing impact on shaping "good politicians," who controlled corruption by monitoring bureaucrats and enhancing economic development (Caselli and Morelli 2004, Besley 2005, Jones and Olken 2005, Halim 2008).

New Institutionalist perspectives on corruption focused on the delineation of formal and informal norms, controls and networks (Lauth 2000, Helmke and Levitsky 2004, Hale 2011). Informal anti-corruption mechanisms referred to bottom-up and internal institutional practices such as merit-based bureaucratic recruitment and mutual peer-supervision. Formal controls, in turn, were institutional practices external to bureaucracies such as control mechanisms based on horizontal and vertical accountability, as well as an overall democratic system (Halim 2008).

The differential impact of formal versus informal means of addressing corruption was the hallmark of the corruption studies from the 2000s onward. Some scholars argued that formal controls were more effective than informal ones in checking corruption (Treisman 2000, Lederman et al. 2001, Montinola and Jackman 2002, Caselli and Morelli 2004). A sub-group among them picked up on the democratization debate over the parliamentary versus presidential systems, and maintained that the latter is more corrupt than the former (Kunicova and Rose-Ackerman 2005), while others argued the opposite (Persson et al. 2003). Still others differentiated between party and electoral systems to maintain that two-party systems in countries with predominantly single-member district electoral formulas, as in the United Kingdom, are less corrupt than multiparty systems using the same electoral formula, as in India, and that proportional representation does not really matter for corruption (Charron 2011). Other scholars went beyond political, party and electoral systems to focus on the relative strength of independent versus less-independent regulatory agencies of corruption. Often more autonomy was associated with less corruption although the type and the degree of autonomy was qualified depending on the different attributes of different administrative contexts (Meagher 2005, Wren-Lewis 2011).[4]

Other scholars stressed the importance of informal over that of formal attributes in effectively preventing and controlling corruption. Such informal attributes included a zero-tolerance culture

(Gong and Wang 2013), lack of legacies of bureaucratic autonomy (Fukuyama 2012),[5] bureaucratic and political coordination and cooperation (Taylor and Buranelli 2007) and positive perceptions of state institutions as conducive to less corruption (Grodeland 2013), and social cohesion, social capital and state legitimacy (Lovseth 2001).[6] Low trust due, in essence, to lack of transparency, was linked with increasing corruption (Uslaner 2008). Still others pointed at the need of using a mix of both formal and informal means depending on the type, degree and source of corruption (Ledeneva 2009).

Both the individual and the institutional perspectives on corruption attempted to adequately operationalize and measure corruption across countries and over time. Quantitative studies of corruption based on the experiences and perceptions of citizens or select groups of individuals and organizations were produced. Objective government performance and experience indicators often consisted of time and fees needed to register a business or obtain a permit; while subjective perception surveys assessed respondents' opinions over the levels and spread of corruption and its types (Knack 2004, Kurer 2005, Arndt and Oman 2006, Camerer 2006, Kenny 2006,[7] Reinikka and Svensson 2006, Kurtz and Schrank 2007, Thomas 2010, Blind 2012).

Corruption prevention also gained in importance in this decade under the rubric of vulnerabilities to corruption (Johnston 2010). Transparency accompanied by accountability conditions such as high literacy, active media and elections were found to be necessary to decrease corruption (Lindstedt and Naurin 2010), even in contexts subject to resource-curse dynamics, which are often associated with rent-seeking economies and high degrees of corruption (Kolstad and Wiig 2009, McFerson 2009). Lack of transparency was deemed to be a signal of corruption while more transparency was associated with its control (Uslaner 2006).

Inclusion of transparency in anti-corruption frameworks brought with it the more holistic purpose of *pro-integrity* rather than *anti-corruption* focus in public governance (Head 2012). The holistic view on corruption as good governance meant the creation of a second generation or aggregate measures of corruption. They took into account both the subjective and the objective measures of corruption using statistical techniques. These quantitative studies generated both praise and criticism in terms of reliability, validity and accuracy of measuring and understanding corruption (Urra 2007).[8]

The holistic view on corruption also led to the adoption of several international and regional agreements to prevent, control and combat corruption. The Implementation of the International Code of Conduct for Public Officials was adopted by the United Nations in 2002, followed by the African Union Convention on Preventing and Combating Corruption in 2003, the United Nations Convention against Transnational Organized Crime and the United Nations Convention against Corruption in 2004. The Organization for Security and Cooperation in Europe (OSCE) put emphasis on the role of good governance and engaged civil society in fighting corruption. It signed a memorandum of understanding with the International Anti-Corruption Academy (IACA) to more effectively prevent and control corruption through deterring money laundering, financing of terrorism and human trafficking (2011, 2012).

CORRUPTION PENTAGON: A CONCEPTUAL TOOL

The chronological overview of corruption definitions shows that corruption studies have moved from unilateral and culturally oriented descriptions of the developing world in the 1960s to multidimensional and analytical analyses of corruption in the developing and developed worlds in the 2000s. Progress notwithstanding, the plethora of *corruption definitions* still exist side-by-side with long lists of *corruption forms* that may be ascribed to myriad *corruption types* with an extensive list of *anti-corruption solutions*. A targeted synthesis of the various causes, controls and consequences of corruption would thus benefit the literature. The following analysis attempts to assemble and sort out this thick conceptual data through the Corruption Pentagon.

The Corruption Pentagon, shown in Figure 4.1, attempts to clarify corruption conceptually through its five pillars. The *Seed* pillar unifies and examines the systemic and internal root causes that may give rise to corruption. The *Feed* pillar assembles and connects the circumstantial and external catalysts that may nourish or discourage corruption. Together, the *Seed-Feed dimension* of corruption consists of value-driven and system-wide corruption, as in the classical definition of corruption.

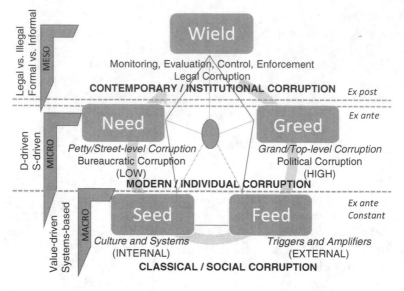

Figure 4.1   Corruption Pentagon

The third *Need* pillar of the Corruption Pentagon analyzes the individual factors that may engender corruption seen from a redistributive policy perspective. The fourth *Greed* pillar looks at the individual and organizational conditions that propagate it, as seen from an extractive policy perspective. Together, the *Need-Greed dimension* of corruption consists of demand- and supply-driven corruption at the individual and organizational levels, as in the modern sense of corruption.

The final *Wield* pillar of the Corruption Pentagon covers the legal/formal and social/informal control mechanisms that may curb corruption after its occurrence. It feeds into the Seed-Feed dimension since ex-post control affects the root causes and the spread of corruption at systemic levels, including before it actually occurs. It also exerts influence on the Need-Greed dimension directly because legal and social restraints shape individual acts and actions, and indirectly, through the Seed-Feed dimension of corruption. As such, the Wield pillar is based on an amalgam of cultural values, system characteristics, individual and organizational incentive schemes, as well as specific anti-corruption rules and regulations.

The Seed-Feed Dimension of Corruption

Not unlike Heidenheimer's "public office" explanation of corruption in the 1970s, and taking it up a notch to encompass public *systems*, some corruption studies of the past two decades have viewed corruption as essentially value-based and systems-driven. In this understanding, corruption is a structural problem that permeates states and societies. It is defined as a lapse by state and society from a standard of goodness due to social degradation and the breakdown of civic loyalty and virtue (Dobel 1978, Johnston 1996).

Corruption defined as a structural problem of state and society could be cultural-specific or universal. Kurer (2005), for instance, maintained that corruption is the violation of the impartiality principle of universal ethics and theories of justice. Accordingly, corrupt states were defined as those that do not treat their citizens equally. Nepotism and bribery were listed as sub-types of systemic corruption: public officials who discriminated in favor of those who are socially close to them were characterized as nepotist, and those who discriminated in favor of those who could pay the highest price were defined as the bribe-takers.

Others, unlike Kurer's (2005) universalist perspective, viewed corruption as a structural phenomenon determined by cultural norms that contradicted the "national integrity systems."[9] Lascoumes and Tomescu-Hatto (2008), for instance, found that the French public was tolerant to petty favoritism in order to get things done. Ko and Weng (2011), on the other hand, demonstrated that the same would be frowned upon and punished in China where dereliction of duty is classified as corruption, even in the absence of private gain. On another end of the spectrum, corruption in India was deemed so rampant that "it often failed to shock" (Gentlemen 2008: 2,[10] Quah 2008).

Among the structural factors found to increase the pervasiveness of corruption, independent of cultural attributes, were: (i) lack of political and economic stability; (ii) large populations with heterogeneous compositions; (iii) complex administrative structures, excessive bureaucratic rules and red tape; and (iv) political regime types with anti-democratic attributes and poverty. Age of democracy, unitary state and openness to trade were often associated with low corruption (Rock 2009). The opposite traits were found to provide opportunities for corruption, break civic loyalties that deter corruption and make the enforcement of anti-corruption laws and regulations difficult (Mauro 1995, Xin and Rudel 2004, Johnston 2010).

Among the structural factors found to engender and propagate corruption in conformity with cultural templates, were: (i) fatalistic world views and religions that could decrease the effectiveness of anti-corruption efforts (Tummala 2002); (ii) colonial legacies with built-in patron–client systems of administration that could propagate corruption, particularly in newly established political systems (Grubisa 2010); and (iii) *un*civic communities with alienated and apathetic subjects (Putnam et al. 1993). British colonial heritage and Protestantism were often associated with low corruption (Rock 2009), and their lack with more corruption.

Corruption understood as a structurally ingrained characteristic of systems could increase, deepen and expand when impacted by certain factors external to the state and society that often arouse circumstantially. These *Feed* factors could be legal, social, economic, political or some combination of any or all of them. They are, *inter alia*, war, privatizations, nationalist revolutions, economic growth or deterioration, decentralization, and the quality, effectiveness, independence and inter-coordination of investigation, prosecution and oversight institutions. War profiteers, for instance, often engage in illicit activities in the post-war period; privatization and decentralization programs that are run based on political loyalties lead to corrupt cycles of favor exchanges; and nationalist revolutions that culminated in overly centralized state authorities perpetuated non-transparent, non-accountable and corrupt dealings.

The Need-Greed Dimension of Corruption

Corruption is not only a state or society's deviation from integrity but also an individual breach of formal and/or informal rules and regulations. Resembling Heidenheimer's "public interest" explanation, corruption in its modern sense was thus explained by individual motives that either push individuals to engage in corrupt transactions or deter them from doing so. In individual corruption, people corrupted systems rather than the other way around. Corruption thus became equated with the organizational loopholes which people exploited to benefit themselves or their private groups at the expense of the public.

In this behavioral understanding, the principal (public) delegated its trust and decision-making power to the agent (public official, politician or the governing agency) who breached the social contract by pursuing his/her private interest through an unauthorized transaction with a third party (client) (Groenendjik 1997). The agent in modern corruption could be a politician or a public servant. If the former, political corruption out of greed, happened at higher levels of government, and corrupt transactions were of significant value. If the latter, bureaucratic corruption, occurred often out of need, at the lower levels of administration, and corrupt transactions were of smaller value.

Both the political and the bureaucratic versions of the modern behavioral corruption were found to be interlinked. Corrupt politicians demanded bureaucratic assistance to extract state resources, or exercise nepotism, such as to provide lucrative contracts or subsidies to politically powerful individuals or groups. Bureaucrats responded to politicians' wishes with technical efficiency and/or access to information by fulfilling the requirements of horizontal accountability (Caselli and Morelli 2004, Besley 2005, Jones and Olken 2005). Grubisa (2010) found that high political corruption brought with it high administrative corruption, but high administrative corruption could happen independently of political corruption.

Bureaucratic corruption was found to originate from the absence of effective legislative measures, and programs and institutions to contain corruption—political and bureaucratic. Some examples of bureaucratic corruption consisted of cheating, bribery, graft, nepotism, misuse of public funds, payments to administrators to shape rules, privileges in taxation, allocation of resources for particular groups and patron–client or rent-seeking types of connections.

Political corruption also included the same forms of corruption but in different contexts—within the framework of the executive, legislative and judicial branches of the government. More specifically, political corruption comprised evasive forms of corruption such as logrolling, influence peddling or trading of favors,[11] votes and donations to politically influential individuals and parties in return for legislative favors, and any other *quid pro quo* including kickbacks. It could also include outright and illegal theft such as looting, embezzlement and extortion, money-laundering, complete violation of non-discrimination laws due to *state capture* and neopatrimonialism, i.e., personalistic rather than legalistic rule (Beekers and van Gool 2012, Dibua 2013).

Table 4.1 includes the short definitions of these various forms of bureaucratic and political corruption starting with the Need pillar of the lower level administrative corruption and going up to the Greed pillar of the higher level political corruption in the Corruption Pentagon. While the degree or the location of any given corruption type may suffice to qualify it as grand and political corruption, the listing attempts to clarify and sort through these terms, which are sometimes used interchangeably in the literature. Although overlapping, bureaucratic and political corruption often require different sets of remedies. For instance, changing the organizational incentives to modify the incentives of individual actors works best for the Need pillar of the Corruption Pentagon, i.e., the associated lower level administrative corruption. For the Greed pillar, i.e., higher-level, grand political corruption, a combination of general democratic reforms along with more targeted anti-corruption laws and sanctions may be more influential. Therefore, both the academic and the policy world can benefit from a categorization of these concepts in terms of their origins, spread, magnitude, consequences and interlinkages.

In administrative corruption, organizational changes toward decreasing excessive rules and discretion, and increasing bureaucratic oversight are crucial because they aim at improving routine and standard procedures and administrative controls. Such organizational realigning may include measures toward meritocratic recruitment,[12] competition among public officials (Rose-Ackerman 1978), performance criteria in public administration (Kaufman 1997), transparency instruments such as the Codes of Conduct as well as accountability instruments such as independent ethics watchdogs, asset and conflict of interest declarations and legal sanctions such as the punishment of specific ethical breaches in courts (Michael 2012).

Political corruption, in contrast, is less permeable to administrative reforms. Several countries have been able to effectively deal with their administrative corruption while their political systems have stayed corrupt.[13] The best ways to deal with political corruption are twofold: specific and credible legal sanctions, and holistic democratic reforms including human rights (Asthana 2012).[14] Specific anti-corruption laws and sanctions are successful to the degree that they are transparent, clear and implemented effectively by a web of governance actors that can cooperate and coordinate with each other.

Table 4.1 Corruption Forms

Bribery, in its active form, is defined as the giving, promising or offering, directly or indirectly, of an undue advantage to any public official for himself or for anyone else for him to act or refrain from acting in the exercise of his duties. Accepting such unfair advantage is passive bribery. Active and passive bribery are associated with petty or street-level corruption although it can assume large proportions in a financial and material sense.

Graft is bribery that, in addition, includes the intention to influence someone in order to fulfil some personal or group interest. It is associated with undeserved gain and special discretionary rights such as the right to have an operation for a patient before the expiration of the usual waiting period in a public hospital.

Nepotism is the favoring of relatives, acquaintances and/or members of exclusive informal groups.

Cronyism is nepotism when corrupt transactions are made to benefit some formal groups such as a political party, interest group or network.

Patron–client or *spoils* system, based on political or kinship loyalties *and rent-seeking* rather than merits and performance, happen when the entire administration is permeated with nepotism and cronyism.

Logrolling is the practice of exchanging favors, especially in politics by reciprocal voting for each other's proposed legislation.

Influence peddling is the illegal practice of using one's influence in government or connections with persons in authority to obtain favors or preferential treatment for another, usually in return for payment.

Kickbacks are illicit payments to stimulate government intervention in specific policy areas.

Looting is stealing or illegally obtaining goods.

Embezzlement is the fraudulent conversion of another's property by a person who is in a position of trust, such as an agent or employee.

Swindling is embezzlement that includes the act of wrongfully obtaining property by a false pretense, such as a lie or trick, at the time the property is transferred.

Extortion is the unlawful and intentional obtainment of a material or non-material advantage through illegal pressure in the form of threat or intimidation.

Money laundering is the process of making illegally obtained money and resources appear legal.

State capture is when a group of corrupt elite subverts the channels of political influence and interest mediation via informal, opaque and preferential channels of access.

Neopatrimonialism is a political system that is entirely captured by influential groups who use the state for personal enrichment and the public resources fail to reach large segments of the population.

Prebandalism or *kleptocracy* are neopatrimonial regimes rampant with corruption and devoid of legitimate and effective political institutions (Acemoglu 2003, 2004).

Source: Compiled from Andvig et al. 2000: 14; UNDP 2008, 8 and U4 – Anti-Corruption Resource Center, Glossary.

Some general reforms of democratization with specific focus on anti-corruption may include:

i) free and fair elections to control politicians' behavior with periodic threats of loss of power (Rose-Ackerman 1999);
ii) institutionalized democratic party politics (Yaday 2012);
iii) effective, independent and non-corrupt judiciary to hold elected and appointed officials accountable;
iv) constitutional structures to hold officials in check in-between elections (Linz and Stepan 1996);
v) right degree of autonomy for the bureaucracy depending on the political culture and institutional settings;
vi) a vigorous civil society that is accountable internally and externally (Hilhorst 2003, Escobar 2004); and
vii) freedom of expression and freedom of press, which allow for civil society activism against corruption (Themudo 2013).

Both bureaucratic and political corruption are about a conflict between the public and private (including family and group) interests, and the consequent *collusion* between corrupt parties who engage in often secret and illegal cooperation to cheat and defraud, and the resulting misuse of public office. Responsibility-focused organizational reforms work to increase efficiency, transparency, effective regulation, cost-effective modes of governance, citizen engagement in decision-making, service delivery, and program monitoring and evaluation. Sanction-focused organizational reforms work to provide credible threats for expected outcomes of corrupt acts while constituting the rule of law pillar of the democratic systems. In this sense, promoting responsibility in administration and imposing sanctions in politics work cross-cuttingly to instill, maintain and reinforce integrity—in public administration as well as in politics.

The Wield Dimension of Corruption

The above analysis of the bureaucratic and political types of corruption and their corresponding forms shows that once corruption becomes scandalous, involving the top-level politicians, holistic democratic reforms and specific legal institutions that wield the authority to punish the wrongdoers become crucial. In other words, accountability measures based on factors such as an increased flow of information, more effective communication, simplification, standardization and the transparency of rules work well to prevent and detect routine corruption in relatively lower-level public administration. Some examples of Wield tools at this Need pillar of the Corruption Pentagon are audits and accounting, public reporting of budgets and political funding, reports by citizens and whistleblowers. When it comes to arbitrary, hidden and grand-level corruption in government and top-level bureaucracy at the Greed pillar of the Corruption Pentagon, democratic measures of institution-building, including elections, (Kaufman 2010) and legal measures of prosecution, sanctioning and conviction that are credible, implemented and respected gain additional importance (Wing-Yat 2013).[15]

Legal anti-corruption measures work better against top-level political corruption than accountability measures because the higher an official's rank, the higher the chances that: (i) he/she best understands the structures of accountability in place to most easily evade and manipulate them (Harsh et al. 2010); and (ii) the indicators of government performance, and other institutional mechanisms to show the vulnerabilities to corruption are within his/her purview so as to be changed relatively easily by a bureaucracy that is horizontally accountable to him/her and with the help of the colluding elite in his/her professional and social network (Popova 2012).

Among the legal means to fight corruption are criminal laws that include anti-corruption clauses under several headings; several anti-corruption agencies, commissions and committees, each with different types and degrees of resources, mandates, autonomy and objectives; the judiciary; the attorney-general; and accountability institutions such as the ombudsmen, auditor general and supreme audit institutions, which may or may not have enforcement and sanction prerogatives. Last but not least, democratic institutions of the presidency, the legislature, the public agencies and the courts have a marked effect on the frequency with which officials engage in corrupt acts (Manzetti 2000).

Some anti-corruption laws can be found under the Criminal Code, Law on Criminal Procedures, Law on Preventing Conflict of Interest, Provisions of the Law on Public Procurement, Law on Financing Political Parties, Law on the Right to Access Information, to name a few. Often, there is no one unified and comprehensive law on the prevention, detection and control of corruption (Grubisa 2010).

While corruption laws have received increasing attention as effective anti-corruption means in developing countries, relying on them exclusively comes with its own risks. They could be used as a façade or implemented improperly. They could also be manipulated by powerful interests (Davis 2012). The longevity and outputs of anti-corruption laws in any given country can give some idea as to the effectiveness of their implementation, hence their real value as anti-corruption mechanisms.

Among the factors that render anti-corruption agencies, commissions and committees[16] effective are: (i) independent prosecutorial powers and strategies of institutionalization;[17] (ii) the right degree of budget and resources, including staff and skills; and (iii) effective coordination and positive interactions with the other anti-corruption institutions—the judiciary, prosecutors, attorney general, parliamentary committees and civil service commissions, police, line ministries like the ministry of finance and the ministry of justice, civil society and the media (Meagher 2005). The effectiveness of anti-corruption agencies also depends on as specific factors as effective use of the Internet (Garcia Murillo 2013) and adequate technological support such as software for tracing assets and detecting advance fee fraud (Parnini 2011)[18] and factors as comprehensive as the overall state capacity (Barcham 2009). The specific attributes of effectiveness in anti-corruption agencies are some of the main reasons why technical anti-money laundering systems based on large quantities of financial data, can be put to use in preventing and controlling financial corruption (Sharman and Chaikin 2009). The more comprehensive attributes of effectiveness of anti-corruption agencies refer to the main structural argument about the necessity to build state institutions and democratize gradually.

It is often repeated in the literature that the anti-corruption agencies are, by themselves, insufficient to reduce corruption and that they work best in democratic settings. Yet, anti-corruption agencies are seldom needed in contexts where rule of law works flawlessly. They are instead needed in less-than-democratic contexts. Therefore— and because their role often extends beyond legal sanctioning, including to education and awareness-raising, prevention of corruption and law-making though bill submissions to the parliament— they can be important components of democratization processes from the start. Coherent national anti-corruption strategies can contribute to the shaping of accountability cultures and the building of state institutions. From such a perspective, tackling corruption early on and in tandem with democratization processes, and doing so integrally, explicitly and with home-grown mechanisms (de Maria 2008, Carr 2009) becomes paramount for both preventing and fighting corruption and for building and strengthening democratic institutions and processes.

Some empirical examples of corruption-democratization linkages are in order. Georgia's Rose Revolution (Kukhianidze 2009) can be given as an example of a failed state context where anti-corruption programs brought a considerable decrease in administrative and political corruption. The example of Thailand is illustrative of how technocratic solutions were instrumental for managing administrative corruption but failed to reach the level of political corruption at the top (Mutebi 2008). The examples of Hong Kong and Singapore can be given as examples where effective anti-corruption laws and institutions reshaped the initial culture of impunity toward integrity in public administration and governance. The sociopolitical turmoil in which Ukraine finds itself today is also very much related to lack of accountability, opaque policy-making and soaring corruption. The question is thus not as much whether anti-corruption laws and institutions should precede or succeed political democratization as it is the degree of the potential for effectively reducing corruption and increasing democratization in the long run, depending on the existence and the timing of introduction of adequate anti-corruption agencies supported by the adequate anti-corruption rules.

An independent and effective judiciary is another important legal anti-corruption institution. A weak and politically dependent judicial system is both a cause and a consequence of corruption (Jain 2001: 72). In a corrupt system, the judiciary is more likely to be mired in corruption, and a judiciary ineffective in tackling petty or grand corruption will only exacerbate corruption. A court system that is independent[19] of the executive and the legislature is often cited as one of the most important factors for corruption control and democratization. An independent judiciary can have the means and the willingness to adjudicate in accordance with the laws, and without pressure from any other third party.[20]

Accountability institutions such as the auditor general, supreme audit institutions and the ombudsmen are also part of the anti-corruption institutions. Although these institutions are often formed for purposes of sharing information and identifying the vulnerabilities to, and signs of corruption ex-ante, rather than for actively investigating and prosecuting corruption ex-post, they are nevertheless influential in changing public expectations about the successful prosecution of corruption cases (Murphy 2009), the public's view of state capability and willingness to control corruption (Uslaner 2006) and the social networks, which form to interact with these institutions and to denounce and control corruption (Ledet 2011).

Accountability institutions also work as effective anti-corruption institutions because they may actually have limited policing power, including pretrial, investigative and prosecutorial mandates. The Ombudsman in the Philippines, for instance, works very much like an anti-corruption agency because it can make binding decisions about administrative law, and prosecute government officials, including its own, directly in a special anti-corruption court. Other ombudsmen around the world are also empowered to bring cases to tribunals to enforce their recommendations, among them the ombudsmen in Ghana and Tanzania (Reif 2004).

The legal sanctioning power of anti-corruption laws and agencies is more robust if accompanied with the informal societal control mechanisms such as an independent media, investigative press, accountability activists, and grassroots citizens' and civil society organizations that exert constant checks on local and national representatives to render them accountable and to make sure that anti-corruption legislations are effectively implemented (Xin and Rudel 2004). In Indonesia, for instance, guilty verdicts in prominent corruption cases involving high-level officials galvanized citizens' groups across the country to open investigations of their respective legislative bodies (Davidson 2007). The same societal activism about transparency in India empowered the urban poor to ask for their welfare rights there (Webb 2012).

Anti-corruption agencies can directly contribute to democratization by empowering marginalized sectors of society. They can also include citizens from all walks of life directly in their structure and modus operandi. Ecuador's Commission on Civic Control of Corruption, for instance, formalizes citizen oversight, with a board selected by civic bodies that directly manages resources (Meagher 2005). Hong Kong's Independent Commission against Corruption also has four citizen oversight boards, known as Advisory Committees. Australia's anti-corruption agency also solicits citizen oversight and input regularly.

In recent years, Supreme Audit Institutions (SAIs) have gained authority as independent controllers of governance. SAIs provide the highest level of external audit of government bodies in a country. They aim at ensuring the proper and effective use of public funds, the development of sound financial management, the proper execution of administrative activities and the communication of information to public authorities and the general public through objective reports.[21] SAIs are assisted by civil society and the legislatures in carrying out their functions (van Zyl et al. 2009). In South Korea, Peru and Honduras, citizens can file complaints directly to the SAIs about suspected corruption cases as well as those they have experienced. In Argentina, they can propose amendments to the annual audit plan. In Colombia, they can become part of the Citizen Oversight Committees of the Comptroller General of the Republic (Nino 2010).[22]

The Wield pillar of the Corruption Pentagon is strong to the degree that the anti-corruption laws and institutions are in conformity with the given national and local integrity systems (Huberts and Six 2012),[23] and are thus not imposed by foreign actors such as the donor countries, or the regional and international (financial) organizations (Barcham 2009, Spector 2012). Regional organizations might be better role models in terms of anti-corruption reforms, rules and institutions due in part to their inter-cultural affinities and smaller membership, which may prove influential in terms of ease of transfer and replication of anti-corruption reforms, and state and societal perceptions over imposition by external entities. They can also enhance south–south cooperation, and contribute to cost saving and healthy growth nationally.[24]

In summary, the Wield dimension of the Corruption Pentagon can be as general as democratic institution-building and rule of law, and as specific as anti-corruption legislation and institutions with different prerogatives. An effective anti-corruption strategy at this dimension could even be more specific to tackle primarily those sectoral niches where actual and/or potential corrupt transactions are most prevalent. Activities and areas which are commonly vulnerable to corruption are state subsidies, public procurement, regulation of business, land use planning, construction standards, safety regulation and environmental protection, public infrastructure, arms industry and extractive sectors (Sadgren 2005, Eicher 2009, Grodeland and Aasland 2011). Well-designed legislation, inclusive regulatory and review processes immersed within an overall democratization process and good governance framework could follow a step-by-step anti-corruption strategy to effectively tackle corruption in all sectors and increase the strength of the democratization process over the long run (Achua 2011).

CORRUPTION AND DEMOCRATIZATION LINKAGES

As with transparency, and less so with accountability, corruption has been linked in different and sometimes contradictory ways with democratization. Ades and Di Tella (1999) failed to find any association between corruption, and the political or civil rights associated with democracy. Conversely, Montinola and Jackman (2002), Goel and Nelson (2005) and Chowdhury (2004) found them to be negatively correlated. Treisman (2000) and Schneider and Schmitter (2004) specified that the inverse relationship was between corruption and the durability of democracy, and not the democratic attributes per se. Others went further to qualify the shape of the inverse relationship in terms of an inverted U curve. Accordingly, Mohtadi and Roe (2003) found corruption to rise initially following a transition from an authoritarian to a democratic regime, and to fall thereafter as democracy endured and consolidated, after about ten to twelve years following the first national elections (445). The relationship was explained in terms of the collapse of systemic and centralized networks of corruption given the higher legal cost of corrupt activities, and their replacement with possibly more dispersed and sporadic corruption.

Street-level corruption in public administration and political corruption at the higher ranks of the government were linked differently with democratization. Administrative corruption analyzed within the *principal–agent model* was linked with *information asymmetries* as its main cause, and *transparency* and *accountability* were underlined as its main solutions toward strengthening the *responsibility* of office holders vis-à-vis the public (Gurgur and Shah 2005)—since they control the opportunities for corruption in routine administrative work (Cohen and Felson 1979).[25] This is the indirect linking of corruption with democratization through good governance.

Political corruption examined within the *crime and punishment model* was linked with the *low risk–high reward* of corrupt acts as its main cause, and the legal sanctions against corrupt officials within democratic structures were stressed as its main solutions toward promoting and maintaining the *answerability* of office holders to citizens (Mohtadi and Roe 2003)—since they determine the terms and consequences of corrupt acts and dealings in extraordinary political scandals.[26] This is the direct linking of corruption with democratization through rule of law and legitimacy.[27]

The associated risks and benefits of corrupt versus non-corrupt acts are also constantly calculated by public officials engaged in street-level corruption. However, both the risks and the rewards are lower in administrative corruption compared to those in political corruption (Graycar and Villa 2011). That is why increasing the income of public officials might control administrative corruption by controlling their *need* to exploit their higher access to information but the same measures often fail at curbing political corruption arising out of *greed* (Rijckeghem and Weder 1997, Gorodnichenko and Peter 2007). With respect to the latter, bribery, extortion, misappropriation and fraud are easily made illegal by the appropriate laws. Legislation and credible legal sanctions are less useful, however, when dealing with more evasive issues such as patronage, clientelism, abuse of discretion and favoritism.

Controlling both administrative and political corruption, however, is best accomplished through a comprehensive package of prevention and sanction, informal and formal, social and legal and individual, organizational and structural means. Within an organization, anti-corruption culture is reinforced with good personnel management, reporting mechanisms for questionable behavior, protection of whistle-blowers and continuous ethics training. The same goes for a country. Good governance and public administration through transparency and accountability, anti-corruption laws, institutions and programs within a coherent anti-corruption strategy and democratization together can tackle effectively the different types, forms and stages of corruption.[28]

CONCLUSION

This chapter brings together a panoply of corruption definitions, types, levels, forms, causes and consequences. It attempts to sort them through the Corruption Pentagon, a conceptual tool that is neither definitive nor exclusive. The Seed-Feed dimension of the Corruption Pentagon gathers and synthesizes the root causes and the main catalysts of *classical corruption* at macro-levels of analysis with focus on value-driven systems and structures. The Need-Greed dimension of the Corruption Pentagon examines the behavioral determinants of *modern corruption* at micro-levels of analysis with focus on demand and supply-driven incentives for individuals, groups and organizations. The Wield pillar of the Corruption Pentagon concerns the institutional attributes of contemporary corruption at meso-levels of analysis with focus on formal and informal rules, laws and sanctions.

The chapter argues that corruption must not be confined to either democratic consolidation or democratic quality phases, debates and policy-cycles of democratization. Instead, corruption must be made an integral part of the overall democratization processes, starting as early as the transitions to democracy. It also maintains that the prevention, detection and the diagnosis of corruption must be covered both formally and informally in democratization processes. For that, transparency and accountability policies and processes with focus on ex-ante vulnerabilities to corruption must be interlinked with the ex-post criminalization of corruption within the framework of continuous democratization. Last but not least, it underlines the endogenous relationship between ex-ante corruption prevention and ex-post corruption control, and urges further corruption research to focus on the middle-level and cross-scalar linkages between the roots, implications and interlinkages of administrative and political corruption.

Vis-à-vis the corruption–democratization linkages more specifically, the chapter recognizes the insufficiency of anti-corruption laws and agencies to deal with corruption by themselves, even when bestowed with the adequate prosecutorial and investigative powers. There is indeed a need for democratic structures in order for anti-corruption strategies to prevail (Mulbah 2012, Simelane 2012). Yet, in cases where authoritarian regimes are supported by corruption, and vice-versa, this argument is nothing more than an excuse for idleness. Democratic structures will not appear and function properly overnight. Proper policies and adequate institutions will be instrumental.

The gist of the argument of the chapter, therefore, is that well-designed, inter-coordinated, credibly enforced and inclusive anti-corruption laws and agencies can be more than just institutional layers to the traditional agents of rule of law, such as the judiciary. They can be the agents of change toward less corrupt and more democratic systems in the long run. In a world where corruption accounts for three to five percent of the world's GNP (Brassilio 2010),[29] there is a need to further examine the role of eclectic and cross-scalar anti-corruption mechanisms and institutions in continuous democratization processes.

CONCLUSION: TOWARD A SUBSTANTIVE DEMOCRACY

Two principal objectives of this book were outlined at the outset: first, as one of constructing a comprehensive synthesis of the notions of democratization, transparency, accountability and corruption; and second, as one of linking democratization processes to the policies of transparency, accountability and anti-corruption. Overall, the book has pondered whether an early and explicit focus on transparency, accountability and corruption control as integral pillars of democratization, rather than as appendages of the quality of consolidating democracies, could lead to healthier and more substantive democratization processes.

Regarding the first aim, multidisciplinary research on the concepts of transparency, accountability, corruption and democratization was conducted and a wealth of information summarized through the use of geometrical heuristics. The *Concentric Circles of Democratization* tracked the progression of explanations of democratization in political science. The *Transparency Triangle* categorized and interlinked the inputs, outputs and outcomes of transparency. The *Accountability Cube* documented the dominant dichotomous definitions of accountability in the literature, and attempted to reconcile them through an alternative and continuous perspective. The *Corruption Pentagon* linked and interlinked the modern and classical definitions of democratization along with its administrative and political dimensions at petty and grand levels, and with focus on ex-ante prevention and ex-post criminalization.

Regarding the second aim, transparency, accountability and corruption control were linked with democratization through direct and indirect means. Directly, the impact of transparency, accountability and anti-corruption focus on democratization has involved potential links ranging from increased information flow, openness and deliberation to strengthened inter-organizational and public responsibility, and a threat or risk of formal/legal sanctioning and informal/social opprobrium in case of deficiencies in any of the three. Indirectly, all three—transparency, accountability and corruption control—have been linked with democratization through their role as the pillars of good (and democratic) governance.

More specifically with regard to transparency, it was shown that while the latter emerged initially as a tool to fight corruption, it was its subsequent pairing with accountability that was found to contribute directly to democratization, starting as early as with the first national elections during democratic transitions, and not before. Especially fueled with the increasing spread and impact of information and communication technologies, transparency has strengthened the basic constitutional freedoms associated with democratic regimes, and has reinforced good governance, of which it is a pillar.

More specifically with regard to accountability, it was found that accountability has contributed to reconciliation in post-conflict societies before and during democratic transitions; electoral accountability has fed into administrative accountability in state-building and democratic transitions, and the underlying deliberative function of accountability has strengthened democratic participation all throughout the democratization process.

Finally, more specifically with regard to corruption, it was suggested that if the latter is thought to be rooted in "information asymmetries," transparency could be instrumental in (ex-ante) preventing the associated administrative/petty corruption through its impact on soft accountability or responsibilities. Conversely, if corruption was deemed to spring from a cost–benefit analysis of the risks versus the rewards of legal and corrupt acts and actions, then accountability supported by transparency was found to be more effective in tackling (ex-post) the associated political/grand corruption, particularly through its impact on hard accountability or answerability.

Overall, as preliminarily shown in Figure 5.1, further research could thus examine when the first transparency (TR1-TR5), accountability (A1-A5) and corruption control laws and policies (CC1-CC5) were undertaken in relation to the stages of democratization, their content and the subsequent enforcement levels in relation to the procedural reforms of democratization, including elections, political parties and civil society. One important factor could be to see if and

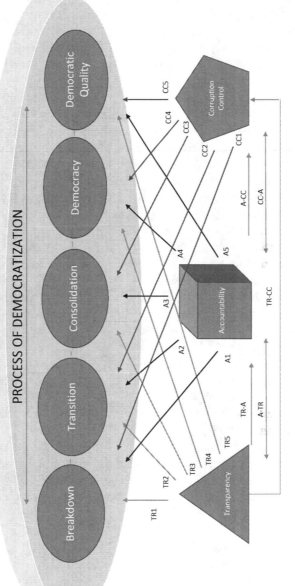

Figure 5.1   Linking Policy with Substantive Democratization

how transparency, accountability and corruption control policies are interlinked (TR-A-CC), and integrated into the procedures and institutions of democracy, both on paper and in practice. Figuratively, this would mean taking the Concentric Circles of Democratization and assessing the TR, A and CC at each layer where a specific country is thought to be situated at any given moment.

The most recent studies of democratization have made the argument, either implicitly or explicitly, that there is a need to shift from theoretical approaches to empirical foci in order to better understand democratization. Policy-driven analysis can be instrumental in realizing such a shift. The definitions of democratization in the Concentric Circles Model have shared, throughout all layers, a common emphasis on the importance of transparent governance, accountable policy making and corruption control. Comparing different policies aimed at democratization through such common areas can help illuminate how the latter may affect democratization outcomes differently in similar structural contexts, and how similar policies may produce similar outcomes in divergent contexts.

"If democracies do not work better to contain crime and corruption, generate economic growth, relieve economic inequality, secure justice and freedom, people will lose faith and embrace (or tolerate) other nondemocratic alternatives," says Larry Diamond (2009) in his *Spirit of Democracy*. Democracies are, by definition, transparent and accountable with minimum degrees of corruption. Therefore, the thrust of this book is that making transparent policy-making, accountable governance and control of corruption part of the democratization processes, legally, institutionally and socially, and from early on, can be the "substantive minimums" of (effective) democracies—in the same way that elections are the "procedural minimums" of (electoral) democracies.

Rock (2009) maintains that "governments do not have to wait until they reach a rather high threshold level of development before they tackle the difficult task of ameliorating corruption and the political delegitimation that accompanies it" (70). This study adds that democratizing governments do not have to wait to be consolidated before they tackle the issues of transparency, accountability and corruption, which are as intertwined with each other as they are with democracy. As such, the proposition of this book is neither groundbreaking nor statistically proven. It is just based on a common-sense review of the appropriate literature and policy developments on democratization. Indeed, if democracy is more than a sophisticated set of procedures and tools, the alternative is not necessarily that it is an intrinsically cultural or ethical template of tolerance and solidarity built over centuries. It could be that a substantive democracy, or at least a viable path to it, is one where governments are able to introduce, implement, maintain and strengthen the cross-cutting democratic principles and policies of transparency, accountability and corruption control.

Clearly, policies on paper will not be enough to democratize any country, or to even improve the procedures of democracy, but they could provide a start, particularly if their implementation is periodically scrutinized. Furthermore, simply paying some or equal attention to the substantive minimums of democratization along with its procedural minimums could be influential in changing the faith of stalled democracies, and help them get back on track for an *oikeiosis democratization*. To retake Kahneman's analogy made in the Introduction to this book, a System II (policy) approach that is more effortful and calculating rather than intuitive and straightforward would require at least the consideration of a *policy-driven approach to democratization*.

NOTES

INTRODUCTION

1. System I is more intuitive and automatic than System II, which is more effortful and calculating. See Kahneman (2013). The analogy drawn here is with the conception of democratization, and not the ways in which analysis was undertaken to arrive at this conception. Explaining democratization through elections, parties, civil society and culture is much more frequent, intuitive and straightforward than accounting for it in terms of policy making. The term policy making covers all policy phases—design, debate, implementation, evaluation and monitoring.
2. Scholars dissatisfied with the limitations imposed by a procedurally minimalist understanding of democratization have come up with "expanded procedural minimums" which, in addition to elections and certain basic rights, cover factors such as the effective power to rule for elected governments. For more, see Collier and Levitsky (1996). Neither "expanded procedural" definitions nor "maximalist" explanations of democracy, which cover socioeconomic in addition to political rights, have accounted for policies pertinent to democratization, nor have they attempted to draw out the substantive minimums of a democracy.

1 THE CONCENTRIC CIRCLES OF DEMOCRATIZATION: TEASING OUT THE COMMON DRIVERS

1. Cosmopolitan, universal or global ethics are defined as "a systematic reflective inquiry into the nature, content, justification and application of a global ethic," itself defined as a "claim about universal and transnational responsibilities, or a set of values and norms universally accepted; or widely shared by people from all over the world." See Dower (2005: 26).
2. Many scholars differentiate between persistence and consolidation drawing boundaries between stability and legitimacy. Often, the arguments for differentiating between the two center on the quality of democracies. See Rose and Shin (2001).

3. In the second volume of *Law, Legislation and Liberty*, first published in 1976, Hayek called the idea of social justice a "mirage." See Hayek (1982).

4. Such a shift in Lasswell's thinking on democracy is remarkable. His earlier work—extending back to his dissertation in 1926—viewed democracy as the ability of the rational political elite along with the scientists to manipulate the irrational masses through symbols and myths. See Lasswell (1926).

5. Rostow's (1964) model of Stages of Growth complemented Lipset's political analysis. It enumerated the steps through which economies must go in order to grow, also based on Western countries' experiences.

6. Other modernization theorists who have explored and posited strong relations between economic development, modernization and democratization are Cutright (1963), Neubauer (1967), Needler (1968), Winham (1970), Coulter (1975), Bollen (1979), Muller (1995), Londregan and Poole (1996) and Przeworski and Limongi (1997).

7. For more on Easton, see Miller (1971).

8. For more, see Coppedge *et al.* (2008).

9. Some scholars referred to a third type as a theoretical tool to study the relationship between state and organized groups in liberal democracies. For more, see Williamson (1985).

10. Bell (1973) divided the modernization phase into the first industrialization and the second post-industrialization phases. The first period was linked with bureaucratization, centralization, rationalization and secularization. The second period was associated with creativity, self-expression and choice, also dubbed as postmodernism.

11. Munck and Leff (1997) categorized Chile as *reform from below*, Huntington (1991) as *transformation*, and Schmitter and Karl (1991) somewhere between *imposition* and a *pact*. Other cases bear similar difficulties of categorization, such as Argentina, Greece, Peru and Zambia.

12. Stradiotto and Guo (2010) demonstrated that the opposition-led cooperative pacts result in higher average levels of democracy in the post-transitional phase compared to other transitional modes, and that they have the greatest survival rate within ten years of transition. Nilsson (2012) found that negotiated settlements following civil war are more conducive to democratization than truces or military victories.

13. O'Donnell (1992) made an additional distinction between the *first transition* starting with the end of the authoritarian regime and the establishment of a *democratic government* through elections; and the *second transition,* equated with democratic consolidation or the effective functioning of a *democratic regime*. Later, O'Donnell (1993) also distinguished between a *democratic regime* and a *democratic state*. A democratic state was a democratic regime or a consolidated democracy that, in addition, included guarantees vis-à-vis citizen rights to fair and equal protection in their social and economic relationships.

14. Terry Karl coined the term "fallacy of electoralism" to refer to the inadequacy of equating democratization with elections alone (Karl 2000, Carothers 2002, Diamond 2002). Committing the fallacy was about adopting an excessively minimalist definition of democracy in which accountability, the broadest meaning of representative democracy according to Schmitter (2004: 47), was relegated to elections. The fallacy instigated numerous and broader definitions and measurements of democracies and democratization (Schmitter and Karl 1991, Munck and Verkuilen 2002). It also led to the distinction between an electoral and a liberal democracy. The latter refused considering systems with enclaves of authoritarianism as democratic even though the overall system was based on fair, free and competitive elections, legitimate constitutions and effective multiparties. It required extended legal and political rights for citizens, and strengthened horizontal accountability among governing institutions (R. A. Dahl et al., *The Democracy Sourcebook*, Boston: The MIT Press, 2003. Available at http://downloads.pavroz. ru/files/democracysourcebook.pdf).

15. For a definition of horizontal accountability, see Chapter 3.

16. Multiparty democracies and proportional representation were associated with more democratic but less pragmatic systems of democracy based on mutual consultation and a legislature with a ministerial vote of no confidence. Two-party democracies and the Westminster system of representation were associated with less democratic but more pragmatic systems of democracy based on turnover of power through periodic elections and a legislature without the ministerial vote of no confidence. Parliamentary systems of governance associated with the first model and the presidential systems associated with the second were not the only two categories analyzed by the democratization scholars. Many different combinations lay in between parliamentarian and presidential regimes, including hybrid semi-presidential regimes where both the President and the Parliament are directly elected by the people, hence the question of dual legitimacy and its associated implications on democratization. For more, see Shugart (2005) and Sedelius and Berglund (2012).

17. Human capital refers to the norms and values held by individuals constituted by formal education and/or organizational skills. For more, see Becker (1993). Cultural capital includes the full range of a society's symbolic resources, from the norms and values that individuals bring to or encounter in interactions with others to the religious, philosophical, artistic, and scientific understandings that frame and interpret reality. For more, see Bourdieu (1990).

18. Three major shifts detectable in the civil society-democratization literature of the decade were: (i) internationalization of civil society—move from a nation-based civil society to globally active civil society; (ii) gender-sensitive civil society—increased emphasis on women's role in civil

society activism; and (iii) policy-driven civil society activism—policies that support or hamper the positive impact of civil society on democratization. In all three focus areas, linkages with democratization were increasingly couched in historical and comparative perspectives.

19. R. O. Keohane et al., "Democracy-Enhancing Multilateralism." *International Organization* 63 (Winter 2009): 1–31. Available at https://www.princeton.edu/~rkeohane/publications/DEMfinal.pdf

20. R. Dominguez, "Diffusion of EU Norms in Latin America: The Cases of Mexico, Venezuela and Honduras," Jean Monnet/Robert Schuman paper series 10, 1 (February 2010), Miami: Florida European Center. Available at http://aei.pitt.edu/15000/1/DominguezEU_LatinAm NormDiffFeb10Edi.pdf

21. F. Decker and J. Sonnicksen, *The Direct Election of the Commission President: A Presidentialist Approach to Democratizing the European Union*, Bonn: Center for European Integration Studies, 2009. Available at http://www.zei.uni-bonn.de/dateien/discussion-paper/dp_c192_ Decker_Sonnicksen.pdf

22. In terms of the unique circumstances of conflict and post-crisis cases, Miller (2012) argued, based on his analysis of 167 countries from 1875 to 2004, that development leads to authoritarianism because it reduces the likelihood of violent leader removal. For Miller, economic development would lead to democratization only if a violent turnover preceded the first democratic elections. In contrast, Fortna and Huang (2012) maintained that peacekeeping in conflict and post-conflict cases does not affect democratization; economic development does.

23. Acemoglu and Robinson (2006) defined economic crisis as an annual growth rate of less than five percent of GDP/capita in any of the preceding five years (65).

24. During economic crises, the private sector, instead of supporting the incumbent regime, cooperates with the lower and middle income groups who protest against the economic grievances. The military also stops supporting the incumbent regime in the face of budget cuts.

25. P. Y. Lipscy, "Democracy and Financial Crisis," Paper Presented at the *Annual Meeting of the International Political Economy Society*, Stanford University, California, November 12, 2011. Available at http://www.stanford.edu/~plipscy/democracycrisis.pdf

26. Albertus and Menaldo (2012) found that the coercive capacity of the authoritarian regime is negatively associated with the likelihood of democratic transitions and the level of subsequent democracy.

27. The use of historical and state–society interaction perspectives were also used to re-examine successful cases of democratization found in the non-Western world. Haddad (2010), for instance, in his analysis of cultural democratization in Japan, demonstrated how traditional institutions changed and adopted to the new circumstances rather than being overhauled and replaced.

28. J. Granato, "Cultural Values, Stable Democracy and Economic Development: A Reply." *American Journal of Political Science* 40, 3 (August 1996): 680–696. Available at http://www.class.uh.edu/hcpp/jimgranato/CulturalValuesStableDemocracyAndEconomic Development.pdf

29. R. V. Jackman and R. Miller, "A Renaissance of Political Culture?" University of Nebraska-Lincoln Political Science Publications 50, 1996. Available at http://digitalcommons.unl.edu/cgi/viewcontent.cgi?article=1050&context=poliscifacpub

30. M. Helbling, "Nationalism and Democracy: Competing or Complementary Logics?" *Living Reviews in Democracy* 1, (2009): 1–14. Available at http://democracy.livingreviews.org/index.php/lrd/article/view/lrd-2009-7

31. Religious endowment to charity with all profit or products going to the poor or other good purposes.

2   THE TRANSPARENCY TRIANGLE: DIFFERENTIATING INPUTS, OUTPUTS AND OUTCOMES

1. This would not apply to the instances when the ruling party perceives its likely loss in the upcoming elections, and thus, supports transparency as a strategy to weaken the winning party. Transparency is also used as a strategy to weaken the political party expected to win the upcoming elections in presidential systems as in South Korea's Sunset provisions, which allow a government to undo the policies of the previous government. For more, see Baum and Bawn (2011).

2. For more on the process and the convention, see European Commission (1998).

3. Confidentiality pressure by national governments who have a monopoly over the information requested by the international organizations has been used to curtail transparency (Keohane 2005).

4. Open Budget Index operationalizes a transparent budget as the presence of a legal and administrative framework, publicly available fiscal information depending on the various stages of the budget cycle, data quality standards, strength of budget oversight institutions such as the legislature and supreme audit institutions, and opportunities for public engagement in budget processes. For more, see Luna-Reyes and Chun (2012).

5. Several scholars have found a robust and negative association between extractive industries and transparency. See McFerson (2010), Williams (2011), Norman (2012).

6. Although some scholars have drawn distinctions between "openness" and "transparency," often pointing at the latter as encompassing the

former, the terms have often been used synonymously. For more, see Heald (2006).

7. Available at http://www.oecd.org/competition/mergers/48825133.pdf

8. Heald (2006) also differentiated between *Transparency Inwards*, when citizens could see inside the operations of government, and *Transparency Outwards*, when subordinates in the government could see outside the government.

9. Required transparency clauses included the investigation of closed sessions, and the optional transparency policies comprised the introduction of codes of conduct, registry of lobbyists and the creation of the office for an auditor general and an integrity commissioner. The municipalities that adopted more than the minimum requirements were often the larger ones that already had policies similar to the voluntary transparency policies suggested by the central government.

10. Wikileaks is an international online non-profit organization that publishes classified information leaked by whistleblowers in public and private institutions. It published confidential information on the Afghan and Iraq wars, and the Guantanomo Bay detention camp from 2010 to 2011. For more, see Margetts (2011).

11. Internal and external transparency divide has also been attributed to the nature of the power holders in ensuring and regulating transparency. External transparency control has been attributed to sociopolitical actors such as elected politicians, civil society and the judiciary. Internal transparency control, in turn, has been associated with internal organizational workings, office heads and auditors. See Moore (2004).

12. FOIA/Ls have often been sponsored by the government agencies themselves, often by diverting agency funds from other projects. FOI offices tend to be understaffed, underfunded and backlogged. In the United States, the 20 days of maximum response provision period is rarely respected by government agencies, and some agencies, such as the State Department, CIA and the FBI, may take much longer to respond.

13. Openness and secrecy are the two halves of one whole in this sense (Cohen 2010: 6) and they are both useful in different issue matters and in different degrees.

14. FOIA/Ls have seldom been consistently implemented across different administrations, let alone different countries. With each change of administration in the United States, a new stand on freedom of information was announced by the Attorney-general of the incoming government. Even though during the Clinton administration, government agencies had to prove harm to justify withholding information, during the second Bush administration, it was acceptable to retain information based on legal justification. As for the differences across countries, some FOIA/Ls as in Zimbabwe and Belarus, might read more like secrecy acts rather than right-to-know clauses. See C. Coglianese et al., *Transparency and Public Participation in the Rulemaking Process,*

Penn.: University of Pennsylvania Law School, 2008. Available at http://www.hks.harvard.edu/hepg/Papers/transparencyReport.pdf.

15. Performance.gov was launched in 2011 to make government agencies' performance plans, reports and annual programs available to civil society. Congressional reports, and testimonies on agencies' performance are available online but not searchable or comparable.

16. Wikileaks transparency is not an entirely positive phenomenon in itself or for democratization. Depending on the nature of the information that is leaked, serious security and privacy concerns may arise and jeopardize the overall freedoms and democracy, including transparency.

17. Regime type and transparency were found to be correlated even after controlling for GDP/capita, IMF participation, country-fixed effects and time trends. For more, see Hollyer et al. (2011).

18. P. Birkinshaw, "Transparency as a Human Right," in *Transparency: The Key to Better Governance?* edited by C. Hood and D. Heald, London: British Academy Publications Online: February 2012. Available at http://www.britishacademypublications.com/view/10.5871/bacad/9780197263839.001.0001/bacad-9780197263839-chapter-3

19. S. Aftergood, "Reducing Government Secrecy: Finding What Works," *Yale Law and Policy Review* 27, 399 (2009): 399–416. Available at http://www.fas.org/sgp/eprint/aftergood.pdf

20. Transparency in elections concerns clear rules for citizen participation, all statutory instruments and ways to deal with electoral malpractice, such as underage registration, vote and polling station results doctoring, and impersonation; and political parties laws. See Debrah (2011).

21. Alt et al. (2002) find that in the United States the individual (fiscal) popularity of policy-makers might be what is making them more transparent, and not necessarily the fact that they were socialized in democratic systems.

22. Although not causally determinant, level of democracy and freedom of press were found to be permissive factors for the emergence, development and spread of transparency.

23. For more, see Hood (2011).

24. De Fine Licht (2011) found that transparent decision-making procedures weaken general trust in public health care.

25. Politics is understood as how conflicting and competing demands are converted into decisions, and policy refers to actions carried out in order for decisions to be perceived as binding in the production of outcomes.

26. Peter Eigen, a manager at the World Bank, became increasingly distressed by the bank's failure to address corruption in its loan-giving to nations, and founded in 1993 with a few of his colleagues, Transparency International (TI), which examines the effects and consequences of corruption across countries (Holzner and Holzner 2006: 188–189). TI publishes its latest audit, annual report, governance process, code of conduct and ethics policy on its website www.transparency.org.

3   The Accountability Cube: Moving from
     Dichotomy to Continuity

1. This chapter uses parts based on the draft version of the previously online published work "Accountability in Public Service Delivery" by Peride K. Blind at http://unpan1.un.org/intradoc/groups/public/documents/un-dpadm/unpan046363.pdf and the unpublished Conference Paper "Linking Civil Society with Democratic Governance through the MDGs" presented by Peride K. Blind at the *World Civic Forum*. Seoul, May 2009.

2. The term accountability does not have a clear equivalent in French, Portuguese, Spanish or Japanese where "responsibility" is the closest term semantically (Dubnick 2002, Harlow 2002). In French, the term *"rendre les comptes"* is relatively new, and has arisen in response to the need to find a better equivalent to the originally Anglo-Norman term of "accountability." For more, see Gordon (2006). Vielajus (2010), for instance, prefers to use the term *"redevabilité,"* for it involves a larger sense of giving accounts than does the term "rendition" or *"reddition de comptes"* (6). In Spanish, accountability is often translated as "control" or *"fiscalización,"* and the literal translation of *"rendición de cuentas"* only approximates but does not equal "accountability" (IFAI 2004: 11). The notion of accountability assumes that an actor is responsible for producing certain outcomes, and is then accountable through oversight to ensure that those responsibilities are met. In this understanding, bureaucrats are responsible to the public but accountable to their superiors and the elected officials. For more, see Boven (2007b) and Blair (2000). In accountability, there is also the notion of answerability. In other words, willingness to be responsible and responsive is not sufficient; also important is the actual procedural phase of control where answers must be provided (Schedler 1999).

3. Although the focus of Lloyd (2008) is on global accountability, his hardware versus software distinction applies to any organization. Global accountability has been used to denote the accountability practices in the international organizations, including the International Financial Institutions (IFIs), Multilateral Development Banks (MDBs), International Non-Governmental Organizations (INGOs) and international organizations such as the United Nations, and its various entities. For more, see the Global Accountability Reports produced by One World Trust. Global accountability has also been used to denote the new norms of international accountability beyond the territoriality of sovereign states, and emanating from the globalization of production, investment and trade patterns (Mason 2005). A specific focus on global accountability is outside the scope of this chapter.

4. Boven (2007b), on the other hand, opts for the hardware approach of accountability dubbing the software as non-falsifiable. For more on falsifiability and concept boundaries, see Popper (1959) and Sartori (1970).
5. This prescriptive dichotomy is paralleled by a methodological one where Boven (2010) refers to "virtue" as the dependent variable, and the "mechanism" as the independent variable.
6. Broadly, good governance describes an open, efficient, effective and legitimate way of conducting public affairs and managing public resources. Good governance accomplishes these goals in a manner essentially free of corruption, and with due regard to rule of law. For many, good governance is synonymous with democratic and effective governance because it is participatory, transparent and accountable. See UNDP (1997a, b). For others, good governance and democratic governance have diverged in the past decade due mainly to the crises triggered by globalization. For such a perspective, see Bang (2008).
7. The more direct link between "accountability as virtue" and "trust in government" is through the link of a "trust culture." A trust culture is where citizens feel that they have a more or less equal and potential chance of making a difference in decision making. For a discussion on trust culture, see Sztompka (1999). For a comprehensive analysis of trust in government and linkages to good governance and accountability, see Blind (2006, 2010).
8. Briefly, "Old Public Management" focuses on hierarchical, rule-oriented and centralized bureaucracies while the "New Public Management" favors an entrepreneurial, performance-driven and decentralized public administration. For more, see Riccucci (2002).
9. Some innovative tools in this shift have included the minimization of several conventional formal oversight mechanisms, such as audits, inspections and performance league tables and the adoption of intelligent commissions by different government agencies and/or third parties, all with extensive citizen engagement and with an eye to engaging the most deprived.
10. Some scholars make a distinction between bureaucratic and political accountability on the grounds that the former concerns accountability to superiors, and the latter accountability to the constituents. For instance, LaFrance shows that, in the case of law enforcement against drunk-driving, the police in the United States display accountability both to the chain of command and the external anti-alcohol lobbies (C. LaFrance, "The Drunk Trap: Bureaucratic versus Political Accountability in Local Law Enforcement Management," *Law Enforcement Executive Forum* 9, 5 (September 2009): 73–87. Available at http://www.academia.edu/366899/The_Drunk_Trap_Bureaucratic_vs_Political_Accountability_in_Local_Law_Enforcement_Management).

Most scholars agree that political and bureaucratic accountability converge on several grounds. Page (2010), for instance, demonstrated that in the case of Sweden, Germany, the United States, France, the United Kingdom and the European Union, political accountability in the form of "ministerial responsibility" dominated and shaped administrative and other forms of accountability, including the legal/judicial and social variants.

11. Boven (2007b) distinguishes among types of accountability based on the nature of the accountability forum, the organizational form of the actor, the nature of the issue of accountability at hand and the nature of the obligation (461).

12. H. F. Ladd, "School Policies and the Black-White Test Score Gap," *Working Papers Series SAN08-03*, Terry Sanford Institute of Public Policy at Duke University, March 2008. Available at http://research. sanford.duke.edu/papers/SAN08-03.pdf

13. Some scholars are satisfied with the accountability weight carried by elections in democratization. Lindstedt and Naurin (2010), for instance, find that devoid of free and fair elections, the impact of information and transparency through education and media is flimsy. Halim (2008) corroborates a similar finding in the developing world.

14. Decreetism is rule-making by decree often involving the bypassing of the legislative branch by the executive. It is often associated with the personalization and concentration of power in the executive and the weakening of legislatures. See O'Donnell (1994).

15. World Bank. "State-Society Synergy for Accountability: Lessons for the World Bank." World Bank Working Paper No. 30. Washington DC: World Bank, 2004. Available at http://siteresources.worldbank.org/ INTPCENG/214578-1116499844371/20524131/297010PAPER0 State1society0synergy.pdf

16. J. Ferejohn, "Accountability in a Global Context," Conference paper presented at the *Normative and Empirical Evaluation of Global Governance Conference*, Niehaus Center for Globalization and Governance, Princeton University, February 2006. Available at http://www. princeton.edu/~pcglobal/conferences/normative/papers/Session1_ Ferejohn.pdf

17. Boven (2007b) finds that, with the transfer of power from the ministers to the heads of agencies, public administrators become more directly accountable to the public than to their political bosses. The decrease in political accountability has thus been paralleled by the increase in legal and social accountability, this further attesting to the higher convergence between accountability types.

18. McCubbins and Schwartz (1984) make the "police patrol" versus the "fire alarm" analogy, the first one referring to rigorous performance targets from above, and the second, to openings of public administration to social pressures from below.

19. Goetz, A. M. "Community of Practice on Social Accountability Launch." World Bank ESSD. Lecture Series: "Reinventing Accountability: Making Democracy Work for All." Washington DC: World Bank, November 2003. Available at http://siteresources.worldbank.org/INTPCENG/1143374-1116506116408/20542842/AMG+speech+for+COPSA,+November+2003.pdf

20. Other scholars have taken a more empirical perspective attempting to discern the different social accountability tools and functions in different environments. See D. Orlansky and N. Chucho, "Gobernanza, Instituciones y Desarrollo: Exploraciones del caso de Argentina en el contexto regional, 1996–2008," *Ponto de Vista* 4 (April 2010): 1–22. Available at http://webiigg.sociales.uba.ar/sepure/Publicaciones/Ponto_de_vista_01abril2010%207.pdf

21. For an analytical analysis of the degree of state support per a given social accountability mechanism (SAM), see Blair (2011).

22. Sarker and Mostafa (2010) are other scholars who affirm that civic engagement processes in enforcing public accountability still stay as piecemeal efforts.

23. With respect to the social accountability tool of citizen councils, some have questioned their autonomy since they tend to be government-funded (Ackerman 2005). Based on his case study of Argentina, Salvochea (2007) distinguishes, for instance, between involving NGOs in such exercises of social accountability where they act as watchdogs over the implementation of public policies, which he finds valuable, and those social accountability functions where they (NGOs) administer public funds, which he advises against for being amenable to patron-client dealings.

24. Within-state accountability to superiors is categorized as vertical or horizontal by different scholars depending on their emphasis on either the "internal/interagency," hence horizontal, or the "hierarchical," hence vertical nature of the relationship.

25. For Boven (2007a), these newer forms of accountability, such as the establishment of ombudsmen, auditors and independent inspectors, are examples of diagonal, and not horizontal accountability because they do not fit within the traditional top-down, principal–agent relationships.

26. Schmitter calls the specific type of accountability linkages between officials and civil society as "oblique accountability" (P. C. Schmitter, *Political Accountability in "Real-Existing" Democracies: Meaning and Mechanisms*. Firenze: European University Institute mimeo, January 2007. Available at http://www.eui.eu/Documents/DepartmentsCentres/SPS/Profiles/Schmitter/PCSPoliticalAccountabilityJan07.pdf

27. The still-developing social accountability literature has often referred to civil society, and more specifically non-governmental organizations (NGOs), as social accountability agents. There is, however, a growing literature on the internal accountability of NGOs, and the accountability of their interaction with state. For more, see Harsh (2010).

28. Some scholars use a reverse terminology. They refer to internal accountability mechanisms as vertical due to their command-and-control nature, and external accountability as horizontal due to the decentralized nature of the accountability mechanisms at the societal level. Boven (2005) is an example.
29. According to Peruzzotti and Smulovitz (2006) social accountability is a relatively new mechanism of vertical accountability.
30. The repeatedly cited cases of vertical accountability success are Brazil/ Porto Alegre's participatory budgeting (1989), Mexico's citizen-run Federal Electoral Institute (1990) and India's Mazdoor Kisan Shakti Sangathan Movement (1990) in Rajasthan. Since these experiences date back to the 1990s, there is an urgent need to research and document more recent, and potentially, more innovative examples of vertical social accountability across the world.
31. According to Stapenhurs and O'Brien, diagonal accountability occurs when active citizens and civil society groups work with elected representatives to enhance the representativeness of the parliaments (R. Stapenhurst and M. O'Brien, "Accountability in Governance," *World Bank Governance Papers*, Washington, DC: World Bank, 2005. Available at http://siteresources.worldbank.org/PUBLICSECTORAND GOVERNANCE/Resources/AccountabilityGovernance.pdf).
32. For a perspective on "New Citizen Engagement" in postmodernism, see Chiou (2000).
33. A basic Google search on "citizen oversight committees," for instance, mostly gives out examples from the educational, health and policing sectors from advanced industrialized countries, and notably the United States. One then would wish that new research tackles diagonal accountability in the developing world.
34. New volumes by Claasen and Lardiés (2011) and O'dugbemi and Lee (2011) are positive steps toward this goal. However, for the most part, they stay as descriptive accounts.
35. E. J. Hernández, "Reinterpretando la rendición de cuentas o accountability: Diez propuestas para la mejora de la calidad democrática y la eficacia de las políticas públicas en España." *Working Paper 145/2009*, Spain: Fundación alternativas, 2009. Available at http://www.academia. edu/3518617/Reinterpretando_la_rendicion_de_cuentas_o_accountability_ diez_propuestas_para_la_mejora_de_la_calidad_democratica_y_la_eficacia_ de_las_politicas_publicas_en_Espana
36. The term "good" governance continues to be controversial and is omitted by many scholars and policy-makers for its unclear and subjective tone and implications. Many equate it with "democratic" governance, and use it as such. Others make a difference between "good" and "democratic" without necessarily opposing one to another. For more, see Bellina et al. (2009).

37. POAS makes all principal officials accountable, including the Chief Secretary, Financial Secretary, Secretary for Justice and heads of government agencies, political appointees chosen by the Chief Executive rather than politically neutral career civil servants. Under the new system, all agency heads become Ministers, members of the Executive Council, a refashioned cabinet. They report directly to the Chief Executive instead of the Chief Secretary or the Financial Secretary.

38. Citizens' stated confidence in their own ability to evaluate a policy proposal substantially affects their willingness to reward or punish a representative for their votes on that policy. Gerber et al. (2011) find that any gap between citizen preferences and policy often reflect citizen deference to "expert" legislators rather than a lack of representativeness.

39. The Westminster system provides various actors with a great potential of increasing their autonomy over others due to the high levels of flexibility. Accordingly, the executive, and particularly the Prime Minister, are able to establish and formulate constitutional traditions (Kumarasingham 2013).

40. Greater media attention, the rise of new controversial cross-cutting issues and the changing cultural attitudes toward higher accountability expectations in Australia may have been at the root of accountability problematic there, not the declining parliamentary and ministerial standards of accountability (Dowding and Lewis 2012).

41. Bridoux and Gerbel (2012) differentiated between a flexible democracy promotion discourse and an inflexible and uncompromising anti-corruption discourse, which together might lead to contradictory policies and processes. They underline that both corruption control and democratization must focus on the ownership and the sustainability of reforms.

42. For more on good enough governance, see Grindle (2007).

43. DDC or *Direction du développement et de la coopération* (2007), for instance, enumerates five principles of good governance including *accountability, transparency, non-discrimination, participation* and *efficacy* (5). These very same terms are also used in defining the term accountability. Accountability, for instance, presupposes transparency because without the latter, accountability will not transpire. Also, accountability breeds transparency and participation (Hernandez 2009, see this chapter, note 35 for details).

44. Council on Foundations and the European Foundation Centre (2007) enumerates seven defining features of accountability in international philanthropy: integrity, empathy, respect, sensitivity, justice, cooperation and collaboration and efficacy.

45. L. Beck et al., *The Enabling Environment for Social Accountability in Mongolia*, Washington, DC: World Bank, 2007. Available at http://www.sasanet.org/curriculum_final/downlaods/EV/Case%20Studies/EE%20CS3.pdf

4   THE CORRUPTION PENTAGON: LINKING CAUSES, CONTROLS AND CONSEQUENCES

1. See United Nations, A/RES/51/191 (1996) and United Nations, A/RES/51/59 (1997) respectively.
2. For more, see Europa (2007).
3. OECD (2008) defines corruption as any activity that involves the offer (active) and the acceptance (passive) of illicit financial or other benefits to a public official in order to incite him/her to violate his/her official duties. See Organization for Economic Cooperation and Development (OECD). Corruption: A Glossary of International Standards in Criminal Law. Paris, 2008. Available at http://www.oecd.org/daf/anti-bribery/41194428.pdf
4. L. Wren-Lewis, "Do Infrastructure Reforms Reduce the Effect of Corruption? Theory and Evidence from Latin America and the Caribbean," *ECORE* Discussion Paper *73*, United Kingdom/Belgium: International Association for Research and Teaching, July 2011. Available at http://www.ecore.be/DPs/dp_1315293840.pdf
5. F. Fukuyama, "Democracy and Corruption." *American Interest*, California (October 5, 2012). Available at http://blogs.the-american-interest.com/fukuyama/2012/10/05/democracy-and-corruption/
6. T. Lovseth, "Corruption and Alienation," Paper presented at the *ECPR joint sessions*. Grenoble, April 2001. Available at http://www.essex.ac.uk/ECPR/events/jointsessions/paperarchive/grenoble
7. C. Kenny, "Measuring and Reducing the Impact of Corruption in Infrastructure," *World Bank Policy Research Paper 4099* (December 2006): 1–42. Available at http://www-wds.worldbank.org/servlet/WDSContentServer/WDSP/IB/2006/12/14/000016406_200612 14120802/Rendered/PDF/wps4099.pdf
8. F-J. Urra, *Assessing Corruption: An Analytical Review of Corruption Measurement and its Problems: Perception, Error and Utility*, Washington, DC: Georgetown University, 2007. Available at http://unpan1.un.org/intradoc/groups/public/documents/apcity/unpan028792.pdf
9. National integrity systems have been in existence for over a decade, and are used to map the integrity of countries across the world. They can be defined generally as institutions, laws, procedures, practices and attitudes that encourage and support integrity in governance (Head et al. 2008, Pope 2000, Sampford 2005). More specifically, they include the legislative, executive and the judicial branches of government, public sector and law enforcement agencies, political parties and electoral management bodies, watchdog agencies and civil society, ombudsman, audit institutions, anti-corruption agencies and the media.

10. A. Gentlemen, "Letter from India: Thin Ray of Light Shines on Dark Ocean of Graft," *The New York Times* (January 7, 2008). Available at http://www.nytimes.com/2008/01/17/world/asia/17iht-letter. 3.9294097.html?_r=2&

11. Even pork-barreling, which might be an essential tool of compromise and balancing different political interests, might be considered corrupt since it is a method of give and take in the parliament.

12. Dahlstrom et al. (2012) found, for instance, that reforms of merito-cratic bureaucratic recruitment reduce public sector corruption even when controlling for a large set of alternative explanations, including public employees' competitive salaries, career stability or internal pro-motion. Others find that meritocratic recruitment does not change corruption nor does education; leadership and good politicians do (Nyblade and Reed 2008).

13. For such an account, see the case of the Slovak Republic by Pawelke (2010), the case of Georgia by Kukhianidze (2009), the case of Bulgaria by Popova (2012).

14. Asthana (2012) finds that awareness of human rights reduces incidence of bribery.

15. Investigations, trials and convictions can be weapons in political strug-gles; visible trends may thus say more about contention among factions than about actual corruption. Indeed, perceptions of a country or city may be made *worse* by serious reforms, as allegations and convictions dominate the news and public discussion. The government needs to gain more public confidence before anti-corruption reforms can strengthen good governance. For more on this stand, see Oyamada (2005) and Johnston (2010). Conversely, anti-corruption reforms and institutions could also decrease the experience of corruption, and hence the percep-tion of it.

16. UNODCCP (2002) differentiates between an anti-corruption agency, which is a standing body established to implement and administer pre-vention and enforcement elements of a national strategy, and an anti-corruption committee or commission, that are intended to develop, launch, implement and monitor the anti-corruption strategy itself. The mandate of an anti-corruption committee or commission could thus call for the establishment of an independent anti-corruption agency and any other necessary entities, the development of legislation, the development of appropriate action plan(s), taking measures to inform the public and foster broad-based support of the national strategy. For more, see Tool 9—National Anti-Corruption Commissions, Committees and Similar in UNODCCP (2002).

17. While the Kenyan Anti-Corruption Commission has been largely inef-fectual, the more autonomous Economic and Financial Crimes

Commission in Nigeria has had a measure of success in fighting corruption. For more, see Lawson (2009).

18. S. N. Parnini, "Governance Reforms and Anti-Corruption Commission in Bangladesh," *Romanian Journal of Political Science* 11, 1 (Summer 2011). Available at http://www.sar.org.ro/polsci/?p=587

19. A judiciary is institutionally insulated from the other branches of government when four conditions are met: (i) Constitution contains guarantees of judicial autonomy and independence; (ii) Judges have life tenure guarantees; (iii) Judiciary is in control of judicial careers—appointment, promotion, discipline, transfers and, if necessary, dismissal of individual judges; and (iv) Judiciary drafts and controls its own budget. For more, see Jain (2001).

20. It is also possible, however, that the institutional insulation of the judiciary contributes to the collusion of a corrupt judiciary with an equally corrupt political elite in an otherwise procedurally democratic setting, as in Bulgaria (Popova 2012).

21. For more on the objectives of public sector auditing, see Lima Declaration of Guidelines on Auditing adopted in Lima, Peru in October 1997 (INTOSAI 1997).

22. E. Nino, "Access to Public Information and Citizen Participation in Supreme Audit Institutions (SAI): Guide to Good Practice," *World Bank Institute Governance Working Paper Series*, Washington, DC: World Bank Institute, 2010. Available at http://siteresources.worldbank.org/WBI/Resources/213798-1259011531325/6598384-1268250334206/Citizen_Participation_SAI.pdf

23. Local integrity systems consist of all the institutions, policies, practices and instruments meant to contribute to the integrity of a given municipality. For more, see Hubert and Six (2012).

24. For an example of regional transfer of anti-corruption initiatives, see Barcham (2009).

25. The premise of routine activity theory is that crime is relatively unaffected by social causes such as poverty, inequality and unemployment because it can be committed by anyone who has the opportunity to do so. The routine activity theory thus examines the factors that render a particular target attractive. For more, see Cohen and Felson 1979.

26. Mohtadi and Roe (2003) assume that democracy increases both the flow of information available to rent-seekers and their access to government officials. Better information about where rents lie and greater access to corruptible government officials increase the returns to rent-seeking. This, in turn, encourages competitive entry into rent-seeking increasing the ongoing rate for bribes, and corruption (451).

27. The direct ways to fight political corruption include: (i) political competition, symbolized by free and fair elections in a democracy, by posing a credible threat to the incumbents of losing office in the

next period (Rose-Ackerman 1999); (ii) constitutional strictures to complement the electoral control of corruption, by keeping the executives in check, especially in between-election years (Linz and Stepan, 1996); (iii) independent and efficient judiciary, by ensuring that the executives and legislatures do not abuse their power; and (iv) civic engagement by monitoring public agencies and officials.

28. Werlin (1998, 2005) underlines a similar notion in his political elasticity theory: Integrating and alternating the political software (linking incentives to persuasion and focusing on policies and practices in governance) with political hardware (including disincentives and coercion and regulatory procedures and sanctions) can control corruption and contribute to democratization, in substance and durability. Wolin (1960) does the same in his 1960 study of the primary versus secondary politics represented by competition and consensus, or partisanship and statesmanship, respectively.

29. M. T. Brassilio, "Corruption," *Powerpoint presentation by the President of the Transparency International—Italia*, Rome, November 26, 2010. Available at http://europeandcis.undp.org/uploads/public1/files/Corruption_Ms_BRASSIOLO_TI.pdf

BIBLIOGRAPHY

Abbott, K. and D. Snidal. "Why States Act Through Formal International Organizations." *Journal of Conflict Resolution* 42, 1 (1998): 3–32.

Abueva, J. V. "The Contribution of Nepotism, Spoils, and Graft to Political Development." *East-West Center Review* 3 (1966): 45–54.

AbuKhalil, A. A. "Change and Democratization in the Arab World: The Role of Political Parties," *Third World Quarterly* 18, 1 (March 1997): 149–163.

Acemoglu, D. and J. A. Robinson. *Economic Origins of Dictatorship and Democracy.* New York: Cambridge University Press, 2006.

Acemoglu, D. et al. "Income and Democracy." *American Economic Review* 98, 3 (June 2008): 808–842.

Achua, J. K. "Anti-corruption in Public Procurement in Nigeria: Challenges and Competency Strategies." *Journal of Public Procurement* 11, 3 (2011): 323–353.

Ackerly, B. A. "Is Liberalism the Only Way Toward Democracy? Confucianism and Democracy." *Political Theory* 33, 4 (August 2005): 547–576.

Ackerman, J. M. "Co-governance for Accountability: Beyond 'Exit' and 'Voice.'" *World Development* 32, 3 (2004): 447–463.

———. "Social Accountability in the Public Sector: A Conceptual Discussion." *Social Development Papers: Participation and Civic Engagement* No. 82 (March 2005).

Ades, A. and R. Di Tella. "Rents, Competition, and Corruption." *American Economic Review* 89, 4 (1999): 982–993.

Adorno, T. et al. *The Authoritarian Personality.* New York: Harper, 1950.

Adsera, A. et al. "Are You Being Served? Political Accountability and Quality of Government." *Journal of Law, Economics & Organization* 19, 2 (2003): 445–490.

Alatas, S. H. *Corruption: Its Nature, Causes, and Functions.* Brookfield: Avebury, 1990.

Albertus, M. and V. Menaldo. "Coercive Capacity and the Prospects for Democratization." *Comparative Politics* 44, 2 (January 2012): 151–169.

Alesina, A. and R. Perotti. "Income Distribution, Political Instability, and Investment." *European Economic Review* 40 (1996): 1203–1225.

Almond, G. and S. Verba. *Civic Culture: Political Attitudes and Democracy in Five Nations.* London: Sage Publications, 1963.

Alt, J. E. and D. D. Lassen. "Transparency, Political Polarization, and Political Budget Cycles in OECD Countries." *American Journal of Political Science* 50, 3 (2006): 530–550.

Alt, J. E. et al. "Fiscal Transparency, Gubernatorial Approval, and the Scale of Government: Evidence from the States." *State Politics & Policy Quarterly* 2, 3 (2002): 230–250.

Amick, G. *The American Way of Graft: A Study of Corruption in State and Local Government.* Princeton: The Center for the Analysis of Public Issues, 1976.

Amin, S. *Le développement inégal. Essai sur les formations sociales du capitalism periphérique.* Paris: Editions de Minuit, 1973.

Amosa, D. U. "Local Government and Good Governance: The Case of Samoa." *Commonwealth Journal of Local Governance* 7, (2010): 7–21.

Anderson, B. R. *Imagined Communities: Reflections on the Origin and Spread of Nationalism.* London: Verso, 1991.

Anderson, L. "The Authoritarian Executive? Horizontal and Vertical Accountability in Nicaragua." *Latin American Politics & Society* 48, 2 (Summer 2006): 141–169.

Ansell, B. and D. Samuels. "Inequality and Democratization: A Contractarian Approach." *Comparative Political Studies* 43, 12 (December 2010): 1543–1574.

Apter, D. *The Politics of Modernization.* Chicago: University of Chicago Press, 1965.

Arat, Z. *Democracy and Human Rights in Developing Countries.* Boulder/London: Lynn Rienner, 1991.

———. "Human Rights and Democracy: Expanding or Contracting?" *Polity* 32, 1 (Fall 1999): 119–144.

Arndt, C. and C. Oman. *Uses and Abuses of Governance Indicators.* Paris: Organization for Economic Cooperation and Development, Development Centre Series, 2006.

Arroyo. D. *Stocktaking of Social Accountability Initiatives in the Asia and Pacific Region.* World Bank Institute Working Papers. Washington DC: The World Bank, 2004.

Ashworth, S. "Electoral Accountability: Recent Theoretical and Empirical Work." *Annual Review of Political Science* 15 (June 2012): 183–201.

Asthana, A. "Human Rights and Corruption: Evidence from a Natural Experiment." *Journal of Human Rights* 11, 4 (October–December 2012): 526–536.

Baccaro, L. "What Is Alive and What Is Dead in the Theory of Corporatism." *British Journal of Industrial Relations* 41, 4 (December 2003): 683–706.

Bachrach, P. and M. Baratz. "Two Faces of Power." *American Political Science Review* 56, 4 (December 1962): 947–952.

Ball, C. "What is Transparency?" *Public Integrity* 11, 4 (Fall 2009): 293–307.

Bang, H. and A. Esmark. "Good Governance in Network Society: Reconfiguring the Political from Politics to Policy." *Administrative Theory and Praxis* 31, 1 (March 2009): 7–37.

Barcham, M. "Cleaning up the Pacific: Anti-corruption Initiatives." *Australian Journal of International Affairs* 63, 2 (June 2009): 249–267.

Barnett, M. and M. Finnemore. *Rules for the World: International Organizations in Global Politics.* Ithaca: Cornell University Press, 2004.

Barro, R. "Determinants of Democracy." *Journal of Political Economy* 107, 6 (Summer 1999): 158–183.

Bartley, R. "The New Public Management in Developing Countries: Implications for Policy and Organizational Reform." *Journal of International Development* 11, 5 (1999): 761–765.

Barzun, J. "Is Democratic Theory for Export?" *Society* 26, 3 (March/April 1989): 16–23.

Baum, J. R. and K. Bawn. "Slowing at Sunset: Administrative Procedures and the Pace of Reform in Korea." *Journal of East Asian Studies* 11, 2 (May–August 2011): 197–221.

Bayley, H. D. "The Effects of Corruption in a Developing Nation." *Western Political Quarterly* 19 (1966): 719–732.

Bearce, D. H. and L. Hutnick, "Toward an Alternative Explanation for the Resource Curse: Natural Resources, Immigration, and Democratization." *Comparative Political Studies* 44, 6 (June 2011): 689–718.

Beck, L. "Senegal's Enlarged Presidential Majority: Deepening Democracy or Detour?" In *State, Conflict, and Democracy in Africa,* edited by R. Joseph. Boulder: Lynne Rienner, 1999.

Becker, G. S. "Nobel Lecture: The Economic Way of Looking at Behavior." *Journal of Political Economy* 101, 3 (1993): 385–409.

Beckman, D. "Recent Experience and Emerging Trends." In *Nongovernmental Organizations and the World Bank: Cooperation for Development,* edited by S. Paul and A. Israel. Washington, DC: The World Bank, 1991.

Bedirhanoglu, P. "The Neoliberal Discourse on Corruption as a Means of Consent Building: Reflections from Post-crisis Turkey." *Third World Quarterly* 28, 7 (October 2007): 1239–1254.

Beekers, D. and B. van Gool. *From Patronage to Neopatrimonialism: Postcolonial Governance in Sub-Sahara Africa and Beyond.* Leiden: African Studies Center, 2012.

Bell, D. *The Coming of Post-industrial Society: A Venture in Social Forecasting.* New York: Basic Books, 1973.

Bellina, S. et al. (eds.). *Democratic Governance: A New Paradigm for Development?* London/New York: Hurst Publishers/Colombia University Press, 2009.

Bellver, A. and D. Kaufman. "Transparenting Transparency: Initial Empirics and Policy Applications." *World Bank Policy Research Working Paper*. Washington, DC: World Bank, 2005.

Benhabib, S. "Models of Public Space: Hannah Arendt, the Liberal Tradition, and Jürgen Habermas." In *Habermas and the Public Sphere*, edited by C. Calhoun. Cambridge, MA: MIT Press, 1992.

Bénit-Gbaffou, C. "'Up Close and Personal'—How Does Local Democracy Help the Poor Access the State? Stories of Accountability and Clientelism." *Johannesburg Journal of Asian & African Studies* 46, 5 (October 2011): 453–464.

Benson, G. *Political Corruption in America*. Lexington: Lexington Books, 1978.

Bentham, J. "Farming Defended." *Writings on the Poor Laws*, vol. 1, edited by M. Quinn. Oxford: Oxford University Press, 2001.

Berg, L. L. et al. *Corruption in the American Political System*. Morristown: General Learning Process, 1976.

Berglund, S. et al. *Challenges to Democracy*. Cheltenham: Elgar, 2001.

Bermeo, N. "Myths of Moderation: Confrontation and. Conflict during Democratic Transitions." *Comparative Politics* 29, 3 (April 1997): 305–322.

Bertelli, A. M. "Credible Governance? Transparency, Political Control, the Personal Vote and British Quangos." *Political Studies* 56 (2008): 807–829.

Besley, T. "Political Selection." *Journal of Economic Perspectives* 19, 3 (2005): 43–60.

Besley, T. and R. Burgess. "The Political Economy of Government Responsiveness: Theory and Evidence from India." *The Quarterly Journal of Economics* 117, 4 (2002): 1415–1451.

Biela, J. and Y. Papadopoulos. "Strategies for Assessing and Measuring Agency Accountability." Conference Paper presented at the *32nd European Group for Public Administration (EGPA) Annual Conference*. Toulouse, September 2010.

Birkinshaw, P. "Freedom of Information and Openness: Fundamental Human Rights." *Administrative Law Review* 58, 1 (2006): 177–218.

Black, H. C. *Black's Law Dictionary*. St. Paul: West Publishing Co., 1979.

Blair, H. "Participation and Accountability at the Periphery: Democratic Local Governance in Six Countries." *World Development* 28, 1 (January 2000): 21–39.

———. "Gaining State Support for Social Accountability." In *Accountability Through Public Opinion: From Inertia to Public Action*, edited by S. O'dugbemi and T. Lee. Washington, DC: World Bank, 2011.

Blaney, D. L. and M. K. Pasha. "Civil Society and Democracy in the Third World: Ambiguities and Historical Possibilities." *Studies in Comparative International Development* 28, 1 (Spring 1993): 3–24.

Blanton, T. S. "The World's Right to Know." *Foreign Policy* 131 (2002): 50–59.

Blind, P. K. "Linking Civil Society with Democratic Governance through the MDGs." Conference Paper presented at the *World Civic Forum*. Seoul, May 2009.

———. "Building Trust in Government: Linking Theory with Practice." In *Building Trust in Government: Innovations in Governance Reform in Asia*, edited by G. S. Cheema and V. Popovski. New York: United Nations Press, 2010: 22–54.

———. "Emergence of the Concept, Evolution of Practices, Current Developments." *Prepared as a Background Document for East West Governance Center.* Honolulu, July 18, 2011.

Bodei, R. "From Secrecy to Transparency: Reason of State and Democracy." *Philosophy & Social Criticism* 37, 8 (October 2011): 889–898.

Boix, C. *Democracy and Redistribution.* Cambridge, UK: Cambridge University Press, 2003.

Bollen, K. "Political Democracy and the Timing of Development." *American Sociological Review* 44 (1979): 572–587.

Bollen, K. and R. Jackman. "Political Democracy and the Size Distribution of Income." *American Sociological Review* 50 (1985): 438–457.

Booth, J. A. and P. B. Richard. "Civil Society, Political Capital and Democracy in Central America." *Journal of Politics* 60, 3 (August 1998): 780–801.

Borshchevskaya, A. "Sponsored Corruption and Neglected Reform in Syria." *Middle East Quarterly* 17, 3 (Summer 2010): 41–50.

Bourdieu, P. *The Logic of Practice.* Stanford: Stanford University Press, 1990.

Boven, M. "Public Accountability." In *The Oxford Handbook of Public Management,* edited by F. Ewan et al. Oxford: Oxford University Press, 2005.

———. "New Forms of Accountability and EU Governance." *Comparative European Politics* 5 (April 2007a): 104–120.

———. "Analyzing and Assessing Accountability: A Conceptual Framework." *European Law Journal* 13, 4 (July 2007b): 447–468.

———. "Two Concepts of Accountability: Accountability as a Virtue and as a Mechanism." *West European Politics* 33, 5 (September 2010): 946–967.

Brahm, E. "Uncovering the Truth: Examining Truth Commission Success and Impact." *International Studies Perspectives* 8, 1 (February 2007): 16–35.

Braibanti, R. "Public Bureaucracy and Judiciary in Pakistan." In *Bureaucracy and Political Development,* edited by J. LaPalombra. Princeton: Princeton University Press, 1963.

Brancati, D. "The 2011 Protests: Were They About Democracy?" *Washington Quarterly* 36, 1 (Winter2012/2013): 25–35.

Bratton, M. "The Politics of Government–NGO Relations in Africa." *World Development* 17, 4 (April 1989): 569–587.

Bridoux, J. and A. Gebel. "Flexibility versus Inflexibility: Discursive Discrepancy in US Democracy Promotion and Anti-corruption Policies." *Third World Quarterly* 33, 10 (November 2012): 1945–1963.

Brinkerhoff, J. "Creating an Enabling Environment for Diasporas' Participation in Homeland Development." *International Migration* 50, 1 (February 2012): 75–95.

Brinks, D. and M. Coppedge. "Economic Globalism and Political Universalism." *Journal of World Systems Research* 6, 3 (Fall/Winter 2000): 582–622.

———. "Diffusion Is No Illusion: Neighbor Emulation in the Third Wave of Democracy." *Comparative Political Studies* 39, 4 (May 2006): 463–489.

Brown, D. S. and W. Hunter. "Democracy and Social Spending in Latin America, 1980–1992." *American Political Science Review* 93, 4 (1999): 779–790.

Broz, J. L. "Political System Transparency and Monetary Commitment Regimes." *International Organization* 56, 4 (2002): 861–887.

Bunce, V. "Rethinking Recent Democratization: Lessons from the Post-communist Experience." *World Politics* 55 (January 2003): 167–192.

Burton, M. G. and J. Higley. "Elite Settlements." *American Sociological Review* 52 (1987): 295–307.

Burton, M. et al. "Introduction: Elite Transformations and Democratic Regimes," in *Elites and Democratic Consolidation in Latin America and Southern Europe*, edited by J. Higley and R. Gunther. London: Cambridge University Press, 1992.

Callamard, A. "Accountability, Transparency, and Freedom of Expression in Africa." *Social Research* 77, 4 (Winter 2010): 1211–1240.

Camerer, M. "Measuring Public Integrity." *Journal of Democracy* 17, 1 (January 2006): 152–165.

Cannon, B. and M. Hume. "Central America, Civil Society and the 'Pink Tide': Democratization or De-democratization." *Democratization* 19, 6 (December 2012): 1039–1064.

Cardoso, F. "Dependent Capitalist Development in Latin America." *New Left Review* 1, 74 (August 1972): 83–94.

Cardoso, F. H. and E. Faletto. *Dependency and Development in Latin America*. California: University of California Press, 1979.

Carnegie, P. J. "Trade-offs, Compromise and Democratization in a Post-authoritarian Setting." *Asian Social Science* 8, 13 (November 2012): 71–79.

Carothers, T. "Civil Society." *Foreign Policy* 117 (Winter1999/2000): 18–40.
———. "The End of the Transition Paradigm." *Journal of Democracy* 13, 1 (January 2002): 5–22.

Carr, I. "Corruption, the Southern African Development Community Anti-corruption Protocol and the Principal-Agent-Client Model." *International Journal of Law in Context* 5, 2 (June 2009): 147–177.

Caselli, F. and M. Morelli. "Bad Politicians." *Journal of Public Economics* 88, 3–4 (2004): 759–782.

Caspersen, N. "Democracy, Nationalism and (Lack of) Sovereignty: The Complex Dynamics of Democratization in Unrecognized States." *Nations & Nationalism* 17, 2 (April 2011): 337–356.

Castells, M. "The Network Society: From Knowledge to Policy." In *Societies in Transition to the Network Society*, edited by M. Castells and G. Cardoso. Baltimore: Johns Hopkins University Press, 2006.

Cees, V. and N. Aarts. "Accountability: New Challenges, New Forms." Conference Paper presented at the *3rd European Communication Conference (ECREA)*. Hamburg, October 2010.

Chambers, P. "Where Agency Meets Structure: Understanding Civil-Military Relations in Contemporary Thailand." *Asian Journal of Political Science* 19, 3 (December 2011): 290–304.

Chandler, R. C., and J. C. Piano. *The Public Administration Dictionary*, 2nd edition. Santa Barbara: ABC-CLIO Press, 1988.

Chang, H. J. *Bad Samaritans, Rich Nations, Poor Policies and the Threat to the Developing World*. New York: Random House Business Books Series, 2007.

Chang, E. C. et al. "Legislative Malfeasance and Political Accountability." *World Politics* 62, 2 (April 2010): 177–220.

Charron, N. "Party Systems, Electoral Systems and Constraints on Corruption." *Electoral Studies* 30, 4 (December 2011): 595–606.

Chen, J. and N. Huhe. "Informal Accountability, Socially Embedded Officials, and Public Goods Provision in Rural China: The Role of Lineage Groups." *Journal of Chinese Political Science* 18, 2 (June 2013): 101–116.

Cheung, C. Y. "How Political Accountability Undermines Public Service Ethics: The Case of Hong Kong." *Journal of Contemporary China* 20, 70 (June 2011): 499–515.

Chien-Kai Chen. "The State-Society Interaction in the Process of Taiwan's Democratization from 1990 to 1992." *East Asia* 28, 2 (June 2011): 115–134.

Chiou, C. T. "The Transition of Public Management Theory in Post-modern Society: From 'New Public Management' to 'New Citizenship Governance.'" *Chinese Public Administration Review* 10, 1 (December 2000): 1–32.

Cho, W. "Accountability or Representation? How Electoral Systems Promote Public Trust in African Legislatures." *Governance* 25, 4 (October 2012): 617–637.

Chowdhury, S. K. The Effect of Democracy and Press Freedom on Corruption: An Empirical Test." *Economics Letters* 85 (2004): 93–101.

Claasen, M. and C. Alpín-Lardiés. *Social Accountability in Africa: Practitioners' Experiences and Lessons.* Cape Town: IDASA, 2011.

Clark, J. *Democratizing Development.* London: Earthscan, 1991.

Cockcroft, L. "Global Corruption: An Untamed Hydra." *World Policy Journal* 27, 1 (Spring 2010): 21–28.

Cohen, J. "The Inverse Relationship Between Secrecy and Privacy." *Social Research* 77, 3 (Fall 2010): 883–898.

Cohen, J. and A Arato. *Civil Society and Political Theory.* Cambridge, MA: MIT Press, 1992.

Cohen, L. and M. Felson. "Social Change and Crime Rate Trends: A Routine Activity Approach." *American Sociological Review* 44, 4 (1979): 588–608.

Collier, D. and S. Levitsky. "Democracy with Adjectives: Conceptual Innovation in Comparative Research." *Working Paper* 230. Kellogg Institute, Notre Dame University, Indiana, August 1996.

Collier, R. B. "Labor and Democratization: Comparing the First and Third Waves in Europe and Latin America." *Working Paper* No. 62 for Institute of Industrial Relations (May 1995): 1–70.

———. *Paths Toward Democracy: The Working Class and Elites in Western Europe and Latin America.* Cambridge: Cambridge University Press, 1999.

Collier, R. B. and D. Collier. *Shaping the Political Arena: Critical Junctures, the Labor Movement and Regime Dynamics in Latin America.* Princeton: Princeton University Press, 1991.

Collier, R. B. and J. Mahoney. "Adding Collective Actors to Collective Outcomes: Labor and Recent Democratization in South America and Southern Europe," in *Comparative Politics: Transitions to Democracy: A Special Issue in Memory of Dankwart A. Rustow* 29, 3 (April 1997): 285–303.

Conaghan, C. M. and R. Espinal. "Unlikely Transitions to Uncertain Regimes? Democracy without Compromise in the Dominican Republic and Ecuador." *Journal of Latin American Studies* 22, 3 (October 1990): 553–574.

Cooper, T. L. "Big Questions in Administrative Ethics: A Need for Focused, Collaborative Effort." *Public Administration Review* 64, 4 (2004): 395–407.

Cooper, T. L. and D. E. Yoder. "Public Management Ethics Standards in a Transnational World." *Public Integrity* 4, 4 (Fall 2002): 333–352.

Coppedge, M., et al. "Two Persistent Dimensions of Democracy: Contestation and Inclusiveness." *Journal of Politics* 70, 3 (July 2008): 632–647.

Coulter, P. B. *Social Mobilization and Liberal Democracy*. Lexington: Lexington Books, 1975.

Crawford, G. "'Making Democracy a Reality'? The Politics of Decentralization and the Limits to Local Democracy in Ghana." *Journal of Contemporary African Studies* 27, 1 (January 2009): 57–83.

Crippa, M. "A Long Path toward Reconciliation and Accountability: A Truth and Reconciliation Commission and a Special Chamber for Burundi." *International Criminal Law Review* 12, 1 (January 2012): 71–100.

Croissant, A. "Provisions, Practices and Performances of Constitutional Review in Democratizing East Asia." *Pacific Review* 23, 5 (December 2010): 549–578.

Croissant, A. et al. "Breaking With the Past? Civil–Military Relations in the Emerging Democracies of East Asia." *Policy Studies* 63 (2012): 72–79.

Crowe, J. "New Challenges for Leadership and Accountability in Local Public Services in England." *International Journal of Leadership in Public Services* 7, 3 (2011): 206–217.

Cutright, P. "National Political Development: Measurement and Analysis." *American Sociological Review* 28 (1963): 253–264.

Dagg, C. J. "The 2004 Elections in Indonesia: Political Reform and Democratization." *Asia Pacific Viewpoint* 48, 1 (April 2007): 47–59.

Dahl, R. *Polyarchy*. New Haven: Yale University Press, 1971.

Dahlstrom, C. et al. "The Merit of Meritocratization: Politics, Bureaucracy, and the Institutional Deterrents of Corruption." *Political Research Quarterly* 65, 3 (September 2012): 656–668.

Davidson, J. S. "Politics as Usual on Trial: Regional Anti-corruption Campaigns." *Indonesia Pacific Review* 20, 1 (March 2007): 75–99.

Davis, K. E. "The Prospects for Anti-corruption Law: Optimists versus Skeptics." *Hague Journal of the Rule of Law* 4, 2 (September 2012): 319–336.

Debrah, E. "Assessing the Quality of Accountability in Ghana's District Assemblies, 1993–2008." *African Journal of Political Science and International Relations* 3, 6 (June 2009): 278–287.

———. "Measuring Governance Institutions' Success in Ghana: The Case of the Electoral Commission, 1993–2008." *African Studies*, 70, 1 (April 2011): 25–45.

de Fine Licht, J. "Do We Really Want to Know? The Potentially Negative Effect of Transparency." *Scandinavian Political Studies* 34, 3 (September 2011): 183–201.

de Maria, W. C. "Délits interculturels: évaluation de la capacité africaine à lutter contre la corruption." *International Journal of Cross Cultural Management* 8, 3 (December 2008): 317–341.

de Mesquita, B. and G. W. Downs. "Development and Democracy." *Foreign Affairs* 84, 5 (October 2005): 77–86.

Denk, T. and D. Silander. "Problems in Paradise? Challenges to Future Democratization in Democratic States." *International Political Science Review* 33, 1 (January 2012): 25–40.

Diamond, L. "Economic Development and Democracy Reconsidered." In *Reexaming Democracy: Essays in Honor of Seymour Martin Lipset*, edited by L. Diamond and G. Marks. Newbury Park: Sage Publications, 1992.

———. *Developing Democracy: Toward Consolidation*. Baltimore: Johns Hopkins University Press, 1999.

———. "Thinking About Hybrid Regimes." *Journal of Democracy* 13, 2 (April 2002): 21–35.

———. *The Spirit of Democracy: The Struggle to Build Free Societies Throughout the World*. London/New York: St Martin's Griffin, 2009.

Diamond, L. and G. Marks (eds.). *Reexamining Democracy: Essays in Honor of Seymour Martin Lipset*. London: Sage Publications, 1992.

Dibua, J. L. *Development and Diffusionism: Looking Beyond Neopatrimonialism in Nigeria, 1962–1985*. New York: Palgrave Macmillan, 2013.

Dobel, J. "The Corruption of a State." *American Political Science Review* 72 (1978): 958–973.

Doig, A. *Corruption and Misconduct in Contemporary British Politics*. Harmondsworth: Penguin Books, 1984.

Doig, A. and S. McIvor. "Corruption and Its Control in the Developmental Context: An Analysis and the Selective Review of the Literature." *Third World Quarterly* 20, 3 (1999): 656–676.

Dominguez, J. "Latin America's Crisis of Representation." *Foreign Affairs* 76, 1 (January/February 1997): 100–113.

Dowding, K. and C. Lewis. "Newspaper Reporting and Changing Perceptions of Ministerial Accountability in Australia." *Australian Journal of Politics & History* 58, 2 (June 2012): 236–250.

Dower, N. "The Nature and Scope of Global Ethics and the Relevance of the Earth Charter." *Journal of Global Ethics* 1, 1 (2005): 25–43.

Dryzek, J. *Deliberative Democracy and Beyond: Liberals, Critics, Contestations*. Oxford: Oxford University Press, 2000.

Dubnick, M. J. "Seeking Salvation for Accountability." Conference Paper presented at the *Annual Meeting of the American Political Science Association*. Boston, September 2002.

Dubnick, M. J. and H. G. Frederickson. *Accountable Governance: Problems and Premises*. Armonk: ME Sharpe Inc., 2011.

Duit, A. and V. Gulay. "Governance and Complexity: Emerging Issues for Governance Theory." *Governance: An International Journal of Policy, Administration and Institutions* 21, 3 (July 2008): 311–335.

Easterly, W. "Democratic Accountability in Development: The Double Standard." *Social Research* 77, 4 (Winter 2010): 1075–1104.

Easton, D. *The Political System: An Inquiry into the State of Political Science.* New York: Alfred A. Knopf, 1953.

———. *A Systems Analysis of Political Life.* New York: Wiley, 1965.

Edel, F. "La Convention du Conseil de l'Europe sur l'accès aux documents publics: premier traité consacrant un droit général d'accès aux documents administratifs." *Revue française d'administration publique* 137–138 (2011): 59–78.

Edwards, B. and M. W. Foley. "Civil Society and Social Capital Beyond Putnam." *American Behavioral Scientist* 42, 1 (September 1998): 124–139.

Eicher, S. (ed.). "Government for Hire." In *Corruption in International Business: The Challenge of Cultural and Legal Diversity.* Surrey: Ashgate Publishing Ltd, 2009.

Ekpo, M. U. "Gift-Giving and Bureaucratic Corruption in Nigeria." In *Bureaucratic Corruption in Sub-Saharan Africa: Toward a Search for Causes and Consequences,* edited by M. U. Ekpo. Washington, DC: University Press of America, 1979.

Embaló, B. "Civil-Military Relations and Political Order in Guinea-Bissau." *Journal of Modern African Studies* 50, 2 (June 2012): 253–281.

Epstein, D. et al. "Democratic Transitions." *American Journal of Political Science* 50 (2006): 551–569.

Escobar, A. "Beyond the Third World: Imperial Globality, Global Coloniality, and Anti-globalization Social Movements." *Third World Quarterly* 25, 1 (2004): 207–307.

Etzioni, A. "Is Transparency the Best Disinfectant?" *Journal of Political Philosophy* 18, 4 (2010): 389–404.

Evans, M. "Beyond the Integrity Paradox—Towards 'Good Enough' Governance." *Policy Studies* 33, 1 (January 2012): 97–113.

Evans, P. B. *Dependent Development: The Alliance of Multinational, State, and Local Capital in Brazil.* Princeton: Princeton University Press, 1979.

———. "From Situations of Dependency to Globalized Social Democracy." *Studies in Comparative International Development* 44 (2009): 318–336.

Evans, G. and S. Whitefield. "The Politics and Economics of Democratic Commitment: Support for Democracy in Transition Societies." *British Journal of Political Science* 25, 4 (1995): 485–514.

Feng, Y. and P. J. Zak. "The Determinants of Democratic Transitions." *Journal of Conflict Resolution* 43, 2 (1999): 162–177.

Fenster, M. "Seeing the State: Transparency as Metaphor." *Administrative Law Review* 62, 3 (March 2010): 617–672.

Ferejohn, J. "Incumbent Performance and Electoral Control." *Public Choice* 50 (1986): 2–25.

―――. "Accountability and Authority: Towards a Model of Political Accountability." In *Democracy, Accountability, and Representation*, edited by A. Przeworski, B. Manin and S. C. Stokes. Cambridge: Cambridge University Press, 1999.

Finkel, E. "The Authoritarian Advantage of Horizontal Accountability: Ombudsmen in Poland and Russia." *Comparative Politics* 44, 3 (April 2012): 291–310.

Finel, B. I. and K. M. Lord. "The Surprising Logic of Transparency." *International Studies Quarterly* 43, 2 (1999): 315–339.

―――. "Conclusion: Power and Conflict in the Age of Transparency." In *Power and Conflict in the Age of Transparency*, edited by B. Finel and K. Lord. New York: St. Martin's Press, 2000.

Finkel, S. E. et al. "The Effects of U.S. Foreign Assistance on Democracy-Building, 1990–2003." *World Politics* 59 (April 2007): 404–439.

Finkelstein, N. "Introduction: Transparency in Public Policy." In *Transparency in Public Policy: Great Britain and the United States*, edited by N. Finkelstein. Houndmills, Basingstoke: Macmillan Press, 2000.

Fisher, J. "Local and Global: International Governance and Civil Society." *Journal of International Affairs* 57, 1 (Fall 2003): 19–40.

Fishman, R. "Rethinking the Iberian Transformations: How Democratization Scenarios Shaped Labor Market Outcomes." *Studies in Comparative International Development* 45, 3 (September 2010): 281–310.

Florini, A. "A New Role for Transparency." *Contemporary Security Policy* 18, 2 (August 1997a): 51–72.

―――. "The End of Secrecy." *Foreign Policy* 111 (Summer 1998): 50–63.

―――. "Does the Invisible Hand Need a Transparency Glove? The Politics of Transparency." Prepared for the *Annual World Bank Conference on Development Economics*. Washington, DC: World Bank, April 1999.

―――. "Increasing Transparency in Government." *International Journal on World Peace* 19, 3 (September 2002): 3–37.

―――. "The Battle over Transparency." In *The Right to Know: Transparency for an Open World*, edited by A. Florini. New York: Columbia University Press, 2007.

Fonchingong, C. C. "The Travails of Democratization in Cameroon in the Context of Political Liberalization Since the 1990s." *African & Asian Studies* 3, 1 (2004): 33–59.

Fortna, V. P. and R. Huang. "Democratization After Civil War: A Brush-Clearing Exercise." *International Studies Quarterly* 56, 4 (December 2012): 801–808.

Fowler, A. *Non-governmental Organizations in Africa: Achieving Comparative Advantage in Relief and Micro-development*. Brighton: Institute of Development Studies, 1988.

————. *Striking a Balance: A Guide to the Management of NGOs.* London: Earthscan, 1997.

Freedman, A. L. "Economic Crises and Political Change: Indonesia, South Korea, and Malaysia." *Asian Affairs: An American Review* 31, 4 (2005): 232–249.

Fritz, V. "Mongolia: The Rise and Travails of a Deviant Democracy." *Democratization* 15, 4 (August 2008): 766–788.

Frost, A. "Restoring Faith in Government: Transparency Reform in the United States and the European Union." *European Public Law* 9, 1 (March 2003): 87–104.

Fung, A. "Infotopia : Unleashing the Democratic Power of Transparency." *Politics & Society* 41, 2 (May 2013): 183–212.

Fung, A. and E. Wright. "Deepening Democracy Innovations in Empowered Participatory Governance." *Politics and Society* 26, 4 (March 2001): 461–510.

Fung, A. et al. *Full Disclosure: The Perils and Promise of Transparency.* Cambridge: Cambridge University Press, 2007.

Garcia-Murillo, M. "Does a Government Web Presence Reduce Perceptions of Corruption?" *Information Technology for Development* 19, 2 (April 2013): 151–175.

García-Sánchez, I. M. et al. "Determinants of Corporate Social Disclosure in Spanish Local Governments." *Journal of Cleaner Production* 39 (January 2013): 60–72.

Gartner, D. "Uncovering Bretton Woods: Conditional Transparency, the World Bank, and the International Monetary Fund." *George Washington International Law Review* 45, 1 (2013): 121–148.

Gasiorowski, M. "Economic Crisis and Political Regime Change." *American Political Science Review* 89, 4 (December 1995): 882–898.

Geddes, B. and A. R. Neto. "Institutional Sources of Corruption in Brazil." *Third World Quarterly* 13, 4 (1992): 641–661.

————. "International Organizations and Government Transparency: Linking the International and Domestic Realms." *International Studies Quarterly* 47, 4 (2003): 643–667.

————. "Transparency of Intergovernmental Organizations: The Roles of Member States, International Bureaucracies and Nongovernmental Organizations." *International Studies Quarterly* 51, 3 (2007): 625–648.

————. Entry for "Transparency." In *International Encyclopedia of the Social Sciences*, 2nd edition, edited by W. A. Darity Jr. Detroit: Macmillan Reference USA, 2008.

Gellner, E. *Nations and Nationalism.* Oxford: Blackwell Publishing, 2006.

Gellner, E. and J. Breuilly. *Nations and Nationalism: New Perspectives on the Past.* Ithaca: Cornell University Press, 2009.

Gentzkow, M. et al. "The Rise of the Fourth Estate. How Newspapers Became Informative and Why It Mattered." In *Corruption and Reform: Lessons from America's Economic History*, edited by M. Gentzkow and C. Goldin. Chicago: University of Chicago Press, 2006.

Gerber, A. S. et al. "Citizens' Policy Confidence and Electoral Punishment: A Neglected Dimension of Electoral Accountability." *Journal of Politics* 73, 4 (October 2011): 1206–1224.

Ghere, R. K. "Network Legitimacy and Accountability in a Developmental Perspective." *Public Integrity* 13, 2 (Spring 2011): 163–180.

Gherghina, S. "The Helping Hand: The Role of the EU in the Democratization of Post-Communist Europe." *Journal of Political Science* 9, 2 (Winter 2009): 65–79.

Gill, G. *The Dynamics of Democratization: Elites, Civil Society and the Transition Process*. New York: Freedom House, 2000.

Githinji, M. and F. Holmquist. "Reform and Political Impunity in Kenya: Transparency Without Accountability." *African Studies Review* 55, 1 (April 2012): 53–74.

Goel, R. V. and M. A. Nelson. "Economic Freedom Versus Political Freedom: Cross Country Influences on Corruption." *Australian Economic Papers* 44, 2 (June 2005): 121–133.

Goertz, A. M. and R. Jenkins. "Hybrid Forms of Accountability: Citizen Engagement in Institutions of Public Sector Oversight in India." *Public Management* 3, 3 (2001): 363–384.

———. "Reinventing Accountability: Making Democracy Work." Conference Paper presented at *World Bank Sustainable Development Lecture Series*. Washington, DC, November 2003.

Goetz, A.-M. "Political Cleaners: Women as the New Anti-corruption Force?" *Development and Change* 38, 1 (January 2007): 87–105.

Goetz, A. M. and J. Gaventa. "Bringing Citizen Voice and Client Focus into Service Delivery." *Institute of Development Studies (IDS) Working Paper 138*. England, July 2001.

Goldfrank, B. *Deepening Local Democracy in Latin America. Participation, Decentralization and the Left*. Penns.: Pennsylvania State University, 2011.

Gong, T. and S. Wang. "Indicators and Implications of Zero Tolerance of Corruption: The Case of Hong Kong." *Social Indicators Research* 112, 3 (August 2013): 569–586.

Good, K. and I. Taylor. "Botswana: A Minimalist Democracy." *Democratization* 15, 4 (August 2008): 750–765.

Goodman, M. "Does Political Corruption Really Help Economic Development? Yucatan, Mexico." *Polity* 7 (1974): 143–162.

Gordon, J. "Accountability and Global Governance: The Case of Iraq." *Ethics & International Affairs* 20, 1 (2006): 79–98.

Gorodnichenko, Y. and K. Peter. "Public Sector Pay and Corruption: Measuring Bribery from Micro Data." *Journal of Public Economics* 91, 5–6 (June 2007): 963–991.

Gortner, H. F. et al. (eds). *Organization Theory: A Public and Non-profit Perspective.* Belmont: Thomson Wadsworth, 2007.

Graycar, A. and D. Villa. "The Loss of Governance Capacity Through Corruption." *Governance: An International Journal of Policy, Administration, and Institutions* 24, 3 (July 2011): 419–438.

Griffith, I. and T. Munroe. "Drugs and Democracy in the Caribbean." *Journal of Commonwealth and Comparative Politics* 33 (November 1995): 360–370.

Grigorescu, A. "Transferring Transparency: The Impact of European Institutions on East and Central Europe." In *Norms and Nannies: The Impact of International Organizations on the International Organizations and Government Transparency Central and East European States,* edited by R. Linden. Boulder: Rowman and Littlefield, 2002.

———. "International Organizations and Government Transparency: Linking the International and Domestic Realms." *International Studies Quarterly* 47, 4 (December 2003): 643–667.

———. "Transparency of Intergovernmental Organizations: The Roles of Member States, International Bureaucracies and Nongovernmental Organizations." *International Studies Quarterly* 51, 3 (2007): 625–648.

Grimmelikhuijsen, S. "A Good Man but a Bad Wizard: About the Limits and Future of Transparency of Democratic Governments." *Information Polity* 17, 3–4 (2012): 293–302.

Grindle, M. S. "Good Enough Governance Revisited." *Development Policy Review* 25, 5 (September 2007): 533–574.

Grodeland, A. "Public Perceptions of Corruption and Anti-corruption Reform in the Western Balkans." *Slavonic & East European Review* 91, 3 (July 2013): 535–598.

Grodeland, A. and A. Aasland. "Fighting Corruption in Public Procurement in Post-communist States: Obstacles and Solutions." *Communist & Post-Communist Studies* 44, 1 (March 2011): 17–32.

Groenendjik, N. "A Principal-Agent Model of Corruption." *Crime, Law & Social Change* 27, 3–4 (1997): 207–229.

Grubisa, D. "Anti-corruption Policy in Croatia: Benchmark for EU Accession." *Croatian Political Science Review* 47, 4 (2010): 69–95.

Grzybowski, C. "Rural Workers' Movements and Democratization in Brazil." *Journal of Development Studies* 26, 4 (July 1990): 19–43.

Gurgur, T. and A. Shah. Localization and Corruption: Panacea or Pandora's Box? *World Bank Staff Research Working Paper* 3486. Washington, DC: World Bank, January 2005.

Habermas, J. *Between Facts and Norms: Contributions to a Discourse Theory of Law and Democracy*. Translated by William Rehg. Cambridge, MA: MIT Press, 1996.

Haddad, M. A. "The State-in-Society Approach to the Study of Democratization with Examples from Japan." *Democratization* 17, 5 (October 2010): 997–1023.

Haggard, S. and R. Kaufman. *The Political Economy of Democratic Transitions*. Princeton: Princeton University Press, 1995.

———. "The Political Economy of Democratic Transitions." *Comparative Politics* 29, 3 (April 1997): 263–283.

Hagopian, F. "'Democracy by Undemocratic Means?' Elites, Political Pacts, and Regime Transition in Brazil." *Comparative Political Studies* 23 (July 1990): 147–170.

———. *Traditional Politics and Regime Change in Brazil*. Cambridge: Cambridge University Press, 1996.

Hale, H. E. "Formal Constitutions in Informal Politics: Institutions and Democratization in Post-Soviet Eurasia." *World Politics* 63, 4 (October 2011): 581–617.

Halim, N. "Testing Alternative Theories of Bureaucratic Corruption in Less Developed Countries." *Social Science Quarterly* 89, 1 (March 2008): 236–257.

Halperin, M. H. et al. *The Democracy Advantage: How Democracies Promote Prosperity and Peace*. New York: Routledge, 2005.

Hanberger, A. "Democratic Accountability in Decentralized Governance." *Scandinavian Political Studies* 32, 1 (March 2009): 1–22.

Haque, S. and P. Pathrannarakul. "The Role of Technology in Enhancing Transparency and Accountability in Public Sector Organizations of Pakistan." *International Journal of Economics Business and Management Studies* 2, 1 (January 2013): 20–24.

Harlow, C. *Accountability in the European Union*. Oxford: Oxford University Press, 2002.

Harris, G. S. "Military Coups and Turkish Democracy, 1960–1980." *Turkish Studies* 12, 2 (June 2011): 203–213.

Harsh, M. et al. "Accountability and Inaction: NGOs and Resource Lodging in Development." *Development & Change* 41, 2 (March 2010): 253–278.

Hartz-Karp, J. "Harmonizing Divergent Voices: Sharing the Challenge of Decision-making." *Public Administration Today* 2 (December-February 2005): 14–19.

Hawes, G. *The Philippines and the Marcos Regime: The Politics of Export*. Ithaca/London: Cornell University Press, 1987.

Hayek, F. A. *The Road to Serfdom*. Chicago: University of Chicago Press, 1944.

———. *The Mirage of Social Justice*. Chicago: University of Chicago Press, 1952.

———. *Law, Legislation, and Liberty: A New Statement of the Liberal Principles of Justice and Political Economy.* London: Routledge and Kegan Paul, 1982.

Haynes, J. "Sustainable Democracy in Ghana: Problems and Prospects." *Third World Quarterly* 14, 3 (September 1993): 451–467.

Head, B. W. "The Contribution of Integrity Agencies to Good Governance." *Policy Studies* 33, 1 (January 2012): 7–20.

Head, B. W. et al. (eds.). *Promoting Integrity: Evaluating and Improving Public Institutions.* Ashgate: Farnham Survey, 2008.

Heald, D. "Fiscal Transparency: Concepts, Measurement and UK Practice." *Public Administration* 81, 4 (2003): 723–759.

———. "Varieties of Transparency." In *Transparency: The key to better governance?* edited by C. Hood and D. Heald. Oxford: Oxford University Press for the British Academy, 2006.

Heard-Laureote, K. "A Transparency Gap? The Case of European Agricultural Committee Governance." *Public Policy Administration* 22, 2 (2007): 239–258.

Hearn, J. "Aiding Democracy? Donors and Civil Society in South Africa." *Third World Quarterly* 21, 5 (October 2000): 815–830.

Heidenheimer, A. (ed.). "Introduction." *Political Corruption: Readings in Comparative Analysis.* New Brunswick: Transaction Books, 1970.

———. (ed.) "Perspectives on the Perception of Corruption." In *Political Corruption: Concepts and Contexts,* edited by A. Heidenheimer and M. Johnston. New Brunswick: Transaction Publishers, 2001.

Held, D. *Models of Democracy.* Stanford: Stanford University Press, 2006.

Hellman, J. and D. Kaufmann. "Confronting the Challenge of State Capture in Transition Economies." *Finance and Development* 38, 2 (2001): 1–8.

Helmke, G. and S. Levitsky. "Informal Institutions and Comparative Politics: A Research Agenda." *Perspectives on Politics* 2, 4 (2004): 725–740.

Heper, M. "Civil-Military Relations in Turkey: Toward a Liberal Model?" *Turkish Studies* 12, 2 (June 2011): 241–252.

Hetland, O. "Decentralization and Territorial Reorganisation in Mali: Power and the Institutionalisation of Local Politics." *Norwegian Journal of Geography* 62, 1 (March 2008): 23–35.

Higley, J. and M. Burton. *Elite Foundations of Liberal Democracy.* New York: Rowman and Littlefield, 2006.

Higley, J. and R. Gunther (eds.). *Elites and Democratic Consolidation in Latin America and Southern Europe.* Cambridge: Cambridge University Press, 1992.

Hilhorst, D. *The Real World of NGOs: Discourses, Diversity and Development.* London: Zed Books, 2003.

Hirsch, W. Z. and E. Osborne. "Privatization of Government Services: Pressure-Group Resistance and Service Transparency." *Journal of Labor Research* 21, 2 (2000): 315–326.

Hirschman, A. O. *Exit, Voice, and Loyalty: Responses to Decline in Firms, Organizations and States.* Boston: Harvard University Press, 1970.

Hirst, P. *Associative Democracy: New Forms of Economic and Social Governance.* London: Polity Press, 1994.

Hollyer, J. R. et al. "Democracy and Transparency." *Journal of Politics* 73, 3 (October 2011): 1191–1205.

Holzner, B. and L. Holzner. *Transparency in Global Change: The Vanguard of the Open Society.* Pittsburgh: University of Pittsburgh Press, 2006.

Hood, C. "Transparency." In *Encyclopedia of Democratic Thought*, P. B. Clarke and I. Foweraker (eds.). London: Routledge, 2001.

———. "From FOI World to WikiLeaks World: A New Chapter in the Transparency Story?" *Governance* 24, 4 (October 2011): 635–638.

Hood, C. and D. Heald (eds.). *Transparency: Key to Better Governance?* London: British Academy, 2006.

Hossain, N. "Rude Accountability: Informal Pressures on Frontline Bureaucrats in Bangladesh." *Development & Change* 41, 5 (September 2010): 907–928.

Huberts, L. and F. Six. "Local Integrity Systems: Toward a Framework for Comparative Analysis and Assessment." *Public Integrity* 14, 2 (Spring 2012): 151–172.

Huntington, S. *Political Order in Changing Societies.* Conn.: Yale University Press, 1968.

Huntington, S. *The Third Wave: Democratization in the Late 20th Century.* Oklahoma: University of Oklahoma Press, 1991.

Imai, K. S. and T. Sato. "Decentralization, Democracy and Allocation of Poverty Alleviation Programs in Rural India." *European Journal of Development Research* 24, 1 (February 2012): 125–143.

Inglehart, R. *The Silent Revolution.* Princeton: Princeton University Press, 1977.

———. "The Renaissance of Political Culture." *American Political Science Review* 82 (1988): 1203–1230.

———. *Culture Shift in Advanced Industrial Society.* Princeton: Princeton University Press, 1990.

———. *Modernization and Post-modernization.* Princeton: Princeton University Press, 1997.

Inglehart, R., et al. "The Theory of Human Development: A Cross-Cultural Analysis." *Journal of Political Research* 42, 2 (2003): 341–379.

———. *Modernization, Cultural Change and Democracy.* Cambridge: Cambridge University Press, 2005.

———. "The Role of Ordinary People in Democratization." *Journal of Democracy* 19, 1 (June 2008): 126–140.

Inkeles, A. "Participant Citizenship in Six Developing Countries." *American Political Science Review* 63, 4 (December 1969): 112–141.

———. "National Differences in Individual Modernity." *Comparative Studies in Sociology* 1 (1978): 47–72.

———. *Exploring Individual Modernity*. New York: Columbia University Press, 1983.

Islam, R. "Does More Transparency Go Along with Better Governance?" *Economics and Politics* 18, 2 (2006): 121–167.

Jabbra, J. G. and P. Dwivedi (eds.). *Public Service Accountability: A Comparative Perspective*. Hartford: Kumarian Press, 1989.

Jain, A. K. (ed.) *Economics of Corruption*. Boston/London: Kluwer Academic Publishers, 1998.

———. (ed.)"Corruption: A Review." *Journal of Economic Surveys* 15, 1 (2001): 71–121.

Johnson, C. "Local Democracy, Democratic Decentralization and Rural Development: Theories, Challenges and Options for Policy." *Development Policy Review* 19, 4 (December 2001): 521–533.

Johnston, M. "The Search for Definitions: The Vitality of Politics and the Issue of Corruption." *International Social Science Journal* 149 (1996): 321–335.

———. "Assessing Vulnerabilities to Corruption." *Public Integrity* 12, 2 (Spring 2010): 125–142.

Jones, B. and B. Olken. "Do Leaders Matter? National Leadership and Economic Growth Since WWII." *Quarterly Journal of Economics* 120, 3 (2005): 835–864.

Jørgensen, B. T. and L. B. Andersen. "An Aftermath of New Public Management: Regained Relevance of Public Values and Public Service Motivation." In: *The Ashgate Research Companion to New Public Management*, edited by T. Christensen and P. Lægreid. Farnham: Ashgate, 2011.

Jørgensen, T. B. and D. L. Sorensen. "Codes of Good Governance: National or Global Public Values?" *Public Integrity* 15, 1 (Winter 2012–13): 71–95.

Joshi, A. "Annex 1, *Service Delivery: Review of Impact and Effectiveness of Transparency and Accountability Initiatives*." Brighton: Institute of Development Studies, 2010.

Kahneman, D. *Thinking Fast and Slow*. New York: Farrar, Straus and Giroux, 2013.

Kaiser, S. "To Punish or to Forgive? Young Citizens' Attitudes on Impunity and Accountability in Contemporary Argentina." *Journal of Human Rights* 4, 2 (April–June 2005): 171–196.

Kaldor, M. and I. Vejvoda. "Democratization in East and Central European Countries." *International Affairs* 73 (1997): 59–83.

Kalinowski, T. "Democracy, Economic Crisis, and Market Oriented Reforms." *Comparative Sociology* 6, 3 (August 2007): 344–373.

Kalyvitis, S. and I. Vlachaki. "Democratic Aid and the Democratization of Recipients." *Contemporary Economic Policy* 28, 2 (2010): 188–218.

Kamrava, M. and F. O. Mora. "Civil Society and Democratization in Comparative Perspective: Latin America and the Middle East." *Third World Quarterly* 19, 5 (December 1998): 893–915.

Karl, T. L. "Dilemmas of Democratization in Latin America." *Comparative Politics* 23, 1 (October 1990): 1–21.

———. "The Hybrid Regimes of Central America." *Journal of Democracy* 6, 3 (July 1995): 72–86.

———. "Electoralism: Why Elections Are Not Democracy." *The International Encyclopedia of Elections,* edited by Richard Rose. Washington, DC: Congressional Quarterly Books, 2000.

Karl, T. L. and P. Schmitter. "Modes of Transition in Latin America, and Southern and Eastern Europe." *International Social Science Journal* 128 (May 1991): 269–284.

Katz, S. N. "Constitutionalism, Contestation and Civil Society." *Common Knowledge* 8, 2 (May 2002): 287–304.

Kaufmann, D. "Corruption: The Facts." *Foreign Policy* 107, 1 (Summer 1997): 114–131.

———. "State Capture" *World Policy Journal* 27, 1 (Spring 2010): 3–6.

Kaufmann, D. and P. Siegelbaum. "Privatization and Corruption in the Transition." *Journal of International Affairs* 50, 2 (1997): 419–459.

Kaufmann, D. et al. "Governance Matters VII: Aggregate and Individual Governance Indicators, 1996–2007." *World Bank Policy Research. Working Paper No.* 4654. Washington, DC: World Bank, 2008.

Keefer, P. and S. Knack. "Institutions and Economic Performance: Cross-Country Tests Using Alternative Institutional Measures." *Economics and Politics* 7, 3 (November 1995): 207–227.

Kelso, A. "Parliament on Its Knees: MPs' Expenses and the Crisis of Transparency at Westminster." *Political Quarterly* 80, 3 (July–September 2009): 329–338.

Keohane, R. "Abuse of Power." *Harvard International Review* 27, 2 (2005): 48–53.

Keqian, X. "Early Confucian Principles: The Potential Theoretic Foundation of Democracy in Modern China." *Asian Philosophy* 16, 2 (July 2006): 135–148.

Kernaghan, K. "Integrating Values into Public Service." *Public Administration Review* 63, 6 (2003): 711–719.

Keyman, F. F. and T. Kanci. "A Tale of Ambiguity: Citizenship, Nationalism and Democracy in Turkey." *Nations & Nationalism* 17, 2 (April 2011): 318–336.

Kickert, W. J. et al. *Managing Complex Networks: Strategies for the Public Sector.* London: Sage Publications, 1997.

Kiki Edozie, R. "New Trends in Democracy and Development: Democratic Capitalism in South Africa, Nigeria and Kenya." *Politikon: South African Journal of Political Studies* 35, 1 (April 2008): 43–67.

Kim, H. J. "Structural Determinants of Human Rights Prosecutions After Democratic Transition." *Journal of Peace Research* 49, 2 (March 2012): 305–320.

Kitschelt, H. et al. *Post-communist Party Systems: Competition, Representation, and Inter-party Cooperation.* New York: Cambridge University Press, 1999.

Klitgaard, R. *Controlling Corruption.* Berkeley: University of California Press, 1988.

Knack, S. "Does Foreign Aid Promote Democracy?" *International Studies Quarterly* 48, 1 (March 2004): 251–266.

Knack, S. and P. Keefer. "Institutions and Economic Performance: Empirical Tests Using Alternative Measures of Institutions." *Economics and Politics* 73, 3 (1995): 207–227.

Knio, K. *Governance and the Depoliticisation of Development.* London: Routledge, 2010,

Ko, K. and C. Weng. "Critical Review of Conceptual Definitions of Chinese Corruption: A Formal-Legal Perspective." *Journal of Contemporary China* 20, 70 (May 2011): 359–378.

Kohler, E. L. *A Dictionary for Accountants.* Englewood Cliffs: Prentice-Hall, Inc., 1975.

Kolstad, I. and A. Wiig. "Is Transparency the Key to Reducing Corruption in Resource-Rich Countries." *World Development* 37, 3 (March 2009): 521–532.

Kopits, G. and J. Craig. "Transparency in Government Operations." *IMF Occasional Paper No.* 158. Washington, DC: IMF, 1998.

Koppell, J. "Pathologies of Accountability: ICANN and the Challenge of Multiple Accountabilities Disorder." *Public Administration Review* 65, 1 (February 2005): 94–108.

Korten, D. *Getting to the 21st Century: Voluntary Action and the Global Agenda.* West Hartford: Kumarian Press, 1990.

Kristiansen, S. et al. "Public Sector Reforms and Financial Transparency: Experiences from Indonesian Districts." *Contemporary Southeast Asia* 31, 1 (2008): 64–87.

Kubal, M. R. "Contradictions and Constraints in Chile's Health Care and Education Decentralization." *Latin American Politics & Society* 48, 4 (Winter 2006): 105–135.

Kuehn, D. and P. Lorenz. "Explaining Civil-Military Relations in New Democracies: Structure, Agency and Theory Development." *Asian Journal of Political Science* 19, 3 (December 2011): 231–249.

Kukhianidze, A. "Corruption and Organized Crime in Georgia Before and After the 'Rose Revolution.'" *Central Asian Survey* 28, 2 (June 2009): 215–234.

Kumar, C. R. "Corruption and Human Rights: Promoting Transparency in Governance and the Fundamental Right to Corruption-Free Service in India." *Columbia Journal of Asian Law* 17, 1 (Fall 2013): 31–72.

Kumarasingham, H. "Exporting Executive Accountability? Westminster Legacies of Executive Power." *Parliamentary Affairs* 66, 3 (July 2013): 579–596.

Kunicova, J. and S. Rose-Ackerman. "Electoral Rules and Constitutional Structures as Constraints on Corruption." *British Journal of Political Science* 35, 4 (2005): 573–606.

Kuran, T. "The Political Consequences of Islam's Economic Legacy." *Philosophy & Social Criticism* 39, 4/5 (May 2013): 395–405.

Kurer, O. "Corruption: An Alternative Approach to Its Definition and Measurement." *Political Studies* 53, 1 (2005): 222–239.

Kurtz, M. J. and A. Schrank. "Growth and Governance: Models, Measures, and Mechanisms." *Journal of Politics* 69, 2 (May 2007): 538–554.

Lamin, A. R. "Building Peace Through Accountability in Sierra Leone: the Truth and Reconciliation Commission and the Special Court." *Journal of Asian & African Studies* 38, 2/3 (August 2003): 295–320.

Lange, S. "The Depoliticization of Development and the Democratization of Politics in Tanzania: Parallel Structures as Obstacles to Delivering Services to the Poor." *Journal of Development Studies* 44, 8 (September 2008): 1122–1144.

Larkins, C. M. "Judicial Independence and Democratization: A Theoretical and Conceptual Analysis." *American Journal of Comparative Law* 44 (1996): 605–626.

Lascoumes, P. and O. Tomescu-Hatto. "French Ambiguities in Understandings of Corruption: Concurrent Definitions." *Perspectives on European Politics and Society* 9, 1 (April 2008): 24–38.

Lasswell, H. *Propaganda Technique in the World War.* Boston: MIT Press, 1926.

———. *Democratic Character.* Glencoe: The Free Press, 1951.

Lathrop, D. and L. Ruma. *Open Government: Collaboration, Transparency, and Participation in Practice.* California: O'Reilly Media, 2010.

Lauth, H.-J. "Informal Institutions and Democracy." *Democratization* 7, 4 (Winter 2000): 21–51.

Lawson, L. "The Politics of Anti-corruption Reform in Africa." *Journal of Modern African Studies* 47, 1 (March 2009): 73–100.

Leblang, D. "Property Rights, Democracy and Economic Growth." *Political Research Quarterly* 49, 1 (1996): 5–26.

Lechner, N. "The Search for Lost Community: Challenges to Democracy in Latin America." *International Social Science Journal* 43, 128 (August 1991): 541–554.

———. "Corruption in Postcommunist Societies in Europe: A Re-examination." *Perspectives on European Politics and Society* 10, 1 (April 2009): 69–86.

Ledeneva, A. "From Russia with Blat: Can Informal Networks Help Modernize Russia." *Social Research* 76, 1 (Spring 2009): 257–288.

Lederman, D. et al. "Accountability and Corruption. Political Institutions Matter." *World Bank Working Paper*. Washington: The World Bank, 2001.

———. "Formal and Informal Institutions: On Structuring Their Mutual Co-existence." *Romanian Journal of Political Science* 1, 1 (2004): 67–89.

Ledet, R. "Correlates of Corruption Rethinking Social Capital's Relationship with Government in the United States." *Public Integrity* 13, 2 (Spring 2011): 149–162.

Leeson, P. and A. Dean. "The Democratic Domino Theory: An Empirical Investigation." *American Journal of Political Science* 53, 3 (July 2009): 533–551.

Leff, N. H. "Economic Development Through Bureaucratic Corruption." *American Behavioral Scientist* 8, 3 (1964): 8–14.

Lerner, D. *The Passing of Traditional Society: Modernizing the Middle East.* Glencoe: Free Press, 1958.

le Van, A. C. "Power Sharing and Inclusive Politics in Africa's Uncertain Democracies." *Governance* 24, 1 (January 2011): 31–53.

Levitsky, S. and L. Way. "Between a Shock and a Hard Place: The Dynamics of Labor-Backed Adjustment in Poland and Argentina." *Comparative Politics* 30, 2 (January 1998): 171–192.

Lewis, C. W. and S. C. Gilman. "Normative and Institutional Currents and Commonalities." *Public Integrity* 7, 4 (2005): 331–343.

Libich, J. "Should Monetary Policy Be Transparent?" *Policy* 22, 1 (2006): 28–33.

Lijphart, A. *Democracies: Patterns of Majoritarian & Consensus Government in Twenty-One Countries.* New Haven: Yale University Press, 1984.

———. *Patterns of Democracy.* New Haven: Yale University Press, 1999.

Lindblom, C. "The Science of Muddling Through." *Public Administration Review* 19, 2 (Spring 1959): 79–88.

Lindblom, C. *Intelligence of Democracy.* New York: The Free Press, 1965.

———. *Politics and Markets: World's Political-Economic Systems.* New York: Basic, 1977.

———. "Still Muddling Through, Not Yet Through." *Public Administration Review* 39, 6 (November–December 1979): 517–526.

Lindstedt, C. and D. Naurin. "Transparency Is Not Enough: Making Transparency Effective in Reducing Corruption." *International Political Science Review* 31, 3 (June 2010): 301–322.

Linz, J. "The Virtues of Parliamentarism." In *Global Resurgence of Democracy*, edited by L. Diamond and M. F. Plattner. Baltimore: The Johns Hopkins University Press, 1993.

Linz, J. and A. Stepan. *The Breakdown of Democratic Regimes: Crisis, Breakdown and Re-equilibration*. Baltimore: Johns Hopkins University Press, 1978.

———. (eds.). *Problems of Democratic Transition and Consolidation: Southern Europe, South America, and Post-communist Europe*. Baltimore: The Johns Hopkins University Press, 1996.

Linz, J. and A. Valenzuela (eds.). *The Failure of Presidential Democracy*. Baltimore: Johns Hopkins University, 1994.

Lipset, S. M. "Some Social Requisites of Democracy: Economic Development and Political Legitimacy." *American Political Science Review* 53, 1 (March 1959): 69–105.

———. *Political Man: Social Bases of Politics*. Garden City: Anchor Books, 1960.

———. "The Social Requisites of Democracy Revisited." *American Sociological Review* 59, (1994): 1–22.

Lipset, S. M. et al. "A Comparative Analysis of the Social Requisites of Democracy." *International Social Science Journal* 136 (May 1993): 155–175.

Ljubownikow, S. et al. The State and Civil Society in Post-Soviet Russia: The Development of a Russian-style Civil Society" *Progress in Development Studies* 13, 2 (April 2013): 153–166.

Lloyd, R. "Promoting Global Accountability: The Experiences of the Global Accountability Project." *Global Governance* 14, 3 (July–September 2008): 273–281.

Londregan, J. B. and K. T. Poole. "Does High Income Promote Democracy?" *World Politics* 49, 1 (October 1996): 1–30.

Luebbert, G. *Liberalism, Fascism, or Social Democracy: Social Classes and the Political. Origins of Regimes in Interwar Europe*. Oxford: Oxford University Press, 1991.

Luna-Reyes, L. F. and S. A. Chun. "Open Government and Public Participation: Issues and Challenges in Creating Public Value." *Information Polity* 17 (2012): 77–81.

Lupel, A. "Tasks of a Global Civil Society: Held, Habermas and Democratic Legitimacy Beyond the Nation-State." *Globalizations* 21 (2005): 117–133.

Maguire, S. "Can Data Deliver Better Government?" *Political Quarterly* 82, 4 (October 2011): 522–525.

Mainwaring, S. "Party Systems in the Third Wave." *Journal of Democracy* 9, 3 (July 1998): 67–81.

———. "Two Models of Democracy." *Journal of Democracy* 12, 3 (2001): 170–175.

Mainwaring, S. and T. R. Scully. "Party Systems in Latin America." In *Building Democratic Institutions: Party Systems in Latin America*, edited by S. Mainwaring and T. R. Scully. Stanford: Stanford University Press, 1995.

Mainwaring, S. and M. Shugart. "Juan Linz, Presidentialism and Democracy." *Comparative Politics* 29, 4 (July 1997): 449–471.

Malena, C. et al. "Social Accountability: An Introduction to the Concept and Emerging Practice." *Social Development Paper 76*. Washington DC: The World Bank, 2004.

Malesky, E. "The Adverse Effects of Sunshine: A Field Experiment on Legislative Transparency in an Authoritarian Assembly." *American Political Science Review* 106, 4 (November 2012): 762–786.

Malloy, J. M. (ed.). "Authoritarianism and Corporatism in Latin America: The Modal Pattern." In *Authoritarianism and Corporatism in Latin America*. Pittsburgh: University of Pittsburgh Press, 1976.

Mamdani, M. *Citizen and Subject: Contemporary Africa and the Legacy of Late Colonialism*. Princeton: Princeton University Press, 1997.

Mamoru, S. and H. Auerbach. "Political Corruption and Social Structure in Japan." *Asian Survey* 17, 6 (1977): 556–564.

Mani, K. "Military Entrepreneurs: Patterns in Latin America." *Latin American Politics & Society* 53, 3 (Fall 2011): 25–55.

Mani, A. and S. Mukand. "Democracy, Visibility and Public Good Provision." *Journal of Development Economics* 83 (2007): 506–529.

Mansrisuk, C. "Decentralization in Thailand and the Limits of the Functionalist Perspective of Institutional Reform." *European Journal of East Asian Studies* 11, 1 (March 2012): 71–97.

Manzetti, L. "Market Reforms Without Transparency." In *Combating Corruption in Latin America*, edited by J. Tulchin and R. Espach. Washington, DC: Woodrow Wilson Center Press, 2000.

Maogoto, J. N. "The 'Good Governance' Crusade in the Third World: A Rich, Complex Narrative--Magic Wand or Smoke Screen?" *International Community Law Review* 9 (2007): 375–385.

March, J. and J. Olsen. *Democratic Governance*. New York: The Free Press, 1994.

Margetts, H. "The Internet and Transparency." *Political Quarterly* 82, 4 (October–December 2011): 518–521.

Martin, R. and E. Feldman. *Access to Information in Developing Countries*. Berlin: Transparency International, 1998.

Martin, S. and A. Webb. "Citizen-Centred Public Services: Contestability without Consumer-Driven Competition?" *Public Money & Management* 29, 2 (January 2009): 123–130.

Martin, L. L. and K. Frahm. "The Changing Nature of Accountability in Administrative Practice." *Journal of Sociology & Social Welfare* 37, 1 (March 2010): 137–148.

Mason, M. *The New Accountability: Environmental Responsibility Across Borders.* London/Sterling: Earthscan, 2005.

Mauro, P. "Corruption and Growth." *Quarterly Journal of Economics* 110, 3 (August 1995): 618–712.

———. "Corruption, Causes, Consequences and Agenda for Further Research." *Finance and Development* 35, 1 (1998): 10–14.

Mazzuca, S. "Democracy and Bureaucracy: Access to Power Versus Exercise of Power." In *Regimes and Democracy in Latin America, vol. 1, Theories Agendas and Findings,* edited by D. Collier and G. L. Munck. Oxford: Oxford University Press, 2007.

McCubbins, M. D. and T. Schwartz. "Congressional Oversight Overlooked: Police Patrols Versus Fire Alarms." *American Journal of Political Science* 28, 1 (February 1984): 16–79.

McFaul, M. "Transition Without Consolidation." *Freedom Review* 28, 1 (January/February 1997): 30–49.

———. "The Fourth Wave of Democracy and Dictatorship: Non-cooperative Transitions in the Post-communist World." *World Politics* 54, 2 (January 2002): 212–244.

McFerson, H. M. "Governance and Hyper-corruption in Resource-Rich African Countries." *Third World Quarterly* 30, 8 (December 2009): 1529–1547.

———. "Extractive Industries and African Democracy: Can the 'Resource Curse' Be Exorcised? Extractive Industries and African Democracy." *International Studies Perspectives* 11, 4 (November 2010): 335–353.

McKoy, M. K. and M. K. Miller. "The Patron's Dilemma: The Dynamics of Foreign-Supported Democratization." *Journal of Conflict Resolution* 56, 5 (October 2012): 904–932.

Meagher, P. "Anti-corruption Agencies: Rhetoric Versus Reality." *Journal of Policy Reform* 8, 1 (March 2005): 69–103.

Merton, R. K. *Social Theory and Social Structure.* New York: Free Press, 1968.

Michael, B. "Issues in Anti-corruption Law: How Can Code of Conduct Laws Be Drafted in Order to Reduce Corruption in a Public Sector Like Romania's." *European Law Journal* 18, 2 (March 2012). 289–322.

Millar, H. "Comparing Accountability Relationships Between Governments and Non-state actors in Canadian and European International Development Policy." *Canadian Public Administration* 56, 2 (June 2013): 252–269.

Miller, E. "David Easton's Political Theory." *Political Science Reviewer* 1 (Fall 1971): 184–235.

Miller, D. *On Nationality.* Oxford: Oxford University Press, 1995.

Miller, M. K. "Economic Development, Violent Leader Removal, and Democratization." *American Journal of Political Science* 56, 4 (October 2012): 1002–1020.

Milton-Edwards, B. "Facade Democracy and Jordan." *British Journal of Middle Eastern Studies* 20, 2 (1993): 191–203.

Minkenberg, M. "Democracy and Religion: Theoretical and Empirical Observations on the Relationship Between Christianity, Islam and Liberal Democracy." *Journal of Ethnic & Migration Studies* 33, 6 (August 2007): 887–909.

Mitchell, R. "Sources of Transparency: Information Systems in International Regimes." *International Studies Quarterly* 42, 1 (1998): 109–130.

Mohtadi, H. and T. L. Roe. "Democracy, Rent Seeking, Public Spending and Growth." *Journal of Public Economics* 87, 3–4 (2003): 445–466.

Mol, A. "The Future of Transparency: Power, Pitfalls and Promises." *Global Environmental Politics* 10, 3 (August 2010): 132–143.

Moncrieffe, J. M. "Accountability: Ideas, Ideals and Constraints." *Democratization* 8, 8 (2001): 26–50.

Montinola, G. R. and R. W. Jackman. "Sources of Corruption: A Cross-Country Study." *British Journal of Political Science* 32 (2002): 147–170.

Moore, B. *Social Origins of Dictatorship and Democracy: Lord and Peasant in the Making of the Modern World.* Boston: Beacon Press, 1966.

Moore, M. (ed.). "Introduction." In *Doha and Beyond: The Future of the Multilateral Trading System.* Cambridge: Cambridge University Press/ World Trade Organization, 2004.

———. "The Limits of Transparency." *Political Quarterly* 82, 4 (October–December 2011): 506–508.

Moran, J. "Democratic Transitions and Forms of Corruption." *Crime, Law & Social Change* 36, 4 (December 2001): 379–393.

Morlino, L. *Democracy Between Consolidation and Crisis: Parties, Groups, and Citizens in Southern Europe.* New York: Oxford University Press, 1998.

Mousseau, D. Y. "Democratizing with Ethnic Divisions: A Source of Conflict." *Journal of Peace Research* 38, 5 (September 2001): 547–567.

Moxon-Browne, E. "Book Review on Political Corruption in Africa by Robert Williams." *International Affairs* 63, 4 (Fall 1987): 699–701.

Mueller, J. "Democracy and Ralph's Pretty Good Grocery: Elections, Equality and Minimal Human Being." *American Journal of Political Science* 36, 4 (1992): 983–1003.

Mulbah, A. S. "The Phenomena of Corruption in Liberian Political System." *Journal of Alternative Perspectives in the Social Sciences* 4, 3 (August 2012): 553–576.

Mulgan, R. "Accountability: An Ever-Expanding Concept?" *Public Administration* 78, 3 (Fall 2000): 555–573.

Muller, E. N. "Economic Determinants of Democracy." *American Sociological Review* 60 (1995): 966–982.

Muller, E. N. and M. A. Seligson. "Inequality and Insurrections." *American Political Science Review* 81 (1987): 425–451.

Mullerson, R. *Democracy: A Destiny of Humankind? A Qualified, Contingent and Contextual Case for Democracy Promotion.* Virginia: NOVA, 2009a.

———. "Democratization Through the Supply–Demand Prism." *Human Rights Revolution* 10, 4 (2009b): 531–567.

Munck, G. "The Regime Question: Theory Building in Democracy Studies." *World Politics* 54 (October 2001): 119–144.

———. "Globalization and Democracy: A New 'Great Transformation.'" *Annals of the American Academy of Political and Social Science* 581 (2002): 10–21.

Munck, R. *Contemporary Latin America.* Basingstoke/New York: Palgrave Macmillan, 2003.

———. "Globalization, Labor and the 'Polanyi Problem.'" *Labor History* 45, 3 (2004): 251–261.

———. "Globalisation and Contestation: A Polyanian Problematic." *Globalizations* 3, 2 (2006): 175–186.

Munck, G. L. and C. S. Leff. "Modes of Transition and Democratization: South America and Eastern Europe in Comparative Perspective." *Comparative Politics* 29, 3 (April 1997): 343–362.

Munck, G. L. and J. Verkuilen. "Conceptualizing and Measuring Democracy: Evaluating Alternative Indices." *Comparative Political Studies* 35, 1 (February 2002): 5–34.

Murphy, D. S. "Las Instituciones Supremas de Auditoría y las Iniciativas de Anticorrupción." *Contabilidad y Negocios* 4, 7 (July 2009): 31–38.

Mutebi, A. "Explaining the Failure of Thailand's Anti-corruption Regime." *Development & Change* 39, 1 (January 2008): 147–171.

Myrdal, G. "Corruption as a Hindrance to Modernization in South Asia." In *Asian Drama: An Enquiry into the Poverty of Nations*, vol. II, edited by G. Myrdal. New York: The Twentieth Century Fund, 1968 (Re-published as chapter 25 in *Political Corruption. A Handbook*, Heidenheimer et al., New Brunswick: Transaction Publishers, 1989).

Nafziger, R. and L. Maak. "Increasing Public Participation, Understanding, and Transparency of the Legislative Process Through the Use of Web Dialogue." *National Civic Review* 212 (Summer 2008): 31 37.

Naím, M. "Latin America: The Second Stage of Reform." *Journal of Democracy* 5, 4 (October 1994): 32–48.

Needler, M. C. "Political Development and Socioeconomic Development." *American Political Science Review* 62 (September 1968): 889–897.

Nettl, J. P. "The State as a Conceptual Variable." *World Politics* 20, 4 (1968): 559–592.

Neubauer, D. "Some Conditions of Democracy." *American Political Science Review* 61 (1967): 1002–1009.

Newsom, G. and L. Dickey. *Citizenville: How to Take the Town Square Digital and Reinvent Government*. New York: Penguin Press, 2013.

Neyland, D. "Achieving Transparency: The Visible, Invisible and Divisible in Academic Accountability Networks." *Organization* 14, 4 (2007): 499–516.

Niblo, S. *Mexico in the 1940s: Modernity, Politics and Corruption*. Wilmington: Scholarly Resources Inc., 1999.

Nilsson, M. "Reaping What Was Sown: Conflict Outcome and Post-civil War Democratization." *Cooperation & Conflict* 47, 3 (September 2012): 350–367.

Norman, M. "The Challenges of State Building in Resource Rich Nations." *Journal of International Human Rights* 10, 4 (Spring 2012): 173–190.

Novak, M. *Catholic Social Thought and Liberal Institutions: Freedom with Justice*. New Brunswick: Transaction Publishers, 1989.

Noveck, B. S. *Wiki Government: How Technology Can Make Government Better, Democracy Stronger, and Citizens More Powerful*. Washington, DC: Brookings Institution Press, 2010.

Nyblade, B. and S. R. Reed. "Who Cheats? Who Loots? Political Competition and Corruption in Japan, 1947–1993." *American Journal of Political Science* 52, 4 (October 2008): 926–941.

Nye, J. "Corruption and Political Development: A Cross-Benefit Analysis." *American Political Science Review* 61, 2 (June 1967): 417–427.

O'Donnell, G. "Bureaucratic Authoritarianism: Argentina 1966–1973." In *Comparative Perspectives*. Berkeley: University of California Press, 1973.

———. "Corporatism and the Question of the State." *Authoritarianism and Corporatism in Latin America*, edited by J. M. Malloy. Pittsburgh: University of Pittsburgh Press, 1976.

———. "Transitions, Continuities, Paradoxes." *Issues in Democratic Consolidation: The New South American Democracies in Comparative Perspective*, edited by S. Mainwaring, G. O'Donnell and J. S. Valenzuela. Notre Dame: University of Notre Dame Press, 1992.

———. "On the State, Democratization and Some Conceptual Problems: A Latin American View with Glances at Some Postcommunist Countries." *World Development* 21, 8 (1993): 1355–1369.

———. "Delegative Democracy." *Journal of Democracy* 5, 1 (January 1994): 55–69.

O'Donnell, G. and P. Schmitter. *Transitions from Authoritarian Rule*, Part 4. Baltimore: Johns Hopkins University Press, 1986.

O'Donnell, G. et al. *Transitions from Authoritarian Rule: Comparative Perspectives*. Baltimore: Johns Hopkins University Press, 1988.

O'dugbemi, S. and T. Lee (eds.). *Accountability Through Public Opinion: From Inertia to Public Action*. Washington, DC: World Bank, 2011.

O'Dwyer, C. and D. Ziblatt. "Does Decentralization Make Government More Efficient and Effective?" *Commonwealth & Comparative Politics* 44, 3 (November 2006): 326–343.

Ojambo, H. "Decentralization in Africa: A Critical Review of Uganda's Experience." *Potchefstroom Electronic Law Journal* 15, 2 (2012): 69–88.

Olsen, J. P. 'The Institutional Basis of Democratic Accountability." *West European Politics* 36, 3 (May 2013): 447–473.

Oquaye, M. "The Process of Democratization in Contemporary Ghana." *Commonwealth & Comparative Politics* 38, 3 (November 2000): 53–89.

Osborne, D. and T. Gaebler. *Reinventing Government*. New York: Addison Wesley Publication Co., 1992.

Otenyo, E. E. and N. S. Lind. "Faces and Phases of Transparency Reform in Local Government." *International Journal of Public Administration* 27, 5 (2004): 2887–2307.

Oyamada, E. "President Gloria Macapagal-Arroyo's Anti-corruption Strategy in the Philippines: An Evaluation." *Asian Journal of Political Science* 13, 1 (June 2005): 81–107.

Page, E. C. "Accountability as a Bureaucratic Minefield: Lessons from a Comparative Study." *West European Politics* 33, 5 (September 2010): 1010–1029.

Pajibo, E. "Accountability and Justice in Post-conflict Liberia." *African Identities* 10, 3 (August 2012): 301–311.

Palma, G. D. *To Craft Democracies: An Essay on Democratic Transitions*. Berkeley: University of California Press, 1990.

Paré, L. "The Challenges of Rural Democratization in Mexico." *Journal of Development Studies* 26, 4 (July 1990): 79–97.

Parsons, T. *The Social System*. New York: Free Press, 1951.

———. "Evolutionary Universals in Society." *American Sociological Review* 29 (1964): 339–357.

Pawelke, A. "Anti-corruption in Slovakia." *Romanian Journal of Political Science* 10, 2 (September 2010): 96–117.

Pelczynski, Z. A. "Solidarity and the 'Rebirth of Civil Society.'" In *Civil Society and the State: New European Perspectives*, edited by J. Keane. London: Verso, 1988.

Pereira, A. W. "Economic Underdevelopment, Democracy and Civil Society: The North-East Brazilian Case." *Third World Quarterly* 14, 2 (1993): 365–380.

Pérez-Armendáriz, C. and D. Crow. "Do Migrants Remit Democracy? International Migration, Political Beliefs, and Behavior in Mexico." *Comparative Political Studies* 43, 1 (January 2010): 119–148.

Persson, T., G. et al. "Electoral Rules and Corruption." *Journal of European Economic Association* 1 (2003): 958–989.

———. "Why Anticorruption Reforms Fail—Systemic Corruption as a Collective Action Problem." *Governance: An International Journal of Policy, Administration, and Institutions* 26, 3 (July 2013): 449–471.

Peruzzotti, E. and C. Smulovitz. *Enforcing the Rule of Law: Social Accountability in the New Latin American Democracies.* Pittsburgh: University of Pittsburgh, 2006.

Peruzzotti, E. "Broadening the Notion of Democratic Accountability: Participatory Innovation in Latin America." *Polity* 44, 4 (October 2012): 625–642.

Peters, B. G. *The Politics of Bureaucracy.* New York/London: Longman, 1989.

Philp, M. "Delimiting Democratic Accountability." *Political Studies* 57, 1 (March 2009): 28–53.

Pilar, D. "Judicial Independence and Judicial Reform in Latin America." In *The Self-restraining State: Power and Accountability in New Democracy*, edited by A. Schedler, L. Diamond, and M. F. Plattner. Boulder: Lynne Rienner, 1999.

Pillay, N. "Establishing Effective Accountability Mechanisms for Human Rights Violations." *UN Chronicle* 49, 4 (2012): 8–11.

Pion-Berlin, D. "The Study of Civil-Military Relations in New Democracies." *Asian Journal of Political Science* 19, 3 (December 2011a): 222–230.

———. "Turkish Civil-Military Relations: A Latin American Comparison." *Turkish Studies* 12, 2 (June 2011b): 293–304.

Piotrowski, S. J. and G. G. Van Ryzin. "Transparency in Local Government." *American Review of Public Administration* 37, 3 (2007): 306–323.

Polanyi, K. *The Great Transformation: The Political and Economic Origins of Our Time.* Boston: Beacon Press, 1944.

Pollitt, C. *The Essential Public Manager.* London: Open University Press/ McGraw Hill, 2003.

Pope, J. *Confronting Corruption: The Elements of a National Integrity System.* Berlin: Transparency International, 2000.

Popkin, E. "Transnational Migration and Development in Postwar Peripheral States: An Examination of Guatemalan and Salvadoran State Linkages with Their Migrant Populations in Los Angeles." *Current Sociology* 51, 3–4 (May–July 2003): 347–374.

Popova, M. "Why Doesn't the Bulgarian Judiciary Prosecute Corruption?" *Problems of Post-Communism* 59, 5 (September–October 2012): 35–49.

Popper, K. *The Logic of Scientific Discovery*. Hutchinson: London, 1959.

Potter, D. et al. *Democratization*. Cambridge: Polity Press, 1997.

Powell, B. *Elections as Instruments of Democracy: Majoritarian and Proportional Views*. New Haven: Yale University Press, 2000.

Przeworski, A. "Some Problems in the Study of the Transition to Democracy." In *Transitions from Authoritarian Rule: Comparative Perspectives*, edited by G. O'Donnell, P. Schmitter and L. Whiteheads. Baltimore: Johns Hopkins University Press, 1986.

———. *Democracy and the Market: Political and Economic Reforms in Eastern Europe and Latin America*. New York: Cambridge University Press, 1991.

———. "Why Democracy Survives in Affluent Societies?" Paper presented in the *New York University Department of Politics Political Economy Seminar*. New York, 2001.

———. "Democracy and Economic Development." In *The Evolution of Political Knowledge*, edited by E. D. Mansfield and R. Sisson. Columbus: Ohio State University Press, 2004.

———. "Self-enforcing Democracy." In *Handbook of Political Economy*, edited by D. Wittman and B. Weingast. Oxford: Oxford University Press, 2006.

Przeworski, A. and F. Limongi. "Modernization: Theory and Facts." *World Politics* 49, 2 (January 1997): 155–183.

Przeworski, A. and I. Wallerstein. "The Structure of Class Conflict in Democratic Capitalist Societies." *American Political Science Review* 76 (June 1982): 215–238.

Przeworski, A. et al. "What Makes Democracies Endure?" *Journal of Democracy* 7, 1 (1996): 39–55.

———. *Democracy and Development: Political Institutions and Material Well-being in the World, 1950–1990*. Cambridge: Cambridge University Press, 2000.

Putnam, R. *Bowling Alone: The Collapse and Revival of American Community*. New York: Simon & Schuster, 2000.

Putnam, R. et al. *Making Democracy Work: Civic Traditions in Modern Italy*. Princeton: Princeton University Press, 1993.

Pye, L. "The New Asian Capitalism: A Political Portrait." In *In Search of an East Asian Development Model*, edited by P. L. Berger and H. H. M. Xiao. New Brunswick: Transaction Publishers, 1988.

———. "Civility, Social Capital, and Civil Society: Three Powerful Concepts for Explaining Asia." *Journal of Interdisciplinary History* 29, 4 (Spring 1999): 763–782.

Quah, J. S. T. "Curbing Corruption in India: An Impossible Dream?" *Asian Journal of Political Science* 16, 3 (December 2008): 240–259.

Quick, S. "Inter-American Development Bank Initiatives Against Corruption." In *Combating Corruption in Latin America*, edited by J. Tulchin and R. Espach. Washington, DC: Woodrow Wilson Center Press, 2000.

Qureshi, A. H. "The New GATT Trade Policy Review Mechanism: An Exercise in Transparency or "Enforcement"?" *Journal of World Trade* 24, 3 (1990): 147–160.

Rabkin, R. "The Aylwin Government and 'Tutelary' Democracy: A Concept in Search of a Case?" *Journal of Interamerican Studies and World Affairs* 34, 4 (Winter 1992–93): 119–194.

Raphael, C. and C. Karpowitz. "Good Publicity: The Legitimacy of Public Communication of Deliberation." *Political Communication* 30, 1 (January 2013): 17–41.

Rashid, S. "Public Utilities in Egalitarian LDCs: The Role of Bribery in Achieving Pareto Efficiency." *Kyklos* 34, 3 (September 1981): 448–461.

Reif, C. L. *The Ombudsman, Good Governance and the International Human Rights System*. Leiden: Martinus Nijhoff Publishers, 2004.

Reinikka, R. and J. Svensson. "Using Micro-surveys to Measure and Explain Corruption." *World Development* 34, 2 (2006): 359–370.

Remmer, K. and G. Merkx. "Bureaucratic-Authoritarianism Revisited." *Latin American Research Review* 17, 2 (1982): 3–40.

Renzio, P. and H. Masud. "Measuring and Promoting Budget Transparency: The Open Budget Index as a Research and Advocacy Tool." *Governance: An International Journal of Policy, Administration, and Institutions* 24, 3 (July 2011): 607–616.

Resler, T. "Dilemmas of Democratization: Safeguarding Minorities in Russia, Ukraine and Lithuania." *Europe-Asia Studies* 49, 1 (1997): 89–106.

Riccucci, N. M. "The Old Public Management Versus the New Public Management: Where Does Public Administration Fit In?" *Public Administration Review* 61, 2 (April 2002): 172–175.

Riley, S. "The Political-Economy of Anti-corruption Strategies in Africa." *European Journal of Development Research* 10, 1 (June 1988): 129–159.

———. "The Political Economy of Anti-corruption Strategies in Africa." In *Corruption and Development*, edited by M. Robinson. London: Frank Cass, 1998.

Ripken, S. "The Dangers and Drawbacks of the Disclosure Antidote: Toward a More Substantive Approach to Securities Regulation." *Baylor Law Review*, 58 (2006): 139–204.

Ritter, J. "Know Thine Enemy: Information and Democratic Foreign Policy." In *Power and Conflict in the Age of Transparency*, edited by B. Finel and K. Lord. New York: St. Martin's Press, 2000.

Robins, S. P. and M. Coulter (eds.). *Introduction to Management and Organization*. Essex: Pearson Education Limited, 2007.

Rock, M. T. "Corruption and Democracy." *Journal of Development Studies* 45, 1 (January 2009): 55–75.

———. "East Asia's Democratic Developmental States and Economic Growth." *Journal of East Asian Studies* 13, 1 (January–April 2013): 1–34.

Rode, M. and J. D. Gwartney. "Does Democratization Facilitate Economic Liberalization?" *European Journal of Political Economy* 28, 4 (December 2012): 607–619.

Rokeach, M. *The Open and the Closed Mind*. New York: Basic Books, 1960.

Romzek, B. S. "Dynamics of Public Accountability in an Era of Reform." *International Review of Administrative Sciences* 66, 1 (March 2000): 21–44.

Rose-Ackerman, S. *Corruption: A Study in Political Economy*. New York: Academic Press, 1978.

———. *Corruption and Government. Causes, Consequences and Reform*. Cambridge: Cambridge University Press, 1999.

———. "The Law and Economics of Bribery and Extortion." *Annual Review of Law and Social Science* 6 (December 2010): 217–238.

Rose, R. and D. C. Shin. "Democratization and Backwards: The Problem of Third Wave Democracies." *British Journal of Political Science* 31, 2 (2001): 331–375.

Rosenau, J. N. "The Illusions of Power and Empire." *History and Theory* 44, 4 (December 2005): 73–87.

Rosendorff, B. P. and J. Doces. "Transparency and Unfair Eviction in Democracies and Autocracies." *Swiss Political Science Review* 12, 3 (2006): 99–112.

Rostow, W. W. *The Stages of Economic Growth*. Cambridge: Cambridge University Press, 1964.

Rother, S. "Changed in Migration? Philippine Return Migrants and (Un) Democratic Remittances." *European Journal of East Asian Studies* 8, 2 (September 2009): 245–274.

Rothstein, B. and J. Teorell. "What Is Quality of Government? A Theory of Impartial Government, Institutions." *Governance: An International Journal of Policy, Administration and Institutions* 21, 2 (2008): 165–190.

Rouquié, A. *The Military and the State in Latin America*. Los Angeles: University of California Press, 1987.

Rowley, D. G. "Giuseppe Mazzini and the Democratic Logic of Nationalism." *Nations & Nationalism* 18, 1 (January 2012): 39–56.

Rueschemeyer, D. et al. *Capitalist Development and Democracy*. Chicago: University of Chicago Press, 1992.

———. "The Impact of Economic Development on Democracy." *Journal of Economic Perspectives* 7, 3 (Summer 1993): 71–86.

Rustow, D. A. "Transitions to Democracy: Toward a Dynamic Model." *Comparative Politics* 2, 3 (April 1970): 337–363.

Sadgren, C. "Combating Corruption: The Misunderstood Role of Law." *International Lawyer* 39, 3 (Fall 2005): 717–731.

Said, A. "The Paradox of Transition to "Democracy" Under Military Rule." *Social Research* 79, 2 (Summer 2012): 397–434.

Salvochea, C. R. "Clientelism in Argentina: Piqueteros and Relief Payments to the Unemployed Plans. An Example of Failure of Civil Society's Role." *Texas International Law Journal* 43, 2 (2007): 287–323.

Sampford, C. "From Greek Temple to Bird's Nest: Towards a Theory of Coherence and Mutual Accountability for National Integrity Systems." *Australian Journal of Public Administration* 64, 2 (June 2005): 96–108.

Sanchez, G. I. M. et al. "Determinants of Corporate Social Disclosure in Spanish Local Governments." *Journal of Cleaner Production* 39 (January 2013): 60–72.

Sandbrook, R. "Transitions Without Consolidation: Democratization in Six African Cases." *Third World Quarterly* 17, 1 (March 1996): 69–87.

Sandholtz, W. and W. Koetzle. "Accounting for Corruption: Economic Structure, Democracy, and Trade." *International Studies Quarterly* 44, 1 (2000): 31–50.

Santiso, C. "Legislatures and Budget Oversight in Latin America: Strengthening Public Finance Accountability in Emerging Economies." *OECD Journal on Budgeting* 4, 2 (2004): 47–76.

Sardamov, I. "Civil Society and the Limits of Civil Society." *Government & Opposition* 40, 3 (Summer 2005): 379–402.

Sarker, A. E. and H. Mostafa. "Civic Engagement and Public Accountability: An Analysis with Particular Reference to Developing Countries." Conference Paper presented at the *14th Annual International Research Society for Public Management (IRSPM) Conference*. Switzerland: University of Bern, April 2010.

Sartori, G. "Concept Misformation in Comparative Politics." *American Political Science Review* 64, 4 (December 1970): 1033–1053.

Savun, B. and D. Tirone. "Foreign Aid, Democratization, and Civil Conflict: How Does Democracy Aid Affect Civil Conflict?" *American Journal of Political Science* 55, 2 (2011): 233–246.

Schamis, H. "Reconceptualizing Latin American Authoritarianism in the 1970s: From Bureaucratic Authoritarianism to Neoconservatism." *Comparative Politics* 23, 2 (January 1991): 201–220.

Scharpf, F. *Games Real Actors Play. Actor-Centered Institutionalism in Policy Research*. Boulder/Cumnor Hill: Westview Press, 1997.

Schedler, A. "Conceptualizing Accountability." In *The Self-Restraining State: Power and Accountability in New Democracies*, A. Schedler, L. Diamond and M. F. Plattner. Boulder/London: Lynne Rienner Publishers, 1999.

———. "¿Qué es la rendición de cuentas?" In *Cuadernos de transparencia* 3. Mexico: Instituto Federal de Acceso a la Información Pública (IFAI), August 2004.

Schillemans, T. " Redundant Accountability: The Joint Impact of Horizontal and Vertical Accountability on Autonomous Agencies." *Public Administration Quarterly* 34, 3 (Fall 2010): 300–337.

———. *Neo-corporatism and the State*. Florence: EUI, 1984.

Schmitter, P. "Still the Century of Corporatism?" *Review of Politics* 36, 1 (January 1974): 85–131.

———. "The Ambiguous Virtues of Accountability." *Journal of Democracy* 15, 4 (October 2004): 47–60.

Schmitter, P. and T. Karl. "What Democracy Is and Is Not." *Journal of Democracy* 2, 3. (Summer 1991): 75–88.

Schneider, C. Q. and P. C. Schmitter. "Liberalization, Transition and Consolidation: Measuring the Components of Democratization." *Democratization* 11, 5 (2004): 59–90.

Scholte, J. A. "Civil Society and Democracy in Global Governance." *Global Governance* 8 (2002): 281–304.

Schumpeter, J. *Capitalism, Socialism and Democracy*. New York: Harper & Brothers, 1942.

Scott, J. M. and C. A. Steele. "Sponsoring Democracy: The United States and Democracy Aid to the Developing World, 1988–2001." *International Studies Quarterly* 55, 1: 47–69.

Sedelius, T. and S. Berglund. "Towards Presidential Rule in Ukraine: Hybrid Regime Dynamics Under Semi-presidentialism." *Baltic Journal of Law and Politics* 5, 1 (June 2012): 20–45.

Seligman, A. B. *The Idea of Civil Society*. New York: The Free Press, 1992.

Shapiro, I. *The Moral Foundations of Politics*. New Haven: Yale University Press, 2003.

Sharman, J. C. and D. Chaikin. "Corruption and Anti-Money-Laundering Systems: Putting a Luxury Good to Work." *Governance: An International Journal of Policy, Administration, and Institutions* 22, 1 (January 2009): 27–45.

Sherman, L. W. *Scandal and Reform: Controlling Police Corruption*. Berkeley: University of California Press, 1978.

Shihata, I. F. "The Role of the World Bank in Combating Corruption." In *Combating Corruption in Latin America*, edited by J. Tulchin and R. Espach. Washington, DC: Woodrow Wilson Center Press, 2000.

Shin, D. C. "On the Third Wave of Democratization: A Synthesis and Evaluation of Recent Theory and Research." *World Politics* 47, 1 (October 1994): 135–170.

Shkabatur, J. "Transparency With(out) Accountability: Open Government in the United States." *Yale Law and Policy Review* 31, 79 (November 2012): 79–140.

Shugart, M. S. "Semi-presidential Systems: Dual Executive and Mixed Authority. Patterns." *French Politics* 3, 3 (December 2005): 323–351.

Simandjuntak, D. "Gifts and Promises: Patronage Democracy in a Decentralized Indonesia." *European Journal of East Asian Studies* 11, 1 (March 2012): 99–126.

Simelane, H. S. "The Swazi Monarchy and the Poor Performance of the Swazi Anti-Corruption Agency, 2006–2009." *Journal of Asian & African Studies* 47, 4 (August 2012): 421–435.

Skocpol, T. *States and Social Revolutions: A Comparative Analysis of France, Russia and China.* Cambridge: Cambridge University Press, 1979.

———. "Bringing the State Back In: Strategies of Analysis in Current Research." In *Bringing the State Back In*, edited by P. Evans, D. Rueschemeyer and T. Skocpol. Cambridge: Cambridge University Press, 1985.

Smith, T. B. "The Comparative Analysis of Bureaucratic Accountability: A Review Article." *Asian Journal of Public Administration* 13, 1 (June 1991): 93–104.

Sniderman, P. *Personality and Democratic Politics.* Berkeley: University of California Press, 1975.

Snow, P. and L. Manzetti. *Political Forces in Argentina.* California: Praeger, 1993.

Snyder, J. L. *From Voting to Violence: Democratization and Nationalist Conflict.* New York: Norton, 2000.

Sorcha, M. and L. Douglas. "Transnational Corporations: Power, Influence and Responsibility." *Global Social Policy* 4, 1 (April 2004): 77–98.

Sosay, G. "Delegation and Accountability: Independent Regulatory Agencies in Turkey." *Turkish Studies* 10, 3 (September 2009): 341–363.

Spector, B. "Negotiating Anti-corruption Reforms in Post-conflict Society: The Case of Afghanistan." *Brown Journal of World Affairs* 13, 11 (Spring/Summer 2012): 45–56.

Spencer, T. "Governance and Civil Society." *Journal of Public Affairs* 1, 2 (February 2000): 1–2.

Spinner-Halev, J. "Democracy, Solidarity and Post-nationalism." *Political Studies* 56, 3 (October 2008): 604–628.

Starr, H. and C. Lindborg. "Democratic Dominoes Revisited: The Hazards of Governmental Transitions, 1974-1996." *Journal of Conflict Resolution* 47, 3 (August 2003): 490–514.

Stasavage, D. "Transparency, Democratic Accountability, and the Economic Consequences of Monetary Institutions." *American Journal of Political Science* 47, 3 (2003): 389–402.

Steffek, J. "Public Accountability and the Public Sphere of International Governance." *Ethics & International Affairs* 24, 1 (2010): 45–68.

Stepan, A. "State Power and Strength of Civil Society in the Southern Cone of Latin America." In *Bringing the State Back In*, edited by P. Evans, D. Rueschemeyer and T. Skocpol. Cambridge: Cambridge University Press, 1985.

Stirton, L. and M. Lodge. "Transparency Mechanisms: Building Publicness into Public Services." *Journal of Law and Society* 28, 4 (December 2001): 471–489.

Stockemer, D. "Does Democracy Lead to Good Governance?" *Global Change, Peace & Security* 21, 2 (June 2009): 241–255.

Stone, D. A. *Policy Paradox: The Art of Political Decision-making*. New York: W.W. Norton, 2002.

Stradiotto, G. A. and S. Guo. "Transitional Modes of Democratization and Democratic Outcomes." *International Journal of World Peace* 27, 4 (December 2010): 5–40.

Surzhko-Harned, L. "Liberal Nationalism, Nationalist Liberalization, and Democracy: The Cases of Post-Soviet Estonia and Ukraine." *Nationalities Papers* 38, 5 (September 2010): 623–646.

Svolik, M. W. "Learning to Love Democracy: Electoral Accountability and the Success of Democracy." *American Journal of Political Science* 57, 3 (July 2013): 685–702.

Sztompka, P. *Trust: A Sociological Theory*. Cambridge: Cambridge University Press, 1999.

Tamir, Y. *Liberal Nationalism*. Princeton: Princeton University Press, 1995.

Tandon, R. and R. Mohanty (eds.). *Does Civil Society Matter? Governance in Contemporary India*. New Delhi/Thousand Oaks/London: Sage Publications, 2003.

Tanzi, V. "Money Laundering and the International Financial System." *IMF Working Paper* 96/55. Washington, DC: IMF, 1996.

Tanzi, V. and H. Davoodi. "Corruption, Public Investment, and Growth." *IMF Working Paper* 97/139. Washington, DC, 1997 (Reprinted in Policies, Institutions and the Dark Side of Economics, edited by V. Tanzi). Cheltenham: Edward Elgar, 2000.

Taylor, C. "Democratic Exclusion (and Its Remedies?)." In *Multiculturalism Liberalism and Democracy*, edited by R. Bhargava, A. K. Bagchi and R. Sudarshan. New Delhi, India: Oxford University Press, 1999.

Taylor, M. M. and V. C. Buranelli. "Ending Up in Pizza: Accountability as a Problem of Institutional Arrangement in Brazil." *Latin American Politics & Society* 49, 1 (Spring 2007): 59–87.

Taylor, L. K. and A. Dukalskis. "Old Truths and New Politics: Does Truth Commission 'Publicness' Impact Democratization?" *Journal of Peace Research* 49, 5 (September 2012): 671–684.

Tedesco, L. "Argentina's Turmoil: The Politics of Informality and the Roots of Economic Meltdown." *Cambridge Review of International Affairs* 15, 3 (October 2002): 469–481.

Themudo, N. S. "Reassessing the Impact of Civil Society: Nonprofit Sector, Press Freedom, and Corruption." *Governance* 26, 1 (January 2013): 63–89.

Thirkell-White, B. "The IMF, Good Governance and Middle-Income Countries." *European Journal of Development Research* 15, 1 (June 2003): 99–125.

Thomas, M. A. "Liberal Republicanism and the Role of Civil Society." *Democratization* 4, 3 (1997): 26–44.

———. "What Do the Worldwide Governance Indicators Measure?" *European Journal of Development Research* 22, 1 (February 2010): 31–54.

Tilly, C. *Democracy*. Cambridge: Cambridge University Press, 2007.

Trechsel, A. H. "Reflexive Accountability and Direct Democracy." *West European Politics* 33, 5 (September 2010): 1050–1064.

Treisman, D. "The Causes of Corruption: A Cross-National Study." *Journal of Public Economics* 76, 3 (2000): 399–457.

Trenz, H. J. and K. Eder. "Democratizing Dynamics of a European Public Sphere Towards a Theory of Democratic Functionalism." *European Journal of Social Theory* 7, 1 (February 2004): 5–25.

Troy, J. "'Catholic Waves' of Democratization? Roman Catholicism and Its Potential for Democratization." *Democratization* 16, 6 (December 2009): 1093–1114.

Tudoroiu, T. "Post-communist Democratization Revisited: An International Relations Approach." *Perspectives on European Politics and Society* 11, 1 (April 2010): 80–108.

Tulchin, R. S. and R. H. Espach. *Combating Corruption in Latin America*. Princeton: Woodrow Wilson Center Press, 2000.

Tummala, K. K. "Corruption in India: Control Measures and Consequences." *Asian Journal of Political Science* 10, 2 (2002): 43–69.

Uhlin, A. "Transnational Democratic Diffusion and Indonesian Democracy Discourses." *Third World Quarterly* 14, 3 (September 1993): 517–544.

United Nations Development Program (UNDP). "Reconceptualising Governance." *Discussion Paper* 2. New York, January 1997a.

———. "Corruption and Good Governance in a Globalised Society." *Discussion Paper* 3. New York, July 1997b.

Uslaner, E. "The Civil State: Trust, Polarization, and the Quality of State Government." In *Public Opinion in State Politics*, edited by J. Cohen. Stanford: Stanford University Press, 2006.

————. *Corruption, Inequality and the Rule of Law.* New York: Cambridge University Press, 2008.

Van Belle, D. *Press Freedom and Global Politics.* Wesport: Praeger, 2000.

Van Doeveren, V. Rethinking Governance, Identifying Common Principles." *Public Integrity* 13, 4 (Fall 2011): 301–318.

Vanhanen, T. *Democratization: A Comparative Analysis of 170 Countries.* London: Routledge, 2007.

Van Rijckeghem, C. and B. Weder. "Corruption and the Rate of Temptation: Do Low Wages in the Civil Service Cause Corruption?" *IMF Staff Working Paper,* WP/97/73. Washington, DC: International Monetary Fund, 1997.

Vermeule, A. *Mechanisms of Democracy: Institutional Design Writ Small.* New York: Oxford University Press, 2007.

Vishwanath, T. and D. Kaufmann. "Towards Transparency in Finance and Governance." *Social Science Research Network Working Paper Series* (September 1999): 1–30.

von Hippel, E. *Democratizing Innovation.* Boston: MIT Press, 2005.

Wade, R. "The System of Administrative and Political. Corruption: Canal Irrigation in South India." *Journal of Development Studies* 18, 3 (1982): 287–328.

Walker, S. "What Have We Learned About Forced Democratization?" *New Zealand International Review* 37, 3 (May/June 2012): 9–12.

Wallerstein, I. *The Modern World-System: Capitalist Agriculture and the Origins of the European World-Economy in the Sixteenth Century.* New York: Academic Press, 1974.

Ward, M. and K. Gleditsch. "Democratizing for Peace." *American Political Science Review* 92, 1 (March 1998): 51–61.

Waylen, G. "Women's Movements and Democratization in Latin America." *Third World Quarterly* 14, 3 (September 1993): 573–587.

Weale, A. "New Modes of Governance, Political Accountability and Public Reason." *Government & Opposition* 46, 1 (January 2011): 58–80.

Webb, M. "Activating Citizens, Remaking Brokerage: Transparency Activism, Ethical Scenes, and the Urban Poor in Delhi." *PoLAR: Political and Legal Anthropology Review* 35, 2 (November 2012): 206–222.

Weber, M. *Protestant Ethic and the Spirit of Capitalism.* London/Boston: Unwin Hyman, 1930.

Weber, R. H. "Transparency and the Governance of the Internet." *Computer Law & Security Review* 24, 4 (July 2008): 342–348.

Welsh, H. A. "Political Transition Processes in Central and Eastern Europe." *Comparative Politics* 27 (July 1994): 379–394.

Welzel, C. "Individual Modernity." In *The Oxford Handbook of Political Behavior,* edited by R. J. Dalton and H. D. Klingemann. Oxford: Oxford University Press, 2009.

Werlin, H. *The Mysteries of Development: Studies Using Political Elasticity Theory.* Lanham: University Press of America, 1998.

Werlin, H. "Corruption in a Third World Country: Why Nigerians Cannot Handle Garbage?" *World Affairs* 168, 2 (Fall 2005): 79–85.

Werner, S. B. "Development of Political Corruption: A Case Study of Israel." *Political Studies* 31, 4 (December 1983): 620–663.

Western, B. "A Comparative Study of Corporatist Development." *American Sociological Review* 56, 3 (June 1991): 283–294.

Weyland, K. "Diffusion Waves in European Democratization: The Impact of Organizational Development." *Comparative Politics* 45, 1 (October 2012): 25–45.

Wiarda, H. J. *Corporatism and National Development in Latin America.* Boulder: Westview, 1981.

Wiener, J. M. "The Barrington Moore Thesis and Its Critics." *Theory and Society* 2, 3 (Autumn 1975): 301–330.

Williams, R. J. "Political Corruption in the United States." *Policy Studies* 29, 1 (March 1981): 126–129.

Williams, A. "Shining a Light on the Resource Curse: An Empirical Analysis of the Relationship Between Natural Resources, Transparency, and Economic Growth." *World Development* 39, 4 (April 2011): 490–505.

Williams, D. and T. Young. "Governance, the World Bank and Liberal Theory." *Political Studies* 42 (1994): 84–100.

Williamson, P. *Varieties of Corporatism: A Conceptual Discussion.* Cambridge: Cambridge University Press, 1985.

Williamson, J. "Seeking Civilian Control: Rule of Law, Democracy, and Civil-Military Relations in Zimbabwe." *Indiana Journal of Global Legal Studies* 17, 2 (Summer 2010): 389–411.

Wing-Yat, E. Y. "Anti-corruption Approaches in Macao: Lawmaking and Legal Enforcement." *Journal of Contemporary China* 22, 79 (January 2013): 93–108.

Winham, G. R. "Political Development and Lerner's Theory: Further Test of a Casual Model." *American Political Science Review* 64, 3 (1970): 810–818.

Wiredu, K. "Society and Democracy in Africa." *New Political Science* 21, 1 (March 1999): 33–45.

Wolin, S. S. *Politics and Vision.* Boston: Little Brown, 1960.

Wollack, K. "Retaining the Human Dimension." *Journal of Democracy* 13, 3 (July 2002): 20–25.

Woon, J. "Democratic Accountability and Retrospective Voting: A Laboratory Experiment." *American Journal of Political Science* 56, 4 (October 2012): 913–930.

Wright, J. "How Foreign Aid Can Foster Democratization in Authoritarian Regimes." *American Journal of Political Science* 53, 3 (2009): 552–571.

Wucherpfenning, J. and F. Deutsch. "Modernization and Democracy: Theories and Evidence Revisited." *Living Reviews in Democracy* (September 2009): 1–9.

Xin, X. and T. K. Rudel. "The Context for Political Corruption: A Cross-National Analysis." *Social Science Quarterly* 85, 2 (April 2004): 294–309.

Yack, B. "Popular Sovereignty and Nationalism." *Political Theory* 29, 4 (2001): 517–536.

Yaday, V. "Legislative Institutions and Corruption in Developing Country Democracies." *Comparative Political Studies* 45, 8 (August 2012): 1027–1058.

Yap, O. F. "A Strategic Model of Economic Performance and Democratization in South Korea and Taiwan." *British Journal of Political Science* 42, 1 (January 2012): 213–239.

Yap, O. F. "Economic Performance and Democratic Support in Asia's Emergent Democracies." *Comparative Political Studies* 46, 4 (April 2013): 486–512.

Young, I. M. *Inclusion and Democracy.* Oxford: Oxford University Press, 2000.

Zirker, D. et al. "The Brazilian Civil-Military Crisis of 2008: A Shift to Monitory Democracy?" *Social Alternatives* 30, 3 (Summer 2011): 31–35.

INTERNET SOURCES

Andvig, J. C. et al. *Research on Corruption: A Policy Oriented Survey.* Mimeograph. Commissioned by NORAD, December 2000. Available at http://www.icgg.org/downloads/contribution07_andvig.pdf

Anticorruption Centre. *Research (U4) Report.* Bergen, Norway, May 2005. Available at www.u4.no/themes/aacc/finalreport.pdf

Bang, H. "Between Democracy and Good Governance." *Journal of Political Excellence* (2008): 2–9. Available at http://jpox.eu/static/bf_pdf/pdfoutput.php?cid=211

Blind, P. K. "Building Trust in Government in the Twenty-first Century: Review of Literature and Emerging Issues." *UNDESA Background Paper*, November 2006. Available at unpan1.un.org/intradoc/groups/public/documents/un/unpan025062.pdf

———. "Perspectives on Corruption Metrics: A Taxonomy." *A United Nations Concept Paper.* New York: UNDESA, 2012. Available at http://unpan1.un.org/intradoc/groups/public/documents/un-dpadm/unpan047377.pdf

Council of Europe. *Resolution (97) 24.* Strasbourg, November 6, 1997. http://www.coe.int/t/dghl/monitoring/greco/documents/Resolution(97)24_EN.pdf

———. European Commission for Democracy Through Law. Venice Commission. "Stocktaking: On the Notions of 'Good Governance' and 'Good Administration.'" CDL-AD (2011) 009 *Study no 470/ 2008* Strasbourg, April 8, 2011. Available at http://www.venice.coe.int/ webforms/documents/CDL-AD(2011)009.aspx

Council on Foundations and the European Foundation Centre. *Principios de Rendición de Cuentas en la Filantropía Internacional.* Arlington/ Brussels, April 2007. Available at espanol.cof.org/pdfs/services_princo-faccountability.pdf

DARA. *L'index de réponses humanitaires: les problèmes liés à la politisation.* Madrid, November 2010. Available at http://daraint.org/wp-content/ uploads/2010/12/HRI-2010-EXE-SUM_fr.pdf

DDC—Direction du développement et de la coopération. *La gouvernance comme theme transversal: guide d'orientation pour sa mise en oeuvre.* Zurich, 2007. Available at http://www.deza.admin.ch/ressources/ resource_fr_156840.pdf

Etienne, G. "United by Corruption." *India Today* June 3, 2011. Available at http://indiatoday.intoday.in/story/cases-of-corruption-in-developing-countries/1/140275.html

Europa. *A Comprehensive EU Anticorruption Policy.* Belgium, 2007. Available at http://europa.eu/legislation_summaries/fight_against_ fraud/fight_against_corruption/l33301_en.htm

European Commission. *The Aarhus Convention.* Denmark, 1998. Available at http://ec.europa.eu/environment/aarhus/

European Commission. "European Governance—*A White Paper.*" Belgium, 2011. Available at http://eur-lex.europa.eu/LexUriServ/site/en/ com/2001/com2001_0428en01.pdf

Global Transparency Initiative (GTI). *Transparency Charter for International Financial Institutions: Claiming Our Right to Know.* South Africa: Institute for Democracy, February 2003. Available at www.article19. org/pdfs/submissions/transparency-charter.pdf

InfoResources. *Remodeler les institutions pour la gestion des ressources naturelles. Direction du développement et de la coopération.* DDC, November 2008. Available at http://www.inforesources.ch/pdf/ focus08_3_f.pdf

International Council on Human Rights Policy (ICHRP). *Corruption and Human Rights: Making the Connection.* Switzerland: ICHRP, 2009. Available at www.ichrp.org/files/reports/40/131_web.pdf

International Monetary Fund. *Transparency.* Washington, DC: IMF, April 2001. Available at http://www.imf.org/external/np/exr/ib/2001/ 042601b.htm

International Organisation of Supreme Audit Institutions (INTOSAI). *The Lima Declaration of Guidelines on Auditing Precepts.* Lima, 1997.

Available at http://www1.worldbank.org/publicsector/pe/befa05/LimaDeclaration.pdf

Karly, T. L. "From Democracy to Democratization and Back: Before Transitions from Authoritarian Rule," in *CDDRL Working Paper*. Calif.: Stanford University, 2005. Available at http://cddrl.stanford.edu/publications/from_democracy_to_democratization_and_back__before_transitions_from_authoritarian_rule/

Kpatchavi, C. A. " Etat des lieux de la reddition des comptes dans les communes de Dogbo, Ouinhi et Sinendé et élaboration d'indicateurs de suivi—évaluation." *Study commissioned by the Netherlands Development Organization (SNV)*, Netherlands Embassy in Benin and VNG International,(July 2009. Available at http://www.gwppnebenin.org/IMG/pdf/Etat_des_lieux__DA_dans_trois_communes_pilotes.pdf

One World Trust. *Global Accountability Reports*. London. Available at http://www.oneworldtrust.org/globalaccountability/gar

Organization for Economic Cooperation and Development (OECD). Glossary. July 2007. Available at http://stats.oecd.org/glossary/detail.asp?ID=7237

_____. "Procedural Fairness: Transparency Issues in Civil and Administrative Enforcement Proceedings." DAF/COMP(2010)11. Available at http://www.oecd.org/competition/mergers/48825133.pdf

Organization for Security and Cooperation in Europe (OSCE). "Joint Declaration by the UN Special Rapporteur on Freedom of Opinion and Expression, the OSCE Representative on Freedom of the Media and the OAS Special Rapporteur on Freedom of Expression. 2004. Available at http://www.cidh.oas.org/relatoria/showarticle.asp?artID=319&lID=1

_____. "OSCE, Anti-Corruption Academy Agree to Co-operate on Fighting Corruption." 2011. Available at http://www.osce.org/eea/76258

_____. Declaration on Strengthening Good Governance and Combating Corruption, Money-laundering and the Financing of Terrorism. Dublin: December 2012. Available at http://www.osce.org/cio/97968

Overseas Development Institute. *World Governance Assessment*. London: ODI, 2009. Available at www.odi.org.uk/projects/00-07-world-governance-assessment

United Nations, A/RES/51/191. *United Nations Declaration Against Corruption and Bribery in International Commercial Transactions*. New York: December 18, 1996. Available at http://www.un.org/documents/ga/res/51/a51r191.htm

_____. "Governance for Sustainable Human Development." *UNDP Policy Document*. New York, 1997. Available at http://mirror.undp.org/magnet/policy

————. A/RES/51/59. *Action Against Corruption*. New York, January 28, 1997. Available at http://unpan1.un.org/intradoc/groups/public/documents/un/unpan010930.pdf

————. "Leveraging E-government at a Time of Financial and Economic Crisis." *United Nations E-government Survey*. New York: DPADM/UNDESA, 2010. Available at http://www.unpan.org/egovkb/global_reports/08report.htm

United Nations Development Programme (UNDP). A Users' Guide to Measuring Corruption. Oslo, Norway: 2008. Available at http://www.undp.org/oslocentre/flagship/democratic_governance_assessments.html

United Nations Office for Drug Control (UNODC). Anticorruption Toolkit. Version 4. November 2002. Available at http://www.unodc.org/pdf/crime/toolkit/f5.pdf

United Nations Office for Drug Control and Crime Prevention (UNODCCP). *Global Programme Against Corruption*. Anticorruption Toolkit 15, 1. Vienna, November 2002. Available at http://www.unodc.org/pdf/crime/toolkit/f1tof7.pdf

United Nations Office of the High Commissioner for Human Rights. *International Covenant on Civil and Political Rights*. Adopted by General Assembly resolution 2200A (XXI) of 16 December 1966 and entered into force in March 1976. Available at http://www.ohchr.org/en/professionalinterest/pages/ccpr.aspx

van Zyl, A. et al. "Responding to the Challenges of Supreme Audit Institutions: Can Legislatures and Civil Society Help?" *U4 Issue 2009*: 1 Norway: Anti-corruption Resource Center, 2009. Available at http://internationalbudget.org/wp-content/uploads/Responding-to-the-Challenges-of-Supreme-Audit-Institutions-Can-Legislatures-and-Civil-Society-Help.pdf

Vielajus, M. "Le défi de la "redevabilité" des agences de développement dans leurs propres pays et face à leurs pairs." *Study commissioned by Agence française de dévelopment*. Institute for Research and Debate on Governance. Paris, June 2010. Available at http://www.oecd.org/dev/devcom/44251172.pdf

World Bank. *Sub Saharan Africa: From Crisis to Sustainable Growth*. Washington, DC: WB, 1989. Available at http://ideas.repec.org/a/eee/agisys/v35y1991i4p473-474.html

Xinhua News Agency. *Unearthed Relics Reveal Corruption 2800 Years Ago*. Beijing, November 20, 2006. Available at http://www.china.org.cn/english/features/Archaeology/189555.htm

INDEX

Printed in the United States of America